RESTING
in the
BOSOM
of the
LAMB

RESTING
in the
BOSOM
of the
LAMB

AUGUSTA
TROBAUGH

The next day John seeth Jesus coming unto him, and
saith, Behold the Lamb of God, which taketh away
the sin of the world.

The Gospel according to St. John, 1:29
The Holy Bible

 BakerBooks

A Division of Baker Book House Co
Grand Rapids, Michigan 49516

© 1999 by Augusta Trobaugh

Published by Baker Books
a division of Baker Book House Company
P.O. Box 6287, Grand Rapids, MI 49516-6287

Paperback edition published 2000

Printed in the United States of America

Library of Congress Cataloging-in-Publication Data

Trobaugh, Augusta.
    Resting in the bosom of the lamb / Augusta Trobaugh.
        p.   cm.
    ISBN 0-8010-1170-1 (cloth)
    ISBN 0-8010-5823-6 (paper)
    1. Afro-Americans—Southern States—Fiction. I. Title.
PS3570.R585R47   1999
813'.54—dc21   98-31305

For current information about all releases from Baker Book House, visit our web site:
http://www.bakerbooks.com

For
John

Prologue

Baby girl, I hope you're listening real good to what I'm gonna tell you about that sure-enough miracle we got us. Had to be a miracle, because in all my born days, I didn't never think it could turn out like this. Didn't never think you'd be sitting right here on this very porch with me, hearing me talk about all us folks you don't know nothing much about yet.

Oh, I sure do wish my sweet mama could've seen it! But she'd been gone to Glory a long, long time when it all happened. I could still feel her with me though, kind of like a sweet little breath of air hovering close. And not just her, mind you. No, indeed! But her very own mama too and all those good, strong women we come from—all the way back to Mama Sunrise herself. And you're truly gonna like hearing all about her, because you've got a lot of her in you. You just don't know it yet.

Back then, I didn't really know that all the folks who came ahead of us are like the brown roots of a big old vine growing close to the porch, and even though those roots are way down deep in the ground where we can't see them, they're still there.

Always.

And we grow from them, our whole lives, and then, if we're lucky, others grow from us. Well, I expect that the ones who came before us—black and white—had things they had to keep still about, too, just like me and Miss Cora. Things we had to do, whether we liked it or not. And then never speak of them again.

So before we got our miracle, I was nothing but a barren old branch, all wore out from not saying things that should have been said right out loud and face-to-face and from still trying to send my own pretty green shoots way up high, to twine all around the gingerbread trim on Miss Cora's big front porch. Twine around and hold on. And grow.

But somehow or other, time got away from me, and I turned into this ugly old woman you see sitting here before you. Hair like cotton left too long in the field, and knees gone all thick and bony, and all these deep lines plowed into my face. Goodness! Me wearing ugly old thick stockings, just to keep me warm—even in the summertime. And my hands—why, you just look at them! Skin like dead leaves and all these big veins roping along so close to the top, like maybe my heart has to pump harder and harder, just to keep me going.

Me nothing but an old black woman sitting in a rocking chair at the very back of Miss Cora's porch. But you're young and you grew up in a different time, so maybe you don't know how black folks always had to sit way in the back. Me and my mama and the ones who came before us, who were really a part of Miss Cora's family for all those years.

But not a part.

Us black and them white and us all tangled up in every sort of way and twined around each other. But still separate. Because that's the way it had always been.

Sitting there together and keeping secrets that pretty much sopped up our whole lives, before we even realized it. It sure cost us something, let me tell you! And—Lord, have mercy on us—it was hard!

Felt like trying to hold onto a piece of ice on a hot summer day.

Because I was born in this house and grew up here with my mama—who cooked and cleaned and took care of things for Miss Cora's family, just like her mama did before her—and when I was a little girl, I used to lurk around, waiting for the iceman to come, those long, hot summertimes. Oh, I'd be so sweaty and sticky, I couldn't think of a thing in this world except snitching me a little piece of that ice and sneaking out to the back porch where I could suck on it without Mama seeing me. Because Mama said snitching was the same as stealing. But I did it anyway.

But you know, almost every single time I managed to get ahold of a little piece, it went and melted right there in my hand before I even got out on the porch with it, and a cold, wet place on my palm was all I'd have left of it. While I'd stand there wondering about it, even that was gone.

That's almost exactly what it felt like all those years I kept my mouth shut about our secrets. Because once my hand warmed up, those secrets almost never crossed my mind again in all creation. And, honey, do you know what that would have meant? Those old secrets would've turned into things that just never happened at all.

But I've always wondered: Where does ice go when it melts anyway? After you've wiped your hand on your apron and your palm is all dry and warm?

*I*t all started in the saddest old November I ever saw. Don't know why it was so sad that year, because it wasn't one bit different from all the other Novembers I've lived through, not that I could tell. Just dark coming earlier and earlier every day, so it seemed like daylight hardly got itself going good before the dark came and ate it all up again.

Long, windy nights, and that old crepe myrtle tree scratching against the side of the house right by my window. A most mournful sound—like old finger bones; and even in the daytime it wasn't much better, because it was always gray and cold, and the windows were all speckled over with rain. There wasn't a thing to see outside anyhow but dead leaves still clinging on that old sycamore and rattling against the cold, gray sky.

Me thinking the strangest thoughts, like how green and hopeful all those leaves were last summer, laughing and fluttering way up there against the blue heavens.

But the saddest thing about that November was that I kept hearing a voice that whispered to me whenever that cold wind tried to squeeze itself under the eaves of the house or around the cotton batting we'd packed into the cracks along the sides of the windows.

And what it whispered was this: *Give . . . me . . . the . . . baby!* Nearly scared me half to death!

First off, I thought it was Miss Cora saying something to me. Because she'll talk and talk to me, when she's way up front in the parlor and I'm in the back hallway or the kitchen, and she thinks I can hear what she's saying all that far away.

"What's that you say, Miss Cora?"

"Pet?" she called back. "You say something?"

"Yes'm," I yelled. "I said, were you talking to me?"

"Didn't say a thing," she hollered back, and then because it's her way, she came to the kitchen doorway in a minute or so and stood there watching me, all suspicious-like.

"You're probably having another one of your spells," she pronounced in that solemn-sounding way she can do. Just like an old judge, I tell you.

"No, ma'am. Just thought you were talking to me, is all."

That's what I said and got myself busy as could be, trying to get the corn bread to come out of the pan in one piece. But I was worried, sure enough. Why, I've read about folks who hear voices that aren't there, and I know what that means—they're crazy.

So I knew better than to say a thing to Miss Cora about that strange voice I heard, but I walked around with goosebumps on me almost all the time and some kind of a heavy hand or something pushing down on my shoulder. And I knew I better watch out, or something bad was gonna sneak up on me in the dark.

Maybe whatever it was that whispered: *Give . . . me . . . the . . . baby.*

Well, Miss Cora had her own way of handling sad feelings whenever they tried to get ahold of her, though I don't think she heard anybody whispering to her, like I did. So that sad November, she just backed herself right out of the here and now, just as pretty as you please, and spent all her days living in the past, reading her "Family Book" and talking nearly all the time about her folks and telling me their stories. Again.

Whenever she got started on that old book, I knew good and well what was gonna happen. She'd get a bee in her bonnet about that old grave she'd been trying to find for years and years, down to Brushy Creek Baptist Church Cemetery. She'd remember it for sure, and then harp on it every single day, until maybe she forgot it again for a little while, and I could have me some peace, until she remembered it again.

So while the wind blew and the rain spattered against the windowpanes, she told me stories out of the old book, and sometimes she even untied the cords that held on that fine leather cover and put in new pages she said we were gonna need when the family started growing again.

Oh, the Family Book's a great big old thing, let me tell you! Old as the hills and almost too heavy for anybody to tote. But the covers are still soft and shiny, from so many folks rubbing their hands over them, I expect. Heaven only knows how many generations of folks have stroked it and written their stories in it and read them aloud to anybody who'd listen.

Because, baby girl, these folks can sure talk and talk and talk some more! Talk all the time, seems to me. And if they sometimes run out of steam or if other folks get all filled up with the stories and just can't listen to one more word, then they take to writing it all down in the Family Book, so they can keep right on talking, you see—just not out loud. And then when they get their steam built back up again, they'll corner anybody they can find and read them the stories.

Why, I guess that book has all the stories of everybody who's ever been in the family. And that's why Miss Cora loves it so much. And that sad November, she hung onto it even harder than usual.

"It's all here, Pet," she said, running her hands back and forth across the pages. "In my great-grandmama's hand and my grandmama's and my mama's and now in mine. And someday, others will take care of it and read the stories and add more to it, and no one will ever forget us. I've even put a little mention about you in here!"

Why, she beamed at me just like she'd handed me the gift of everlasting life!

"And we'll pass the Family Book on to the ones who come after us, so they'll know who we were, and they can put their own stories in here for the ones who come after them."

Not gonna be a living soul coming after us. Not gonna be any new stories, either. That's what I thought; but, of course, I didn't say a thing.

Because Miss Cora thinks we're maybe like the trees—that we can lose all our leaves in the fall and then grow new ones the next spring. And if that's what she wants to think, I'm sure not gonna be the one to spoil it for her. No harm I can see in her dreaming about the family going on and folks coming after us to read our stories and tell their own.

But the truth was, there wasn't nobody but old folks left in this big house back then. Me and Miss Cora, of course—and Wynona and Lauralee too. They're the daughters of Miss Cora's sister, Miss Emma, and they've lived with us since . . . well for a long time.

And there wasn't nary a soul going to be coming after us. Or so I thought.

But I can sure remember way back to a time when we were just brimming over the rim with hope, even going back to when Wynona and Lauralee were little girls and started spending their summers with us, right here in this very house. They lived the rest of the time with their mama and papa in a little sharecropper's shack on Mr. Bondurant's land. And even further back than that—to the very day Wynona was born. Because my mama told me all about it, so it was just like I was there myself.

Mama was the one who brought Wynona into this world, because neither Miss Anne—Miss Cora and Miss Emma's mama—nor any of the aunts would've gone out to the Bondurant place themselves. They were still mad as fire about Miss Emma up and running off with Mr. Sam, and her just a girl of sixteen years! They said she'd married so far beneath her, and that a gentleman—which, of course, they said he wasn't—wouldn't have encouraged a child like Emma to run off with him like that in the first place, and he sure wouldn't have gotten her with child until she'd had a chance to settle in as a married lady. A respectable length of time, you see. But Wynona was born exactly nine months after they ran off to Burke County and got married.

My mama said the funniest thing she ever did see in her whole life was Miss Anne trying to count backwards without using her fingers! Of course, it certainly did add up to nine months, just barely, but Miss Anne and the aunts always snorted anyway, whenever anyone mentioned Mr. Sam to them.

So when it came Miss Emma's time for having Wynona, they sent my mama in a wagon out to that little slat house on Mr. Bondurant's place to take care of her.

And the whole time Miss Emma was having that baby, Mr. Sam sat in the other room and said not a word. Once in a while, Mama could hear him putting more wood in the stove, but aside from that, she never heard a sound out of him. One time, she asked him to go get more water and set it to boil, and she said he seemed to be so happy for someone to tell him what to do to help. Way back in his family there was a Bixley, you see, and for the most part, Bixleys don't like feeling helpless or waiting for someone else to do what needs to be done.

Mama always said he put more store in Miss Emma than anybody gave him credit for. Oh, he may have been a hard man and poor, and he didn't know how to do things folks would have called "charming," but he sure loved Miss Emma in his own way. Maybe he never could quite believe that a real lady like her would care about somebody like him, and maybe, too, he was thinking about how he was the one who caused Miss Emma to hurt so bad like that. Because some men feel that way when they find out what all a woman has to go through to bring a child into this world.

Mama said it took a good, long time for Wynona to come, but finally she did, and she was just as strong and stout as a little oak tree. Crying and red-faced and hungry. But Miss Emma was all used up by the birthing, and when my mama finally got her to hold Wynona in her arms, Miss Emma let out a terrible sigh like maybe feeding and taking care of that baby was just one more chore she had to manage.

Like to have broke Mama's heart, that sigh did, so when she drove the wagon back home, all she could do was cry for the little girl baby who had come into the hard, hard world that little shanty held onto. But even with crying like that for Wynona, Mama said she was praising Jesus all the way home, that her own baby—me—was going to be born into a good, strong house full of good, strong folks.

She just didn't expect me to come that very same day. But come, I did.

It was six long years later, after Wynona and I were both born, that Miss Emma had another little girl, Lauralee. But after me, my mama never had another child.

"You're the last little fruit off this tired old tree," she used to say to me. And I always did like to think of that—being my mama's fruit.

So when Lauralee was born, I was old enough that Mama took me with her out to Miss Emma's, but she wouldn't let me or Wynona go in the room where Miss Emma was. We just sat on the floor outside the closed door.

After a long time, we heard that little baby cry, and we were so surprised! Wynona and I hugged each other and smiled and hugged some more, and when Mama came out carrying Lauralee, she took the baby over to Mr. Sam and showed her to him, then came back and stooped down and put Lauralee right into Wynona's arms.

Well, Wynona took that little baby just as easy as you please, like she'd been holding babies all her life, and from that very day, she loved Lauralee more than anything else in this whole world.

She'd always been a good one for taking care of creatures, Wynona had—baby squirrels and baby coons and, one time, even a little runt pig. But that was Mr. Bondurant's pig, and after Wynona fed it with a bottle and raised it by hand, he butchered it right along with the rest of the pigs and never even had the kindness to offer her a bit of sausage or anything, though he would have lost that pig for sure, if she hadn't fed it and taken care of it and kept it warm. But that's the kind of thing can happen when a man works other folks' land and raises other folks' pigs. Because Mr. Sam was just a tenant farmer, the very thing Miss Anne held against him so hard.

But anyway, Wynona took to that little baby right away, just the way she'd taken to that poor little pig. So I guess her babying all those animals made her feel comfortable with any kind of baby.

Of course, I wished Mama had let me hold the baby, but she sure knew what she was doing, giving it right to Wynona like that. And Wynona did let me hold it for a few minutes while she went and got a pan of warm water for bathing it.

I'll never forget what that was like, holding Lauralee. I guess I thought a baby would feel like an old rag doll or something, but she was lots heavier than a doll and warm and moved around and opened her eyes and looked right at me! I sat there looking at that red, round face and those pretty blue eyes like I could never get enough of seeing her, and then she tried to suck on her fist, but she kept waving it around so much, she couldn't get a hold on it. That was right funny, I thought.

16

When Wynona came back with the pan of warm water, we took the baby into Wynona's room and put it on the bed and unwrapped its covers, and I let it hold onto my finger while Wynona bathed it. And sang to it.

Mama said she knew Wynona would always take good care of Lauralee, and Lauralee sure did need taking care of, because even though Miss Emma was a good lady her whole life, she wasn't one to sing to a baby or even hold it, except for when she had to feed it. And she didn't seem to be a bit more interested in Lauralee than she had been in Wynona. I don't know why that was. Maybe things had just been too hard on her. Or maybe her own mama had never done any singing or anything like that to her.

There was lots of work for them to do on Mr. Bondurant's land in exchange for them living in that shack and getting to plant a vegetable garden, but no matter how hard she worked, Wynona always had time for Lauralee. I remember going out there to get some fresh-churned butter from Miss Emma and seeing Wynona chopping weeds from the garden with Lauralee tied up in a big shawl and slung over her back. And the way Wynona was bending and straightening, bending and straightening, she had rocked Lauralee right to sleep.

Whenever Wynona wasn't working, she played with Lauralee just like she was a big old doll, dressing and undressing her and bathing her and singing her to sleep at night. Every time I went out there to get more butter, Wynona let me hold Lauralee, and I loved that more than anything else in this whole world. I used to beg Mama to put more butter in my grits, just so we'd use it up faster, and I could walk out to the Bondurant place for more . . . and get to hold Lauralee.

So that's the way three or four years passed, and Lauralee was the most beautiful little girl anyone had ever seen. Sweet too.

Once a year, Miss Anne and the aunts drove out to see Miss Emma and the girls on a Sunday afternoon, but they wouldn't even get out of the car, and when they came back, all they could do was talk about how hard everything was on Miss Emma and those little girls. And how it was all Mr. Sam's fault.

Maybe that's why Miss Anne got it in her mind that Wynona and Lauralee should come spend their summers with us in town, because she said if we didn't do something, those girls would grow up to be just as ignorant as dirt. They wouldn't ever be proper young ladies, not living out there in that shack, and they wouldn't ever learn to crochet or have good table manners or be able to go into a library and find a book to read.

Oh, they did go to school, I guess. Because no matter how hard Mr. Sam was, he wouldn't have let them grow up ignorant; but the school was just a little one way out in the country, and Miss Anne said that even if they did learn to read and write, they wouldn't learn how to be proper young ladies.

I never did know how the idea got put up to Mr. Sam, but it did, and I waited and waited, praying so hard that he'd let Wynona and Lauralee come here and live in this house in the summertimes. I daydreamed all the time about what games we were gonna play and how much fun we were gonna have. I was so dreamy that finally Mama had to say something to me about it.

So I tried my best to stop daydreaming all the time, but I sure enough couldn't get that smile off my face, no matter how hard I tried.

'Specially when I found out that all Miss Anne's pestering had worked!

But it was only the beginning of what all we went through together. The kind of things that only get shared when you get to spend your whole lifetime with people you love so much and want to keep safe from anything or anybody that could hurt them.

Now, Wynona had her own way of dealing with sad old November. She started in on a crusade about cleaning something—anything—and that year it was the pantry. Miss Cora and I had done a right good bit of canning toward the end of summer, putting up jars of tomatoes and butter beans and corn from the garden and blackberry jam and good cucumber pickles, so that the pantry shelves were loaded to the hilt with all those beautiful jars with the red and green and yellow and deep purple fruits of our labor. We were neat and clean as could be, of course, but, as usual, it wasn't good enough for Wynona.

So one day when she went into the pantry for something or other, she stuck her head back out and looked at us with a face like a thundercloud! I knew that granite-jawed look, sure enough!

"Uh-oh," I whispered to Miss Cora. "She musta found a little sticky spot on one of our jars!"

So we just got out of Wynona's way, because we knew what was coming. And sure enough, Wynona mumbled and grumbled and got herself a big bucket of warm, soapy water, and then she muttered the whole time, going at that pantry with a vengeance—stripping off the old shelf paper, scrubbing the shelves, putting on new paper, and wiping off each and every jar and the top of every single can.

I always thought maybe all that mumbling she did was just her mama's voice still talking to her, telling her how to do the job just right. Because Miss Emma sure had been picky about things.

"Cleanliness is next to godliness," Miss Emma always said; and she'd say it over and over again while she swept off those half-rotten steps and scrubbed the cracked windowpanes and spread their raggedy quilts out in the sunshine, where they grew warm and sweet-smelling. Of course, she finally wore herself down with it all, but I guess she left some of it with Wynona.

The whole time Wynona scrubbed and wiped and muttered, Lauralee sat at the kitchen table, watching her. She'd pulled her chair back just far enough so she could see her sister, and Lauralee didn't seem to need much more than that—just to be where she could keep Wynona in her sight.

So that's how we passed the first part of November that year. Us trying to stay busy so we wouldn't have time for looking out of windows. Miss Cora put lots more new pages in the Family Book, and, when Wynona got done with the pantry, it sure did look nice, what with all that fresh shelf paper and each and every jar gleaming. I started in crocheting me a little collar to go on a new dress I'd made, and then Wynona found a speck of tarnish on one of the teaspoons, and that set her into another tizzy. She got out all the silver and sat at the kitchen table, polishing and polishing. Lauralee helped her a little bit, but mostly she just looked at Wynona with those beautiful sad eyes and smiled, just the least little bit.

And over everything, Miss Cora's voice going on and on, telling us the old stories.

Again.

"I feel it in my bones," I finally whispered to Wynona in the kitchen. "Miss Cora's gonna get started about that old grave any day now, and I expect we'll wind up having to take her down there to look for it *again*."

Wynona sighed and kept right on polishing the silver. "Weather's too bad. Maybe we'll have to wait until spring?" she added hopefully.

But like everything else we hoped for, it didn't happen that way. The dark, low-hanging clouds scudded off to the east the very next day and took the rain and the chilly air with them. In their place came a sweet little warm spell, with a high, pale blue sky and big, whipped-cream clouds up from the Gulf of Mexico and beautiful autumn sunshine to beam on all the yellowed leaves on the ground around the big sycamore. Wynona looked out the dining room window and cut her eyes sideways at me. Because if Miss Cora said something then about us all going down to the cemetery, we wouldn't have the weather to blame.

So for the next few days, Wynona and I kind of walked on eggshells around Miss Cora. But even with us worrying about that, I felt ever so much better because I didn't have to listen to the rain and some voice whispering about a baby. Not as long as the wind was quiet.

But what I didn't know was that I'd be hearing a lot more than whispers, sure enough. And without a speck of wind! And *seeing* things as well!

How clearly I remember—a Wednesday evening, when it was Wynona's turn to go to evening prayer meeting and mine to stay home with Miss Cora and Lauralee. And because of that warm spell, we went to sit out on the porch early that evening, right after Wynona left. We wore sweaters around our shoulders and rocked in the old chairs, Lauralee looking off into some distant place and Miss Cora and me just leaning back in our chairs and gazing across the street at the lighted windows in Miss Addie's house.

Now, sweet old Miss Addie was some kind of distant relation to Miss Cora—a three-times-removed family mess that neither one of them could ever quite figure out. But they sure did have a good time trying to untangle that knot of ancestors, and that's the truth! Many's the time I've heard them go on and on about, "My great-aunt Lucy's older brother was the one who married your grandmama's second cousin."

Gave me a headache sometimes! But I loved Miss Addie, just the way I loved Miss Cora, so I didn't really mind.

Sitting there looking at her house across the street that evening, I got to remembering how ever since I was a little thing, I thought Miss Addie's house looked just like a big, white wedding cake, what with the way the second story was stepped back a little from the front porch—and all that fancy, gingerbread trim. And it painted snowy white, whereas our house was just the natural color the wood had always been.

When I was little, sometimes my mama would take some fresh biscuits hot out of the oven over to Miss Addie, or some butter beans, when she'd cooked an extra plenty, and I always went along, walking behind Mama and going up those wide steps to the screened porch around back. And when Mama knocked on the door, I could hardly wait for Miss Addie to come, because she was always so kind and good and happy to see us, even back in the days when white ladies usually held themselves far above black servant-women and their baby girls—like Mama and me. And no matter what we brought to her, she always acted so surprised and delighted.

"Why, Dilsey!" she would laugh. "What have you brought to me this time?" And then she would say what she always said: "I declare, you're simply an angel! Simply and purely an angel!" Then she would always put her hand on Mama's shoulder and turn her just a little bit, pretending to look for wings.

And they would both look at me and laugh.

But I really didn't know what was so funny. Wouldn't have surprised me one little bit did Mama have wings. And Miss Addie too!

"I better go over and see about Addie tomorrow," Miss Cora said. Because Miss Addie had taken sick again, and even though I'd gone over with some good chicken soup I made special for her, Miss Cora needed to see for herself.

"Thompson's with her tonight," I said. "She'll be all right."

Miss Cora snorted at the mention of Miss Addie's grown son.

"Well, I've sure had her on my mind this day." Miss Cora heaved a sigh. "And another thing I've been thinking about is going back down to the cemetery at Brushy Creek before the weather gets cold again, so I can find that grave—the one without a headstone. I've been pondering on it, and I remember now that it's west of the great oak. That's exactly where it is. I can find it. This time, I'm sure of it."

Lord, have mercy! I was thinking. *All our tiptoeing around, and she remembered it anyway!*

Because the only thing she was going to find down there was the blues, and we'd have an awful time helping her feel better, and just when we'd think we'd gotten her over it, she'd turn right around and forget we'd gone at all and start in to harping about it all over again.

And besides, her mentioning the great oak set me to wondering if maybe her mind wasn't *gone,* sure enough!

She didn't say anything else, and it took me only a few minutes to figure out that while she was on her way to that same old story about the unmarked grave, she must have finally remembered about the great oak being gone. Bet that surprised her sure enough, finding out she'd forgotten something so important.

She glanced over at Lauralee, who was leaning a little in her chair, staring down at the toe of her shoe and tapping it lightly against the bottom banister, as if nobody had said a thing. Then she tilted her head toward where I was sitting in the far back corner of the porch, but I didn't say anything, so she probably figured I'd dozed off, like I do sometimes. Anyway, she made the prettiest U-turn you ever saw in your life—away from the story of the unmarked grave and right into the story of the great oak and the night it fell over.

Well, I'd heard that one a thousand and one times too, going all the way back to when Miss Anne told the same story. So I knew every single word by heart, but I guess I was right glad to hear it again, and besides, maybe it would keep her from trying to find her way to the story about the old grave. That one was lots longer, and besides, I'd heard it more than any of the other stories.

"Such a wild and windy night it was," Miss Cora started out. "Darker than any night has ever been. My mama just a young thing and me just a baby. All of us staying the night with Mama's mama and papa out at the farm. Right after midnight was when the storm waked Mama up, and Papa wasn't there because he and Grandpa had taken the cow over to the other side of Zebina, to Mr. Jackson's fine bull. And when they saw the storm clouds coming up, they stayed the night at the Jackson place. Said they knew we were in a good, stout house and had nothing to fear from the wind.

"And Mama heard that terrible storm coming down on us. Lightning crackling all around and the wind howling and her looking through the window and seeing strange, blue lights in the cemetery down at the bottom of the hill. And right at that very moment, the night train coming through the Zebina crossing, blowing its whistle like always, and the great oak starting to fall as soon as the whistle blew . . ."

Here, Miss Cora's voice dropped almost to a whisper, and I braced myself for all the goosebumps I knew were gonna come up on me.

". . . Looked just like a big old spider, Mama said, with all its branches clutching at the sky. Oh, that tree tried so hard not to fall! But fall, it certainly did, and when it tore apart, Mama said it sounded . . . just like a woman screaming."

I sat there on the quiet porch, all goosebumped and quiet and seeing that big tree falling over. Watching those shocked, white-lit branches grabbing at the black sky.

"Papa said it must have been a scientific thing—that whistle having just the right pitch to it—for shattering the very heart of that tree."

Miss Cora's voice startled me a little, because I'd been watching that tree so hard, I thought I was standing right down in that old cemetery, with the wind whipping my hair and lightning flashing all around.

"I never did know whether it was scientific or not, but I do know it was something my mama never forgot. Those strange lights in the cemetery and that tree screaming like a woman."

Miss Cora was silent, and I was thinking: *Please, dear Lord, don't let her get started about the grave!*

I guess the Lord answered my prayer, because Miss Cora didn't find her way to the story about the grave, but she did turn right around and start in on the great oak story *again*.

"Such a wild and windy night it was," she started out, with me wondering how on earth she could forget so fast that she'd just told it. But I didn't say anything, of course—just sat there and

23

listened to it all over again and worried about how absentminded Miss Cora was getting, telling us the same things over and over again. And worrying too about Miss Addie across the street. Wishing with all my heart she could come over and sit with us like she used to do almost every evening, even all those long years ago, when Miss Anne was the one telling us the great oak story.

Miss Cora's voice going on and on, and me beginning to notice how she sounded exactly like her mama used to. Her saying the very words her mama said and just the way she used to say them, even rocking her chair the same way—slowing down as she talked, and at the last, forgetting to rock at all.

Maybe that's why I got the strangest feeling that Miss Anne was right there with us on the porch that evening—and Miss Addie too, though I could look across the street and see the light in her bedroom window and know full well she was sick in bed. Them sitting there smiling, and me just like a bump on a log and with my mouth hanging open.

And, all of a sudden, there were all kinds of other folks right there on the porch with us—all the old ones from so long ago. My own sweet mama, sitting in the same chair behind the trellis, and me sitting at her feet and resting my head against her knees. And Miss Cora, a young lady. And Lauralee and Wynona, just little girls, about the same age as when they first came here to spend their summers in this house.

Then somehow or other—and I know there's not a way in this world to explain it—my grandmama showed up and Mama Sunrise too—my great-grandmama, and the one I was named for. I'd never seen her before, because she passed on long before I was born, but I knew who she was that evening. I sure did. Her bigger than most grown men I'd ever seen, rocking and laughing and showing her big, strong teeth.

She's the one I say you're so much like, so you ought to be real happy about that.

But anyway—that just turned out to be the most crowded porch I was ever on! Like a big old family reunion, with us all there together—us like we are now and us like we were way back then—and all the folks who have gone on ahead of us. Everybody talking at once, telling the old stories over and over again and smiling to beat the band! Voices spinning back and forth, looping around and knitting us together, until that whole porch was glowing with all the voice-threads, tying us together into one wonderful, shining something.

I got so dizzy, I felt like I was everywhere at once, looking down on us from way above—like I was hanging from the light fixture upside down just like an old bat. Looking up at us too, peering through the porch banisters from deep down among the vines and close to the ground, like a snake. And looking out from behind every chair, my own included, though I knew as surely as day was coming that I was sitting in the very chair I was looking out from behind!

And remembering the old things. How when Wynona and Lauralee—grown ladies then—came back here to live with Miss Cora and me for good, it took all the old stories and all the strength we'd inherited to make it through what we had to get through. This good house sheltering us then just like it had done for my mama and her mama before her, and Miss Anne and her mama before her, and all the ones who had come before us.

Our turn then to carry the burdens, to go in and out of the old rooms, reaching up on the topmost shelf of the pantry to find that crystal cake-stand at Christmastime, just like our folks had done before us, and passing our nights with our heads on our grandmothers' pillows. And how, because of all the stories they told us, we knew how to do everything that needed to be done.

More than that too, but I can't say it the way it really is. Just that it's who we are and who we come from. That's the most important thing—who we come from—because that's who we really are.

What a strange and wonderful thing it was! Me just as dizzy as could be, but knowing it sure wasn't just a dream I was having, that I was wide awake. Listening to all the voices and the stories and watching Mama Sunrise smiling when I think she said to me, "Daughter, it's coming time for you to lay your burden down."

I almost opened my mouth and said, "Why, Mama Sunrise! What *do* you mean?" but thank goodness, I caught myself, because Miss Cora would have heard me and tattled to Wynona, telling her I'd had a spell, sure enough, me sitting on the porch talking to folks who weren't really there. And Wynona would have started watching me all the time, like maybe she thought I was crazy.

So I said not a word, just sat and watched and listened for a long time—and wondered if maybe I should be worried about *myself,* as well as about Miss Cora and Miss Addie—until very slowly, the faces and the voices faded away one by one, leaving just me and Miss Cora and Lauralee together in the here and now, and the wind shifting a little so I could hear the closing hymn from Wynona's prayer meeting at the Baptist Church down at the corner: "In the sweet by and by, we shall meet on that beautiful shore. . . ."

We shall meet. . . . Well, that was sure something to think about. But you had to be dead to meet on that beautiful shore, and I sure wasn't dead yet. That much I knew. So I was wondering what on earth got me started in to imagining all those folks on the porch.

Give me the baby.

There it was again! Someone whispering to me, and this time, the wind wasn't blowing one little bit. But I didn't have time to worry about it, not after what all I had just seen and heard.

Miss Cora's voice was still going on and on and me thinking how wonderful it was to have my mama and Mama Sunrise there with me and wishing with all my heart that they could really be sitting there with me again. So I just gave myself to the old pull of blood, reached out, and took into my own hands the wonderful gift of memory my mama held out to me:

Mama and me in bed in the tiny room off the back porch. Me snuggling up against her and whispering, "What's my name, Mama?" Because it's a game we always play before we go to sleep.

"Why, your name's Pet," she says, making her voice sound real surprised. Because that's part of the game too.

"No'm, Mama," I giggle. "What's my real name?"

"Why, your name's Patricia, same as your great-grandmama."

"No'm, Mama," I persist. "What's my name? And her name too?"

Then Mama whispers the name, her breath all soft and warm against my ear. Whispers the forbidden name, the one from Africa that was Great-

Grandmama's real name. The name somebody got a bad whipping for,
back in slave times, for saying out loud.

I never did know why we were still whispering it years and
years later. Maybe because by then, it was kind of a tradition, a
way to be reverent about what all our people had suffered. And
I'd long ago forgotten exactly what that word was. But it was
very beautiful, just the sound it made.

"And what's my name mean, Mama?"

"It means Sunrise."

And even though I was an old woman that Wednesday evening in November, I could still hear my mama whispering to
me and feel her warm breath against my ear.

Wynona came strolling out of the dark at the edge of the yard
just as Miss Cora started in on yet another telling of the great
oak story. Miss Cora paused for a moment, watching Wynona
come up the steps. "Wynona, have I ever told you the story about
the night the great oak fell?"

"Yes, ma'am, you sure have," Wynona said, glancing at me,
rolling her eyes up to where the porch light burned high above,
and silently mouthing, *over and over and over again.*

"Y'all have a good service?" I asked.

"Sure did," Wynona said. "Right good crowd too."

". . . Papa said it was a scientific thing. That whistle having
just the right pitch to it for shattering that tree's very heart . . ."
Miss Cora was going on and on.

"We better get her to bed," Wynona said real low to me. "It's
getting chilly out here, and she's all wound up tonight."

"She's not the only one," I said, but Wynona didn't hear me.

While we were trying to help Miss Cora get ready for bed, she
took it in mind to find a string of beads that had belonged to her
mama. She looked through two or three dresser drawers and
started fretting when she couldn't put her hands right on them,
but Wynona finally got her to go to bed by promising she'd help
find them first thing in the morning.

"She'll forget all about them by then," Wynona said, as she
closed Miss Cora's door.

"Maybe," I said. "And maybe not."

Because what I'd found out during that strange evening was that forgetting things isn't always something we choose. And remembering them isn't either.

Wynona went to Lauralee's room to see that she was ready for bed, and I went on to my room off the back porch—the same little room where I was born and where my mama used to whisper my real name in my ear. Coldest room in the house in the wintertime, but I never minded that, because I had my mama's big feather bed to snuggle down into. And besides, my room was where Miss Cora kept all the things that didn't seem to go anywhere else but that were too good to give away. So maybe that was one reason why I never forgot about what happened to us. Not completely anyway. Because in my room there were all kinds of wonderful things I could touch and smell and look at for remembering the early times when things were so good for us. Why, there was a cedar chest full of old letters on fine, stiff paper and a chifforobe chock-full of those pretty dresses Wynona and Lauralee used to wear when they were children—some of them dresses I remember watching my mama iron. And an old dresser that used to be in their room and still had things of theirs in it from when they were young ladies. Hairbrushes and hairpins and a powder jar with powder still in it.

So that sometimes when I was almost asleep, I thought I could still see those two girls, Wynona and Lauralee, laughing together just like always, with their hands over their mouths and their eyes bright. Like two beautiful white birds.

Maybe there's some way for old rooms to hold onto things from the past, so that wherever Wynona and Lauralee were—the girls they used to be, I mean—time could rise up under their feet once in a while just like a dream-bridge and bring them right back to me, so I could see one of them sitting at the dresser and the other standing behind her, smiling into the mirror. And they wore white dresses with little pearl buttons on them and flowers in their hair, and their arms were like white marble, reflected in the glass.

*W*ynona turned out to be right about the beads, because Miss Cora didn't say a thing about them the next morning. Only thing she seemed to have on her mind was Miss Addie. I could tell that without her saying a word, so I did the only thing I knew to do right then—made a double batch of biscuits, buttered them, wrapped half a dozen up in a heavy linen napkin, and took them across the street, telling Thompson to be sure his mama had some while they were still hot.

Then I came back and put the bowl of grits and the platter of sausage patties and scrambled eggs on the table.

"How's she doing this morning?" Miss Cora asked.

"Pretty good, I think. Thompson said she slept well."

Miss Cora stirred some milk into her coffee. "I'll go over right after breakfast."

I was clearing the table when there came a knock at the back door.

"Minnie Louise, probably," Miss Cora said, getting up and going toward the dining room. "Ask her can Delia please let us have an extra dozen eggs this week. I've had such a taste for some good deviled eggs lately; maybe Addie would like some too. And I'm going on over there now," she added.

Minnie Louise, my second cousin, worked for Miss Delia, who lived way out on the Waynesboro Highway and had the best flock of laying hens in the whole county. Too, Miss Delia was also probably the only soul left—besides me and Miss Addie, of course—who remembered anything about what happened to us all those years ago. And Minnie Louise always told me whenever Miss Delia started trying to talk about it.

But she couldn't very well remember what little she used to know, because she hadn't had anyone to talk to about it in a long time. Her family was gone now, except for two grown-up granddaughters, and they didn't come see her very often. Even when they did come, they always brought the children—"to see Mee-Maw"—or so they said, and all they did the whole time was fuss at the children. Hollering things like "TAYLOR TREDWELL MARTIN! How many times have I told you to quit that!" or "You give that back to your sister this very minute, or I'll go get a switch! This very minute, you hear?"

So what with all the yelling and the terrible thumping, thumping of children's feet stomping up and down the front porch—"Just like wild animals, I tell you!" Miss Delia said—she never could remember much of the story, much less get a chance to tell it to anyone. Which was a blessing, sure enough!

Still, she sometimes tried to bring it up to Minnie Louise, who came to her place every morning to feed the chickens, gather up the eggs, help Miss Delia take a sponge bath, and cook her a hot dinner. But Minnie Louise wouldn't go along with such talk.

Polite but disinterested . . . that was the way she tried to handle it, of course.

"You remember it, Minnie Louise? When Wynona and Lauralee came to live with Cora and Pet for good? Young ladies, they were, and that Lauralee the prettiest thing you ever saw in your whole life. Sweetest thing anyone ever knew."

"No'm, I don't remember it, 'cause my people lived over to the other side of Sparta back then. I didn't get over here til nineteen hundred and twenty-six, when I come to do cooking and day-cleaning for you. Don't you remember that?"

"Indeed I do!" Miss Delia snorted. "I'll never forget the day you walked right up to my front door, just as bold as brass! Why,

I nearly fainted dead in my tracks! Figured I'd go right on down to Cora's and ask that Pet what on earth she meant, sending me some uppity colored girl didn't know enough to come around to the back door, and I didn't care if you *were* Pet's very own cousin, you should've known better than that. You coming right up to the front door just as bold as brass! I never did get over it."

"Well now, Miss Delia, it's been a long time, and we worked out all right, didn't we?"

"We sure did that," Miss Delia admitted. "But it was still a big shock for me, because that's not the way things were done back then. You know that as well as I do."

Minnie Louise raised an eyebrow but didn't say anything.

"Anyway," Miss Delia went on, "it must have been just before you came that Wynona and Lauralee moved in with Cora and Pet for good. Not like when they were children and came during the summers, but when they came to stay. Grown young women, they were, and seems to me there was something about Wynona's husband passing on, but I can't recollect what it was. She'd only been married about a year or so, as I recall. And what was his name? Wynona's husband?"

"Don't matter none, something that long ago."

"I suppose you're right," Miss Delia said, reluctantly. "But I sure do wish I could remember what it was about that. Maybe some-time or other I'll ask Pet. I'll bet she remembers."

"I don't think I'd go asking her about it, if I was you," Min-nie Louise offered.

"Well now, I certainly don't know why not. Pet knows every-thing that's ever gone on in that house. Born right there under that very roof, she was. I'll bet you didn't know *that.* Right in what they used to call the preacher's room in the old days, because all the big houses had such rooms so circuit-riding preachers could stay the night, before they went on to the next church.

"And I even remember a long time before that, when Cora's papa himself moved Dilsey—Pet's mama—under his own roof. Now that sure did cause some eyebrows to shoot up in this town, I tell you! But it was a bitter, bitter winter, and Dilsey had been living in that old shanty down at the end of the kitchen garden.

"'I'll not stand by and see her freeze to death when there's a perfectly good room under my roof and it going unused.' That's what Cora's papa told Miss Anne. And even though Miss Anne tried her dead-level best to make him see how it was going to look to folks, he wouldn't budge an inch."

Miss Delia drew her eyebrows together. "Dilsey never did move out again, and so when Pet was born, it was right there in that room. And it was Cora herself who brought Pet into this world."

"I didn't know *that*," Minnie Louise admitted, warming to the story a little, in spite of herself.

"Reason I remember it," Miss Delia continued, "was that Pet's an exact age with Wynona. Born the very same day. Because Miss Anne sent Dilsey out to the old Bondurant place, where Emma and Sam were living, you see, to help Emma when Wynona was born. Miss Anne wouldn't have gone out there herself, because neither Anne nor any of the aunts would have put one foot in that little sharecropper shack. They never did get over the way Emma ran off like that and married somebody like Sam—him a tenant farmer and so ignorant and all. So it was Dilsey they sent, and as soon as she got back home from bringing Wynona into this world, she went straight to childbed and had her own baby, Pet.

"Seems to me there was some criticism from folks, about Anne sending her way out there in that old wagon, what with her being so close to having a baby herself. All that jouncing around, you see. But whatever it was caused Pet to come, she did—and fast! They didn't even have time to get Dilsey's mama there, so it was Cora herself brought Pet into the world. Only thing Miss Anne and the aunts did was wring their hands and run around, bumping into each other. But Cora stayed with Dilsey the whole time, wiping off the sweat and cleaning up the blood and tending to her in every way. And Cora hardly more than a child herself—only fifteen or so, if I remember right.

"So it was Cora's own sweet hands first touched that little baby. Tiniest little thing—black or white—anybody had ever seen. That's how come everybody to call her Pet, you see. Because she was so little, she could have fit into a grown man's hand.

"Seems to me her name was supposed to be Sunrise—after Dilsey's grandmother or somebody like that. Not Sunrise, but maybe an African word for *sunrise,* supposed to be. Still, it didn't matter in the long run, because Pet is what everybody's always called her. So you see, Minnie Louise, I know all of that—and I'll bet you anything Pet remembers every single thing ever happened to any of them."

"Yes'm."

"I sure do wish I could remember what it was about Wynona's husband that time."

"Yes'm."

So that was the first thing Minnie Louise told me about when she came that morning. "Miss Delia's been talking about when Wynona and Lauralee came to live with you and Miss Cora for good. And trying to remember about it. You know that?"

"I knew somebody or other was thinking about it, besides me," I said. "Been feeling it in my bones."

"Well, I thought you ought to know."

"Yes," I said. "I ought to know." And I did know, I guess, but I hadn't thought about it in so long, it was like I'd wrapped up the memories in a quilt and put them way in the back of the closet, so they were snuggled down among pillows that smelled of old talcum powder.

Or maybe it was like waking up in the middle of the night in the dark and turning on the radio, just for a little company. Turning the dial to find something you want to listen to, and, once in awhile, hearing a radio station very faint and from very far away. Some man singing about his woman leaving him, maybe, or just a few banjo notes before it begins to fade away. I think it's one of the saddest things in the world, it fading off like that and leaving you all alone in the dark, wondering where that little bit of sound came from. Maybe from far away over mountains and it turning into no sound at all. Nashville, maybe? Or some lonely little place in Alabama? And who else was listening to it and what were they thinking about? So sad and far away, like someone talking and you can't quite hear them. Or something like that.

33

"I figure you'll tell me all about it, one of these days," Minnie Louise muttered, and her voice was strangely unexpected in my ears.

"One of these days," I said. But, of course, I was just being polite.

"Well, I made some of my good chicken mull last night, 'cause I heard Miss Addie was sickly."

"I'll heat it up and take it over for her dinner," I said. "That was right good of you to fix it for her."

But Minnie Louise never did know what to do with a compliment, so she just ignored it.

"I told Thompson I could come stay with her, afternoons," Minnie Louise said with some gruffness in her voice. "But he never did call me."

"Guess he figures between us and him and his wife, Maude, it's enough," I said.

"Hmph!" she grumbled. "Well, I better get on along. Miss Delia don't like it when I'm late getting there. Says all she can think about is me being splattered all over the highway somewheres. Youall need eggs?"

"Yes, please. An extra dozen, can she spare them. I'll see Miss Addie gets the mull."

"Tell Thompson I could come afternoons," Minnie Louise repeated.

After Minnie Louise left, I worried a little about Miss Delia trying to remember things. But then I thought that if Miss Cora herself could forget something as important as the great oak being gone—and lots more besides—surely Miss Delia could forget to wonder about what happened to us all them years ago. And besides, she didn't know the whole story. I was the only one who knew that.

And Miss Addie.

True to my word, I heated up Minnie Louise's good chicken mull and took it over to Miss Addie's right around noontime. Miss Cora was just coming down from upstairs.

"She's been sleeping off and on," she whispered. "Is that some of Minnie Louise's chicken mull?" she asked, lifting the cover of the dish and sniffing.

"Sure is. She brought it over this morning and more than aplenty, so I've left some heated up for you at home. It's on the back of the stove. Wynona's made some corn bread to go with it."

"Good!" Miss Cora said, because she sure did love Minnie Louise's mull. Everybody did. "I'll be back in a little while."

"Minnie Louise says she can come stay with Miss Addie afternoons, if Thompson wants!" I called through the screened door, as she went across the porch and down the steps. She waved her fingers to let me know she'd heard and then hurried on across the street to Minnie Louise's good mull and Wynona's fresh-baked corn bread.

I went up the stairs and tapped on Miss Addie's door.

"Ye-es?" she asked, with that familiar lilting voice, because Miss Addie could pack more syllables into her words than anybody else in the whole wide world.

"It's Pet, Miss Addie."

"Oh, ye-es! Come right on in!" Why, she sounded so bright and cheerful, I wondered if maybe she was feeling lots better. But when I saw her lying there in that great big old four-poster bed, I knew she wasn't better at all. Her eyes were sunken and not a speck of color in her cheeks and the room with that musty-sweet kind of perfume to it, where someone very old and very precious is ill.

"I brought you some of Minnie Louise's good chicken mull," I said. "She made it special for you and brought it over to me this very morning. You think you can enjoy a taste of it?"

"Maybe a little later," she said. "Just put it on the dresser, if you please."

So much for that, I thought.

"Sit with me a while, Pet?" Miss Addie asked, lifting herself a little out of the feather bed and indicating a boudoir chair nearby.

"Yes'm." Because I would have done anything in this world Miss Addie asked me to do, and there was so much between us we had never talked about. But when we sat together, even in silence, it almost felt like we were saying it all. Just not out loud.

We stayed silent for a long time, and I'd just started casting around in my mind for some kind of gentle small-talk when she said, "It's getting close to time, Pet."

"Ma'am?" I asked, and my heart lurched hard against my ribs.

"It's getting close to time," she repeated, and I was thinking, *No, please! Don't you talk about dying, Miss Addie. I can't bear it!*

But dying wasn't what she meant to talk about, and I should have been relieved, except that what she said next surprised me so, I could hardly hear the words.

"Time for you to make Cora remember," she said. "About Hope."

When I heard that name, it set my head to spinning. "And about you," she breathed.

What could I say? Except "yes'm."

"She needs to know the family's going to go on."

"Yes'm."

"You *have* to make her remember."

"Yes'm."

"Will you?" she asked. A direct question this time and aimed right at me.

"I'll try," I mumbled, and all kinds of things were racing through my mind and bumping into each other hard and falling down and dusting themselves off and getting back up. Like every single thing inside my head just got the living daylights scared out of itself.

"Will you?" Miss Addie repeated, somewhat louder.

I hesitated for only a moment before I gave the only answer I could give to anything she asked of me.

"Yes'm."

She nodded and closed her eyes and drifted back into sleep. I watched the covers rising and falling with her gentle breathing and thought about how, a long time ago, Miss Addie did something for me that no one else in this world would ever have done.

So I whispered low, "I'll do anything you ask, Miss Addie." And then I added, "But I think you're wrong about the family going on."

I took the bowl of mull, tiptoed downstairs, put it in the refrigerator, and straightened things up a bit for Miss Addie. There was a pot soaking in the sink, and I scrubbed it until it was shining. I rinsed out her dish towels, hung them out to dry on a little clothesline on the back porch, ran a dust rag over the dining table, and straightened the tea set on the buffet. Then I sat out on the back porch and waited for Miss Cora to come back, and wondered how on earth I was gonna be able to do what Miss Addie made me promise. But thinking about that hurt my old heart so bad, I shifted myself over to wondering if Thompson would give in and get Minnie Louise to come help. But that probably wasn't going to happen, so Miss Addie being sick again meant that Thompson, or Maude, or one of us would be staying with her.

I never minded it, myself, and Wynona was good about it, except she worried it would upset Lauralee. But when Miss Cora stayed the night, she'd be awful tired out the next day. I don't think she ever went to bed in the room next to Miss Addie's but sat up all night in a chair right by her bed. So I was a little bit worried about that.

But when Miss Cora came back after lunch, she was smiling.

"Thompson's on his way back over here," she said. "And I made him promise me he'd get Minnie Louise to come stay afternoons."

Then her smile suddenly disappeared. "It's the least he can do!" she snorted. "His very own mama! And I just had to say something to him about it because she's my own kin, as well. I think it was my great-aunt Lucy's older brother who married her grandmama's second cousin."

She stumbled to a halt and rubbed her forehead. "Or something like that," she added.

*M*iss Addie started getting better right away, and Minnie Louise said it was her good chicken mull had done it. I think she was right about that, because I'd seen Minnie Louise's you-eat-this-all-up kind of sweet-talking before, and it was a wonder to behold—how she could come across a sick room with a bowl cupped in both hands like it was full of rubies or something, her just beaming and chanting, "M-m-m-m! Here comes the very best chicken mull in the whole world, and it's just for you!"

Why, anybody with a speck of life still left in them couldn't help but rise up out of the bed and grab the spoon!

It was a harder time Minnie Louise had with Miss Addie, but Minnie Louise won anyway, like I knew she would. She just sat there beside Miss Addie's bed for as long as it took to get a good dinner into her, one spoonful at a time, sing-songing nonsense things like, "This here's a little bluebird just wanting to sing his heart out. You gobble him up and see don't he start singing inside you!" And "Well, look at this! Here's a pair of little red dancing shoes sitting in this spoon, and they can't wait to get down to your feet and set 'em to dancing up a storm!"

That's the way Minnie Louise got little bits of nourishment into Miss Addie. Because that Minnie Louise was always so good with children and old folks. And babies? She was the very best with babies. I knew that for a fact.

The doctor said that sometimes older folks just seem to rally for no reason. I didn't tell that to Minnie Louise.

We were just so happy she was better, we really didn't care about the *why* one little bit.

That's the way November finally ended. The rain didn't come back, but the air got colder and colder every single day, with the high dome of heaven such a pale blue and all the yellow leaves on the ground turning brown.

About two weeks before Christmas, we got our first real bitter-cold weather, and it came late enough that we knew good and well we wouldn't get any more warm spells until winter was over. So we went ahead and closed off the parlor.

That big room was always cold as a barn, and we could never get it warmed up the least little bit in bitter-cold weather, not even after Miss Cora had gas heaters put in the house some years ago. So we gathered up our tatting and crocheting and the books we were reading and Miss Cora's African violets and took them into the dining room. We brought out the Family Book too, because Miss Cora would have had a fit if we'd forgotten it.

Then we took one last good look around the room, just to make sure we hadn't overlooked something we couldn't do without until spring, and we shut the big door. I used a nut-pick to pack strips of old sheets and cotton batting good and tight into every crack, so that for the whole long winter, the parlor would stay sealed away, all dim and cold beyond the door.

There was always something special about knowing Miss Cora's mama's Queen Anne side chairs were waiting there under their icy velvet, with the heavy drapes sometimes moving in drafts from the window, like old eyelids twitching in a dream, and the whole time, we were in the cozy dining room and the kitchen and making such good things to eat—biscuits and country ham for breakfast and fried chicken and corn bread for dinner in the warm kitchen.

Once sure-enough, honest-to-goodness winter arrived, I never felt one bit sad anymore, the way I always did in fall. Because there couldn't be anything nicer in the whole world than the way we all sat around the gas heater in the dining room. Just like little sparrows fluffed out and huddled together and chirping away and just being happy—and doing plenty of cooking, so as to keep the kitchen warm, and always hurrying across the street to take something good to eat to Miss Addie before it got cold.

It was nice for us to just sit and listen to Miss Cora's stories from the Family Book and tat and crochet together in the dining room where Miss Cora's mama's Seth Thomas clock ticked its steady tock on the mantelpiece.

Miss Addie even got to feeling good enough to enjoy watching Wynona and me put up a Christmas tree for her and decorate it, and when we plugged in the cord and that beautiful tree came alive with all those colorful lights, Miss Addie laughed right out loud, and we laughed too.

She sure did look pretty that day, sitting there with a wool lap robe over her knees and her silvery hair all soft—like a halo—and shining in the lights from the Christmas tree.

On Christmas morning itself, we gathered up a whole big basket of groceries and all our presents and went over to Miss Addie's, where I fixed us a great big breakfast—sausage and country ham and grits with red-eye gravy and scrambled eggs and fresh-made, hot biscuits with plenty of fig preserves—and orange marmalade, a special treat because of it being Christmas morning.

After breakfast, we opened our presents. Miss Addie liked the pillowcases I'd edged with tatting for her, and Miss Cora and Wynona laughed when they opened their gifts from me—because I'd given them all the very same thing. Lauralee didn't laugh, of course, but she ran her fingers over the tatting and looked at me so sweet-like, and that was enough.

Miss Cora gave Miss Addie some lovely, china egg cups that were a beautiful robin's egg blue on the inside. Miss Addie gave Miss Cora some knee-warmers in the most shocking shade of pink any of us had ever seen.

"I'm sorry, Cora," Miss Addie said. "I guess you can tell I had to get Maude to do my little bit of shopping for me."

"Well, they *are* right bright," Miss Cora admitted. "But they're sure going to feel nice and warm this winter. Probably keep my knees from hurting me in this cold weather."

Miss Cora gave me some of the prettiest embroidered hankies, and while I was opening the present, I noticed Miss Addie looking back and forth from Miss Cora to me and smiling and nodding her head.

Yes'm.

We stayed all morning, to give Thompson and Maude a little rest. But when they got to Miss Addie's around noon, we went on home, even though I could tell Maude was hoping we'd stay awhile. But Miss Cora said it was time for us to go, so I expect she was thinking of Lauralee, because she'd had about all the excitement she could handle in one day.

Miss Addie kept on feeling good after Christmas and right on through most of that long winter. And such a long winter it was! Day after day of bitter cold, so the trees outside the dining room window looked like they were frozen stiff against the gray sky. My fingers went through all the right motions with that little silver tatting shuttle, but my thoughts tumbled around in the long-ago things and Miss Addie and what she'd said it was getting time for me to do, and how maybe Miss Addie was thinking she was ready to pass on, so it was something like a last wish she'd handed over to me. So I had a reprieve—seeing as how she was feeling so much better. But it wasn't a reprieve that would last forever, so I sat and thought and worried myself and tatted enough lace to edge about a thousand pillowcases.

Lauralee did some crocheting, with Wynona helping her when she dropped a stitch. Like always, Wynona was good and patient, but I could tell she was getting restless, what with the parlor shut off where she couldn't clean and dust and the bedrooms too cold for much of anything except making up the beds in the mornings. Finally, she went to the dimestore and bought herself a thousand-piece puzzle and started putting it together on one end of the dining table.

But she went at that puzzle with a vengeance, the same way she cleaned the pantry or polished the silver, and that big old puzzle had about three hundred dark, streaky little pieces that were supposed to be a line of bare trees in wintertime and about seven hundred tiny pieces that were for a pale blue sky over the trees and blue-tinted snow beneath them. Couldn't tell the difference in the sky and the snow.

Liked to have driven her crazy. And me too, the way she kept tapping her foot against the table leg and biting her lip and muttering to herself. Miss Cora just went on reading through the Family Book, and Lauralee drew her eyebrows together and worked away at her crocheting. But it sure bothered me.

And to add to everything, Miss Cora turned a page of the book one afternoon and said, "Look—here's some of the old Hezekiah Longwood story, written by my grandmama's very own hand! I'd forgotten it was here!"

Wynona kept on trying to fit a piece of snow into the sky—or vice versa—and Lauralee didn't look up, so I was the only one left to answer. I smiled at Miss Cora, because what else could I do? She was gonna tell us that story anyway, whether we wanted to hear it or not. So she took my smile to be an invitation and started reading, but then she forgot to read and just told us the old story. Because she knew every story in that old book by heart. And so did we.

"It started with old Miss Liza, who was my great-great-grandmother on my mama's side, who was the only daughter of Hezekiah Longwood, you know. He was just a young man when he walked all the way up here from Savannah, after his papa threw him out of the house for 'carousing'—might have had something to do with a woman, you know.

"But it was a fine morning when he got this far, and that after he'd spent most of two days wading through that bog to the south, through tangled vines and black mud, so he was all covered in sweat and mud and tears; and he never could see where his feet were going, so he was just solid goosebumps and thinking he saw scaly things and feeling hot-needle fangs stinging his ankles.

"He was so worn-out, he just couldn't go any farther. So he slept in the bushes right beside the creek for a while and then got himself cleaned up as best he could—took a bath in the creek and tried to clean his clothes. Then he walked on until he came to town and got himself a job at the sawmill. Let on that he didn't have any money, and that's how he got to sleep in a storeroom and fatten himself up on the good food the other millworkers' wives sent to him because they felt so sorry for him.

"That old Hezekiah! He was sure enough fooling folks, because he turned right around in only a few months and paid cash for some good land that bordered on that very creek he'd rested beside. Bought it with money most folks said he stole from his papa and some he'd been able to save from the sawmill, what with sleeping in the storeroom and letting everybody else feed him. Then he built himself a right good house, worked hard at the sawmill, and even joined the church—which is where he met his future bride, Eliza Bixley.

"But only a year after their nuptials, she died in childbirth, leaving him a baby daughter to raise. Eliza's brother took the baby to his own wife, who'd just had an infant girl herself a few weeks before and could feed it, you see. And those two newborn little girls were to be the last of the old and honored Bixley line—almost.

"Sad to say that Hezekiah turned his back on his daughter and on the church. Turned out to be the coldest papa and the biggest backslider anybody ever heard of—and I'm sure sorry to have to say that about somebody who's our own kinfolk, but it's the truth.

"By the time that little baby was old enough to go back to Hezekiah, he'd taken up company with some trashy woman and was living with her openly and . . ."—Miss Cora lowered her voice, as she always did when she came to that part of the story—". . . without benefit of clergy! Well, when Eliza's brother heard about it, he said he'd not see that innocent little girl raised by a *harlot,* so he went to court and adopted her himself, and Hezekiah never said a word about it."

Here, Miss Cora heaved a deep sigh and ran her hand across the page before her. I guess it was her way of maybe stopping for a little minute to breathe a silent prayer for the saving of his soul.

Then she heaved her shoulders up and went on with her story: "In fact, no one ever heard anything from him—until forty years later, when he died and left sixty-seven acres of his land, bordered on the south by Brushy Creek, to his daughter, Eliza Rose Longwood. She'd been named after her sweet mama, you see, and of course, Hezekiah didn't know her name had been changed to Bixley when she was adopted, but the judge soon worked out the legal kinks, and Miss Liza, who was already a matron of over forty and a spinster as well, attracted—because of her sudden land-wealth, most folks said—a husband, one Thomas Jehosophat Thompson, an old widower with four grown sons.

"So Miss Liza and old Mr. Thomas and his sons and their wives—and two of those wives already in a family way—moved to the land, built a big old rambling house, and started clearing and plowing and planting the land.

"When the first Thompson grandson was born on Miss Liza's land, he was baptized Adam Jerome *Bixley,* and that was when folks began to figure out why Miss Liza married an old man who had nothing to offer her except mighty prolific sons. She was out to preserve the Bixley name, and she sure did that. Of all the male children born on her land, the first and every other one after that was to have the surname of Bixley, and all that weren't Bixleys got to stay Thompsons. To help Miss Liza keep them straight, all the Bixleys had first names from the Old Testament and the Thompsons from the New.

"There were sure plenty of babies—one every six months or so, among the four sons and their wives: Adam Bixley, Paul Thompson, Elijah Bixley, Andrew Thompson, Abel Bixley, Matthew Thompson, and Enoch Bixley, and a lot of others whose names I don't remember hearing about. Once in a while, of course, there came along a Martha, Elizabeth, or Sarah, but the girls were all Thompsons—because they couldn't carry on a name anyway, even though Miss Liza found a way. She sure did!

"Then one spring, twin boys were born, but their mama had to have a midwife, who said she'd been so busy getting those babies born, she couldn't for the life of her remember which one came first. But one of the babies had a little bit of red hair, and that reminded Miss Liza of her dear departed mama—the way she had been described to her, you see—and so she said he would be the Bixley. At the same time, she was feeling real pleased by the big, noisy family all around her and contented and very well-fed too, from the good land her papa had left to her, and she was ever so happy about those twin boys—like getting two for the price of one, she said. The Thompson baby was named Mark, but she named the Bixley baby Isaiah Longwood Bixley. To be called Longwood, for the daddy she never even knew.

"Now the Longwoods—and actually, they weren't really Longwoods, not church-blessed, that is, but they thought of themselves that way—all that time had gotten along quite well themselves, five of Hezekiah's born-on-the-wrong-side-of-the-blanket sons staying on those remaining two hundred acres of good rich land and marrying and starting families of their own. But they were sure mad about their papa leaving all that good land to Miss Liza, and it bordering on the creek. So when they heard about her naming that baby Longwood Bixley, they turned right around and named their next male child Bixley Longwood—to be called Bixley for his given name.

"Because they said, 'If she kin use our name, we kin use hers'n.'

"But it was strange how it all turned out. The War, you know, and so many boys never coming back. Not Longwood Bixley or Bixley Longwood. Maybe that's why somebody or other started telling a story about how those two young men got their names because their families loved each other so much, and then everybody started believing it, so it got to be the truth.

"But what I started out to say is this: They both died at Bull Run, and only one of them got brought back home—Bixley Longwood or Longwood Bixley—I don't know which. And the stonecutter got the name wrong, so that if it was Longwood Bixley who got buried at home, he carved it Bixley Longwood.

"Or vice versa."

Wynona was looking at me, with that little puzzle piece still suspended, and I was looking back at her, because we both knew what was coming next, Heaven help us!

"Then somebody or other, a Longwood or a Bixley, tried to chisel a comma in the stone between the names, to get things right before everybody was gone who knew how it was really supposed to be, and he hit the chisel with one light tap, and that whole stone just shattered to pieces. Nobody ever did get around to having another one made, maybe because both families wanted to think it was their boy had gotten brought home.

"And now, no one remembers. Not even me. And no one knows where that grave is anymore. Not even me."

Wynona and I sighed almost in unison, and Miss Cora smiled at us as if in appreciation of what she took to be our expressions of sympathy. Then she heaved a deeper sigh than either of us and said, "Now listen—I want to go back down to the cemetery and look for it again. Just as soon as the weather warms up a bit. Now don't you let me forget it, you hear?"

She cast a pretty vicious glance at me and Wynona, because she knew good and well how we dreaded taking her down to the cemetery. Seems like all that ever happened was her getting upset, and she never could find that old grave anyway.

"Because," Miss Cora went on, like she was thinking up a way to butt heads with us, "there's just nothing in the world as sad as a grave everybody's forgotten about, and him our very own kin! I know I can still find it, unless more trees have fallen, for I remember it was near two big cedar trees that stood at the end of the stone wall of the old slave cemetery. And when we find it, we'll order a brand-new stone and have it carved right.

"Just as soon as I can rightly remember which way the name is supposed to be."

"Yes'm," Wynona and I both said at the same time, and Lauralee looked up, a little surprised at how we'd chimed in together and almost smiled before she went back to her crocheting.

So from something as bothersome to me and Wynona as Miss Cora's wanting to go back down to that old cemetery, we all smiled that winter afternoon, and that certainly made it something special.

Within minutes, of course, we had all gone back to what we were doing. Miss Cora was writing something or other in the Family Book, maybe even something about Lauralee almost smiling; Wynona was back at her puzzle, but her shoulders looked a little more relaxed, and instead of muttering under her breath, she was humming some little tune without even knowing it.

And I went back to my tatting, like there wasn't a thing in this world going through my mind except that silver shuttle and the thread between my fingers.

Truth of the matter was, though, that little moment we'd passed together with Lauralee was so sweet, it set me to thinking back on how good things had been for us those long years ago:

Because that first summer they came, Wynona was at that awkward stage all girls go through, with legs as long as a colt's and knees grimy and hands rough. And Lauralee just as pretty as a teacup. A mighty big change they had when they came here, especially that first summer, because at home, their papa worked them just like they were boys, chopping cotton and carrying firewood and shelling tough old dried corn for feeding the chickens, and helping Miss Emma in the house, too—scrubbing floors on their hands and knees and using lye soap to do it with. Yes, and Lauralee learned to do it all, and her hardly more than a baby.

And when harvest time came, they had to help in the fields again as well.

But soon as Miss Anne—God rest her soul!—got her way and brought them here to this house that first summer, she and the aunts scurried around and bathed those little girls with sweet-smelling soap and shampooed their hair and got out all the snarls and put it up in rags, for making curls. And they dressed Wynona and Lauralee in those pretty white frocks with tucks and little pearl buttons down the front.

I was Wynona's exact age of course and old enough to know I better stay out of the way until all the flurry died down a bit. But watching what all went on, I was thinking maybe those two little girls just went from one kind of hard work to another, what with the way they had to learn how to sit still and be quiet and have good manners. Be proper young ladies, you see.

But after the first few days, things eased off a bit, and Wynona and Lauralee got to come to the kitchen, where my mama was fixing dinner, and we sat around the kitchen table together—Wynona, Lauralee, and me—and Mama told us stories and taught us songs to sing while she worked.

And right from the first time they came into the kitchen, and we did all that laughing at Mama's stories and all that good singing too, we were never, ever timid around each other.

We played and played and had the very best time. And Miss Anne took it in her mind that Wynona and Lauralee needed dancing lessons—to help improve their posture and teach them how to be graceful, she said—and when they'd come back from their lessons, we'd go out on the back porch so Wynona could teach me the steps they'd just learned and help Lauralee practice them too.

Of course, I sure didn't have me any little pink satin slippers or stretchy kinds of dancing suits like they did, but I didn't care. I got to where I could point my toes inside my old sandals right well and make a proper curtsey when I finished doing one of those fast, twirl-around steps I liked so much.

Other times, we played Mama and babies, and sometimes I got to be the mama and Lauralee was my baby and Wynona my other little girl. And then sometimes I'd be the other little girl and Wynona would be the mama to me and Lauralee.

We played school too, but Wynona always got to be the teacher. I never did get me a single turn at that. But Wynona was sweet and patient when I got stuck on adding numbers and Lauralee got her letters crooked and outside the lines. Still, she was downright determined we'd learn our lessons, and learn is what we had to do! But it was always fun.

Whenever Miss Anne took Wynona and Lauralee to the library, they sneaked their books to me, so I could read them too. Because back then, the black folks had their own library, and it was too far away for me and Mama to walk. But Mama had already taught me to read, using the good old King James Bible. Gave me such a love for words!

There were other things Wynona and Lauralee and I had to learn that didn't make much sense to us. But we had to learn them anyway.

How, when it was almost time for dinner, Miss Cora would take Wynona and Lauralee into the bedroom and bathe their faces and hands, brush their hair, put them in dresses freshly ironed by my mama, and take them into the dining room.

But I stayed in the kitchen, because that's where I was supposed to stay.

Sometimes, Mama let me carry the big bowl heaped with her good potato salad into the dining room, where Miss Anne and the aunts and Miss Cora and Wynona and Lauralee were sitting silently at the big mahogany table, waiting for their dinner to be served.

Such careful steps I took, just like I was walking on eggs; and I'd be so proud when I got that big old bowl all the way to the table without dropping it and put it on the snowy white tablecloth in the room where those heavy drapes were shut against the summer sun, so that it was always cool even in the hottest part of the summer, and quiet too, in a very special kind of way.

I didn't look at Wynona or Lauralee, because we'd been friends and playmates until only a few minutes before dinner, and it was hard on us when things changed so fast. But we knew they'd change right back, soon as dinner was done.

But we couldn't look at each other, not in the dining room, because we always wanted to giggle. And Miss Anne wouldn't allow that! She said it was fine for us children to play together in the kitchen or on the back porch, but when it came to the dining room, that was another thing.

One time I heard her telling Mama to make sure I "remembered my place." That meant no giggling, and more than that too, but I was too young to know much about it.

Once in a while, when I brought in the potato salad, Miss Anne would say, "Why, little Pet! Has your mama made potato salad again?" And she'd say "again" so that it rhymed with "rain" and wrinkle up her nose like maybe the potato salad didn't smell quite right.

I smiled when she did that, because I knew they wouldn't eat much of it, and I could have all I wanted after the table was cleared and the bowl came back to the kitchen.

"And, little Pet," Miss Anne would say. "Tell your mama I said you're to wear a clean apron when you come into the dining room. Can you remember that?"

"Yes'm, I can remember that."

Because it's the most important thing in the world for us to remember. Why, if we forget, we lose things forever, and then no matter what window we ever look out of, it's always gonna be a gray, rainy day. So I know how to remember.

But I know how to keep quiet too. I learned that when I was a little girl. Because being quiet is what got me plenty of potato salad.

So that even years later, during that long winter when we sat together in the dining room, I knew those long-ago summers were still hanging in the air somewhere. Because you don't lose things like that. The years come and go in this house, each with its own sounds and smells, but sooner or later they all get mixed in with each other, just the way Wynona and Lauralee and I got made into one something. That's what I was thinking about during that long, cold winter—a winter we thought would never end.

But it did, and in a way we sure didn't want.

Because Miss Addie got awful sick again, and the doctor told Thompson she'd probably had another little stroke and just to keep her warm and quiet. Every morning, Wynona or I would stay with her, until Minnie Louise got done at Miss Delia's, and then she would come and stay until Thompson and Maude got there for the evening. And Miss Addie never even opened her eyes. Sometimes, we'd get her to take a little sip of hot tea, and she was always good about letting us give her the medicine she needed, but other than that, she just slept. Even Minnie Louise couldn't get her to eat more than a little bite or two, no matter what kinds of wonderful things she said were in the spoon.

Then one evening Thompson came to our door.

"Come on in the dining room, Thompson," Miss Cora invited. "It's too cold in this old hall."

"No, ma'am; thank you, though. I've got to get on back and see to Mama, but I was wondering if maybe you all could please spare Pet to come over and stay with her tonight, so's me and Maude could go home and get some rest."

I was in the dining room, but I heard what he said, so I went into the kitchen and put on a clean apron and then went out into the hall.

Miss Cora looked at me. "Well, I guess it's all right with you, Pet, so it might as well be all right with us too. Tell Addie we hope she feels better, and you be sure to call us if you need us during the night."

"Thank you, Miss Cora," Thompson said. "And thank you too, Pet."

The very minute I saw Miss Addie that evening, I knew she was very close to passing over, and when that great miracle finally happened, I was right there with her, holding her hand.

I never tried to tell how it happened, because nobody would have understood.

"Lord, have mercy! Pet's having another spell!" That's what Miss Cora would have said, and Wynona would look at me in that stone-cold stare of hers, and I'd be able to see all those worried little bird-thoughts flying around behind her eyes.

So I never tried to tell them how, right before dawn, Miss Addie waked up because she heard something.

"Addie? Baby?"

I sat real still, waiting and listening to a far-away-sounding laugh that got louder until I was sure it was right there in the room with us. Then it faded away, and nothing was left but me and Miss Addie and the whirring sound from Miss Addie's grandmama's mantel clock just before it struck the quarter-hour.

Me sitting and listening while those old brass hammers pounded on my eardrums.

"Addie? Baby?"

"What?" I watched Miss Addie rise up out of her warm sleep and turn her face to the window.

"Addie?"

"WHAT!" she yelled, fussing like the dickens, the way she did years ago when Thompson was a little boy and went through a stage where all he did was chant, "Mama! Mama! Mama!" in that high-pitched voice of his. All the time and at the very top of his lungs.

I thought that was right funny, how vexed she sounded about it.

And I guess there's nothing in this whole world as beautiful as folks who're getting ready to cross over. Miss Addie was so close that the least little breeze could have lifted her up and sailed her right out the window, and she'd just fly away, and that worn-out body she didn't need no more would float down right into the dwarf azalea bushes, like a spiderweb you can't see unless it's real early in the morning and there's still dew caught in it.

So I wasn't worried one bit about Miss Addie, because I knew what kind of a treat she was in for. I'd seen Death before, and I already knew how beautiful he can be.

Because when I was just a little thing, I was sitting out on the back steps eating a biscuit when Death came for my grandmama. And in the blink of an eye, the light went all funny, like a cloud passing in front of the sun, making the shade into something that doesn't seem real anymore, and right then I saw a coal-black horse with big wings and just as silent as a ghost come out from behind the carriage house at a full gallop. Foam streaming out of his mouth and blood glowing in his nostrils.

51

Just like a stone, I sat there. Couldn't have moved a muscle to save my life. He rushed past me, and his wings were bigger than a barn, and they touched me and felt just like the lightest downy feather you could ever imagine! Along the side of the house, he galloped, right to my grand-mama's window, and he stopped so fast that sparks flew up from his hooves.

Me still sitting there, holding my biscuit and watching while my grand-mama climbed out the window and onto his back. Seeing his dark neck and his blood-red breath and Grandmama's white nightgown flowing out just like the veil on a bride. Her holding tight to his mane and laugh-ing up a storm, and when they swept past me, she looked back at me and blew me a kiss.

But when Death came for Miss Addie, he wasn't a horse at all, but her very own papa, who walked along right down the mid-dle of the street, whistling a tune and stopping in front of her house and calling, "Addie? Papa's here."

So I just sat there and watched Miss Addie, where she was lying in that *big high bed her papa made for her mama—with his own hands—as a wedding present. The same bed where they spent their wed-ding night and where Miss Addie was born all those years ago. And where Miss Addie spent her wedding night when she and her sweet husband came together for the first time in that special way God made for hus-bands and wives.*

Miss Addie so lovely-looking, wearing that hand-embroidered, white nightdress her grandmama made of the very softest batiste anyone had ever seen.

The nightdress Miss Addie later wrapped in tissue paper and put away in the bottom drawer of the dresser. Because it was a long, long night of tender shame and innocent shock, even just her knowing the warmth of his skin.

The same bed where Thompson was born that terrible and wonder-ful Sunday morning when Miss Addie could hear church bells ringing, and she thought for sure she'd already died, and her screams were the bells, louder and louder, until one final iron-on-iron screaming and scraping no one could hear but her, and the last push against that old bell-wheel that turned and tore with every stroke. And Addie's feet, just like her mama's feet, against the footboard, sliding around in sweat until she felt

a vacuum somewhere near her heart and a wetness and then her hear-
ing the baby's first cry, something more beautiful than all the bells in the
whole world! And that tiny baby so warm and slippery against her.

The same bed where she would pass away at last, after all the good
things that can happen to us and the bad things as well—every single thing
that being alive brings to us—if we're lucky.

So here it was then.

And I sat right there and held her hand until at last she pulled it away,
ever so easy, and she reached out and took her own papa's hand and
walked away with him, just as that new day's dawn got itself untangled
from the branches of that big pecan tree in her front yard.

The last thing I did in those solemn moments was tell Miss
Addie I wouldn't forget what I'd promised her, and I decided
right then and there I just wouldn't think about what was going
to happen when I made Miss Cora remember everything. I had
to trust Miss Addie for knowing what was best.

So I thanked her again, one last time for what she'd done for
me that long-ago day—oh, that terrible, terrible day!—when she
held me in her arms right in front of God and everybody. A day
when I needed somebody to hold me, sure enough, and she said
I mustn't blame myself—looked me right in the eyes and said
it wasn't my fault, and she's the only one ever figured out how
hard I'd been blaming myself.

So I thanked her for that. But it wasn't something I could have
said to her before.

Afterwards, I called up Thompson on the phone and told him
to come, and when he got there, he was as white as a sheet and
with his eyes all red around the rims, wide and unbelieving, like
it couldn't really be true.

Maude stood on the porch, wringing her hands and with her
hair all done up in fat, pink rollers and her dress on wrong-side-
out. Thompson stared at me for only a moment before he rushed
past me, running up the stairs two at a time, just like—if he hurried—he'd find his mama still there to smile at him.

I walked back across the street in that pretty pearl-gray light
of morning, across grass wet with dew, so that it darkened the
toes of my shoes and started me in to wondering, as I always
wondered—just where does it come from? Dew, I mean. And

where does it go, after the sun gets everything warmed up and dried off? Maybe up into the clouds to be held onto for dropping onto the grass another morning? Maybe even falling into Brushy Creek where it runs through town right behind Bill's Dollar Store and washing on down under the bridge at Old Quaker Road and in and around all the curves between the fields and under shady places where the trees grow tall? And past the cemetery where that old grave is just sitting there somewhere or other, waiting for Miss Cora to find it?

I came up the front porch steps and sat down in the nearest chair—Miss Cora's chair—and stayed there for the longest kind of time, just me and that chilly, brand-new day together there, and the light on Miss Addie's porch still burning and glowing in the morning light, like a brooch on the front of a lady's dress.

After a while, Miss Cora came out to the porch, wearing her nightgown and bedroom slippers but with a coat thrown over her shoulders and her hair in a thin, stiff, little braid over her shoulder. She didn't say a thing about me sitting in her very own chair but sat down in Wynona's chair right beside me.

"She's . . . *gone* . . . isn't she?"

"Yes'm."

"When?"

"About an hour ago. It was a peaceful going she had."

Miss Cora sat there, looking for all the world like a little girl sitting in a chair that was too big for her and with her toes not even touching the floor, and for some reason, I was remembering the first time I fixed her hair for her, *when I was just a little thing. Fixed it for her just the way my mama showed me how to do. And being in that bedroom where there were bees humming in the bushes just on the other side of the screen and that sweetest smell of tea olive coming in on a breeze that pushed the curtains out into the room like white arms. Some old dog barking far off and sunlight coming across the floor and touching the edge of Miss Cora's robe. And that thick braid of her shining, chestnut hair so heavy in my hand and the clean-warm smell of it.*

Wishing I could put my arms around her and comfort her now, but knowing she wouldn't allow it.

So instead, I said, "After a while, I'm going back over, to get that pretty white nightdress and fix it up so Thompson can take it to the funeral parlor for her."

"Nightdress?" Miss Cora asked.

"The one she wore on her wedding night. The one her grand-mama made her."

"I never knew anything about that," Miss Cora said, staring at me for a long time before she added, "Maybe it's all been too much for you. You're probably just having one of your little spells."

Then she didn't say anything else, and neither did I.

*S*uch a long, sad morning that was. Wynona tried to make sure Miss Cora and Lauralee stayed in the kitchen at the back of the house until Mr. Grower from the funeral parlor could come and get Miss Addie. No need in them having to see that awful, black hearse—especially Lauralee.

But I watched through the curtains when that terrible old hearse pulled into Miss Addie's driveway and Thompson came out onto the porch, with his mouth hanging open, like he never dreamed in all his born days he'd see that thing coming to get his very own mama. A few minutes later, I watched that long, black car leave, carrying its precious burden, and then Thompson and Maude left too.

That's when I went back over to Miss Addie's to get me that nightgown so I could fix it up for her just right. I felt so strange, going into that silent house; and to save my life, I couldn't go up the stairs without announcing myself, though I knew there wasn't a living soul up there.

"It's Pet here," I called out, making goosebumps come up on my arms; and I really thought I'd hear Miss Addie call back to me, "Ye-es?"—like she always did.

But like I said, it was a silent house.

When I got upstairs, the door to Miss Addie's room was closed, and I started to knock on it but stopped myself, took a deep breath, and turned the doorknob. That heavy old door swung open all by itself, creaking a little on its hinges, and I was right back in Miss Addie's room, where I'd been such a short time before. But, oh, how different it all was.

And maybe I'd been able to keep myself from knocking on the door, but I sure couldn't keep myself from going on tiptoe all the way across the room to Miss Addie's dresser. I eased open the top drawer. Gloves in all different lengths, a little pair of gold-framed glasses, and a small, tasteful bunch of silk violets for pinning on the front of a summer dress.

"I'm sorry, Miss Addie, to be going through your things," I whispered, closing the drawer. "But I mean to find that night-dress and fix it up just right for you."

Opened the next drawer. Cotton stockings, tatted-edged pil-lowcases I'd given her for Christmas, and a scattering of yel-lowed calling cards, each with "Mrs. William James Barker (Addie Thompson Barker), Hairdressing" written on them in old ink that was turning brown. No nightdress.

I opened the third drawer, and there was something wrapped in smooth, old tissue paper, and I picked it up almost reverently and opened it. Yes, I'd found it, and when I touched it, the lace was warm against my fingers. I wrapped it back up and placed it on top of the dresser, and then I stripped the bed and put fresh, crisp linens on it, so everything would be ready when Mr. Grower brought her back home for the lying-in. Because that's the way it was still done in our little town, bringing folks back to their own beds so family and friends could say good-bye under the same roof where so many of the memories were made.

I took the gown and went downstairs, but before I left Miss Addie's house, I cleaned out the fireplace, dusted the living room furniture, ran the sweeper over the rugs, and washed up the few dishes that were in the kitchen sink. Because Thompson and Maude hadn't done a very good job of keeping things nice, and neither had Minnie Louise. But I couldn't fault her; she'd spent all her time just trying to get Miss Addie to eat something.

Well, at least I felt better that day, having done a last some-thing for Miss Addie. Besides what I had promised her, that is. And, goodness knows, straightening up her house and fixing up the nightdress were a whole lot easier to do than what I had waiting ahead of me.

I washed, dried, and ironed the nightgown in my own room, so nobody would have to watch me taking care of that, and for the rest of the day, we pretty much tried to go about doing the same things we always did. But it was hard going. Every once in a while, Miss Cora sighed and shook her head. I guess maybe she was trying to convince herself that Miss Addie was really gone.

And me, I just moved about in that big old house like I've always done, doing up the breakfast dishes and making the beds and using some red oil to polish the dining table. But no matter what kind of usual things I did, I couldn't get away from what I knew—that nothing was ever gonna be the same.

But I argued with myself about that. Because everything . . . and I do mean everything on this earth . . . has to end sometime or other.

Even all those good, long-ago summers when Wynona and Lauralee were with us.

Summer after summer went by; we got a bit more grown-up and weren't content with playing Mama and babies or school anymore. So we used to spend rainy afternoons in the bedroom, with pictures from movie magazines spread out and trying to make Wynona's hair look like a movie star's. But it was hard, because her hair was so fine and sort of had a mind of its own too, about which way it wanted to be fixed. Lauralee would watch us doing Wynona's hair, and then, sooner or later, she would just ease in and sit beside Wynona on the bench in front of the mirror, and then we would both get to fixing Lauralee's hair, because it had some curl to it, and we could make it into long ringlets just by brushing it around our fingers. That's how we were here together every long, hot, and endless day in this good house, living our lives together in rooms with high ceilings and wallpaper with faded roses as big as cabbages on it.

And something or other happened to us over those summers. Maybe for Wynona and Lauralee, it was learning what it was like to be loved the way children are supposed to be loved. Because whatever those girls did or said, there was always Miss Anne or one of the aunts or Miss Cora to smile and look at them like their eyes could never get enough of seeing them. Not so much for Wynona, maybe, as for Lauralee, but that never caused any trouble between them. If somebody had ever come right on out and said that Lauralee was nice to look at, Wynona would have agreed with them. But that's how they came to know who they were and how they fit into this world.

Like how when Lauralee was around eight, they were all at the dinner table one evening and one of the aunts looked at Lauralee and said, "You know, Anne, I believe you're right about her having the Bixley chin. For just now, the way the light was on her face, Lauralee's chin was so much like my own grandmama's, it just gave me goosebumps to see it. Goose-bumps, I tell you!"

They all stopped and looked at Lauralee's chin, and Lauralee stopped too and turned red under their gazes.

"Yes," Miss Anne said. "I was absolutely right about it. She certainly has the Bixley chin."

Later, when I was helping Mama clear the table, I saw Lauralee looking at herself in the long, narrow mirror on the back of the buffet, turning her head this way and that way and studying her chin from all angles, as if she'd never seen it before.

"What does it mean, Pet? And why does it matter?" she asked me.

"Well, it's who you are, that's all."

I knew about things like that from my mama, because of my name being the same as her grandmama's. Because Mama said the minute I was born, she could tell I was the spitting image of her grandmama. So my name was her name, and somehow or other that I could never explain but that I've always known, is that I'm a part of her. That's how come I knew what it meant about the Bixley chin. But it isn't anything you can really say. Even when your mama whispers it in your ear.

But Lauralee must have felt it, even if she didn't understand, because she took to stroking her chin with one finger, even when she didn't know she was doing it. That's her habit to this very day, and I guess the thing we couldn't say then—and we can't say even now—is that you're always stamped with something from your ancestors, even if you don't know what it is. Something that goes back further than you and that's going to go forward further than you. All of a piece, you see.

And what happened to me was that I loved them both with all my heart, and I used to pretend that they were my honest-to-goodness sisters. Family. That's what we were, all of us.

Well, those good summers kept on coming and going, and I guess no one thought much about Wynona getting to be a young lady. Of course, Miss Anne and the aunts tried once or twice to introduce her to other young people in town, but it didn't work, because too many folks could never understand why somebody like Miss Emma ran off and married a dirt farmer like Mr. Sam. So the mamas of all the other young folks said there must be a wild streak in the family. They were scared of that, sure enough.

Then, when Wynona and I were around fifteen, she didn't come during the summers anymore. Said her mama needed her too much at home. Lauralee came once by herself, but after that, we couldn't get her to come, not without Wynona.

So it was all over too fast, those summers we spent together. But I haven't ever forgotten them, and I know Wynona and Lauralee haven't forgotten either. Even though they don't know that. Because if it hadn't been for those summers we spent together here in this house, I truly believe they couldn't ever have survived what came to them later. They would never have known—ever!—that they deserved something better than what Wynona's husband gave them. I wouldn't either, and that's what made all the difference.

So even if the summers were gone forever, all the good things we got from them never went away.

I needed to think that way about Miss Addie. Because what she'd done for me was gonna stay with me to my dying day.

I made us an extra good dinner at noon, trying to cheer everybody up a bit—salmon croquettes, steamed rice, fried okra, and even some deviled eggs, like Miss Cora said she'd been wanting. But none of us was very hungry.

We were sitting at the table, kind of picking away at our dinner when Miss Cora spoke up, right out of the blue, and we all jumped at the sound of her voice. But I was happy to have somebody saying something—anything—because that silence was so sad.

"Addie always did have a weak heart, you know," Miss Cora said.

Of course, we did know, and we knew what story was coming, and oh, what a comfort to hear it again!

"Her widowed so young," Miss Cora went on. "And right when she was expecting Thompson. Why, all she had left in the whole world was that baby coming and the big house her papa left to her. She decided right off she wasn't going to lose that house, no matter what, so she had to find a way to make a living. Because there was no money, you see."

We saw. We had always seen.

"After Thompson came, Addie learned how to cut hair and put in permanents, and that's how she kept the house. But she was always delicate after that, because of all those things that happened to her when she was too young for them. But Addie was a Thompson by blood, and everybody knows that Thompsons will never give up. That's why she gave Thompson her maiden name as his Christian name. Because she wanted him to know who he was.

"So once Addie got everything set up for her hairdressing business, she took some of her mama's lovely engraved calling cards out of the desk, and on the backs of them she wrote, 'Mrs. William James Barker,' and in parentheses, 'Addie Thompson Barker—Hairdressing.' The next Sunday afternoon, she strolled up and down the street, pushing Thompson in his buggy and stopping to visit at each and every house, and when she was ready to leave, she slipped one of those cards onto the table beside the pitcher of iced tea or lemonade and never said a thing—just lifted Thompson's hand out of his covers and made it seem like he was waving good-bye.

"After she'd gone, those good folks—most of them old friends of Addie's mama—were gladdened to see the old, familiar name on the card. Then they turned it over and saw the handwritten message on the back and knew that Addie was going to do right by the house her papa left her and by Thompson as well.

"So all the ladies in town started going to Addie for having their hair done—to help her out, you see. But it was so hard for them to have Addie's aristocratic fingers working the perfumed lather into their hair. They almost died from the embarrassment of it—what with her being such a lady and all. But it was the only way they could help her keep her dignity and her house and provide for her son—her mama's grandson."

Miss Cora paused, and we didn't say anything, because we knew that story wasn't over yet. And what with Miss Addie being gone now, it was so good to hear Miss Cora telling us her story. Again. Made it almost seem like she wasn't gone after all.

"Over the years, when the older ladies—the ones who'd known Addie's mama—passed on one by one, their daughters kept going to Addie, because it was a tradition for them, and that's something you can't change. When the young ones sat under the dryer, they knew that their own mamas had sat there as well, and maybe it was more than that. Because even though you could always smell that strong lotion Addie used when she gave permanents to folks, there were always other aromas in that house that nothing could cover up—old wood and beeswax polish and that kind of familiar perfume grand, old houses always have about them. Dusting powder and silk fans and rugs that have been walked on for a hundred years. That sort of thing.

"Sometimes, Addie needed a little extra cash, when taxes went up or the roof needed fixing—such as that. So she sold off some of her mama's furniture. In the late 1950s and the early '60s, there were a lot of rich folks from Atlanta had a fashion of driving out into small towns on the weekends, looking for antiques they could buy real cheap. Of course, those people weren't really Atlantans, or even Georgians at all. Mostly, they were from up north and just trying to make their big, new houses in Atlanta look as if their families had lived there for generations and actually had that kind of furniture to leave to them.

"The bad thing about that kind of pretending is when the ones doing it really begin believing the furniture was left to them, and no one is there to say any different. Not unless those same folks could invent some ancestors for themselves—and all the stories they would have told.

"So Addie, who really had ancestors and who was a grand lady, sold her mama's rosewood chairs to Yankee women to sit on while they poured tea for their other Yankee women friends in those tacky, big houses in Atlanta."

Miss Cora paused and sighed deeply. Wynona and I sighed as well, in sweet, deep contentment at hearing Miss Addie's story again. But then, Miss Cora added more, and I wasn't expecting that.

"It's what I've had on my mind this whole morning long. How Addie did what she had to do to get along in the world and never complained. Not once. That, and the first Christmas after Thompson was born, because he was so beautiful, and she was so proud of him. Goodness knows, she'd been through a lot and still had more to get through, but the most important thing in the whole world was right there in that little baby. He was one thing she could understand—because he had Addie's pretty blue eyes and Addie's mama's forehead and Addie's papa's chin, and he was going to last.

"That's all that matters, you know. The ones we leave behind us, so it all keeps going on and on, after us."

Lauralee, who'd been sitting quietly, with her hands around her cup, looked up at me when Miss Cora said that, and I almost saw something or other flicker in her eyes.

Oh, Lord! I prayed silently. *Please help me find a way to do what's gotta be done. And without hurting Wynona and Lauralee!*

Somehow, we made it through that whole long day, and I was so glad when it was time for us to go to bed. We needed darkness and quiet, and I needed to be alone with my thinking, the worst in the world.

In my own room, I hung up my apron and my dress and put my shoes in the bottom of the chifforobe, and just as I pulled my nightgown over my head, I thought I heard somebody say something, so I was prepared to hear that whispering, *Give me the baby!*

But even though I stood there listening for a long time, I didn't hear another thing, and I was grateful for that. So I got in bed, thinking of how we would have to get through Miss Addie's funeral in a couple of days and remembering my promise to her and thinking about what happened to Wynona—and to Lauralee—that finally led to everything we went through together.

Because Wynona was already in her late twenties when she finally had a suitor come calling on her, a Mr. Adkins, a widower who'd opened a hardware store and who was new in town. He was older—almost of an age with Mr. Sam, in fact, and one evening, he came driving up in Mr. Sam's

63

yard and got out and walked over to the front porch and stood there for a long time saying nothing.

Took him quite a while to get around to telling Mr. Sam why he'd come—he wanted to call on Wynona, and of course, he knew he had to ask Mr. Sam first.

Sure was a big surprise for Wynona, because she'd been in his store lots of times, buying lids for her canning jars or some nails for her papa; but in all that time, Mr. Adkins never said one single word to her.

Later, Wynona told me she was real mixed up about Mr. Adkins wanting to call on her, because she wasn't one bit unhappy with her life just the way it was. She liked waking up in the morning in the same room and with the window just starting to turn gray with the new light. And in spring, there were birds in the crepe myrtle tree right outside her window and an old rooster that stood on top of the chicken house, crowing to beat the band.

But still, Mr. Adkins' attention was flattering to her. And different.

The evening Mr. Adkins first came right out of the blue to talk with Mr. Sam, Wynona and Lauralee were in the bedroom, peeking through the door, listening to what Mr. Adkins and Mr. Sam were saying on the porch. That was when Wynona and Lauralee both remembered about how Mr. Adkins sometimes put sticks of peppermint candy in the sack with the new jar lids, though he said not a word at the time. When Wynona found the candy, she thought he meant it for Lauralee, who'd been standing at Wynona's elbow the whole time, wearing a light blue cotton dress that brought out the color of her eyes.

But of course, once Mr. Adkins came to call, Wynona knew it had been more than just an older man's kindness for a sweet, pretty, little girl, and that he meant it for Wynona all along.

I guess that was the only time in Wynona's whole life that somebody paid more attention to her than to Lauralee, but Wynona wouldn't have known that's how she felt. Maybe I'm wrong about that anyway. Wynona was always too sweet to be jealous of Lauralee. And besides, she loved her too much for anything like that.

So Wynona and Lauralee stood there at the bedroom door, hardly breathing as they tried to listen to every word, and then they scampered away when they heard the screen door open and their papa coming toward their room. Mr. Sam pushed the door open and looked in to where they were sitting on the edge of the bed, just as innocent as baby mockingbirds.

"Wynona, Mr. Adkins from town is here; he wants to know if you'll sit and talk with him a while. Says his wife's been gone a right long time, and he's lonely. I told him it's all right with me, if you're willing."

"Yes, Papa," Wynona answered in a whisper, because she'd never thought such a thing could happen, and she told me later that even a little chance that Mr. Adkins may have thought she was pretty just crossed out everything from her mind. When Mr. Sam closed the door again, those two girls stared at each other for a few seconds, and then they muffled their laughter and rolled around on the bed with their hands over their mouths, both of them maybe thinking of fat Mr. Adkins and his bald head and his round, red face. Miss Anne would have said it was shameless for them to behave that way, but then, they never really had a chance to play and get those kinds of things out of their systems, so maybe they did act just a bit silly.

Anyway, they finally stopped giggling, and they rushed around, brushing Wynona's hair until it was shining, and looking for a scarf to pin inside the collar of her Sunday dress and pinching her cheeks to put some color in them and smoothing her eyebrows with their fingers. And then Wynona went out to the porch and sat in the swing with Mr. Adkins for nearly an hour.

That was the first of lots of visits by Mr. Adkins, and he always brought a present—a little brown bag filled with hard candies from the big glass jars in his store or a bouquet of flowers from his garden or a package of handkerchiefs. Once, he even brought a box of chocolates that were all wrapped in silver and red foil and were so beautiful to look at and smell, Wynona and Lauralee could hardly stand to eat a single piece. And after every visit from Mr. Adkins, Wynona came back inside the house and went straight to the bedroom and showed Lauralee whatever gift he'd brought and told her every single thing he said.

They thought it was so sad that his wife died and left him all alone and him such a kindly man and so generous with gifts, and one night Wynona told Lauralee she thought Mr. Adkins was close to asking her to marry him. So the next time he came, they fixed up a plan where Lauralee would slip out the back door and tiptoe along the side of the house and hide in the bushes near the porch so she could hear Mr. Adkins' proposal, if he made one. Or at least, so she could hear for herself all the pretty words he said to Wynona.

But when a sputtering Mr. Adkins suddenly lurched out of the swing and fell on his knees in front of Wynona, it was so startling, both for

Wynona, who could see it, and for Lauralee, who could only imagine what was going on, it was more than either one of them could stand.

But I'll say this much to Wynona's credit: She struggled hard to keep her face straight, even though she was looking at the fat, red face looking up at her from the level of her knees, and maybe she could have controlled herself if she hadn't, right at that very minute, heard a strangled giggle coming from Lauralee in the bushes at the end of the porch. So Wynona started smiling and smiling, and then her lips couldn't stay closed over her teeth, and she started grinning and she couldn't stop to save her life! All that time, Mr. Adkins must have taken her grinning to mean that she was so happy about it all.

But there was a terrible, terrible snicker caught in her throat, and finally, it escaped, and there wasn't a blessed thing she could do about it. She just laughed and laughed—couldn't help it one little bit. By the time she could finally wipe her eyes and get a hold of herself, Mr. Adkins was gone, and she didn't even remember seeing him leave.

Of course, she knew right away what a mean and cruel thing she'd done, but she hadn't done it on purpose. So the next day, Wynona went to town to Mr. Adkins' store and made her apology. She told me later that's when she said she'd marry him, and her words were as much of a surprise to her as they were to him, for they seemed to just fall out of her mouth before she even knew that they were there. Seemed like it was something she had to do. To make up for her awful bad manners.

But even though Mr. Adkins said he forgave her, I guess he always carried it around with him. Because from that very day, there was something cold about him. Of course, that was only a few weeks before he got into kind of a fever about religion and went all brimstone-hot about it. After that, it seems to me he just got meaner and meaner for the rest of his life.

And I wish I'd known what was coming for Wynona. And for Lauralee. So maybe I could have saved them. And me as well.

On the evening before Miss Addie's funeral, we peeked through the curtains as car after car came along ever so slowly and quietly and parked along the side of the street. The men got out, hitched up their pants, and opened car doors for the ladies, who all carried bowls of salad, or cakes or pies, or platters of fried chicken, and then they moved almost on tiptoe across Miss Addie's yard on a little path of light that came from the front porch. Almost every one of them glanced up, as if they thought Miss Addie would be there, waving and welcoming them, just like always. We understood that feeling, sure enough, because the whole evening, we'd halfway expected to see her come out on the porch for a little minute and wave at us. But that hadn't happened in a long time—not since she'd taken sick. And now, it wasn't ever going to happen again.

We'd gone over earlier, to take a high, white coconut cake I'd made just like my mama used to make and put it on the table and climb those wide, curving stairs, following Thompson up to the quiet room and that high bed where Miss Addie was lying so peaceful-like, wearing that beautiful old gown I'd hand-washed and dried and ironed so carefully. The lace at the neck touched one strand of Miss Addie's hair, and her hands were folded, quiet and pure.

I thought it wanted for words the worst in the world, but I didn't know any to say it with, so I just stood close to Miss Cora, and we whispered about how peaceful Miss Addie looked. Like she was having a good nap. Then we came back downstairs and nodded our heads to other folks who had come along after us. Miss Cora and Wynona took the plates Maude handed to them and moved quietly around the dining table, serving themselves apple and raisin salad and cheese biscuits with thin slivers of ham in them and small slices of the cake we'd brought.

I stood back, waiting until Miss Cora and Wynona took their plates and went into the parlor, and then I fixed my own plate and went through the back hallway to the kitchen, where Minnie Louise was sitting alone at the kitchen table, dunking a cheese biscuit in her coffee and humming a mournful tune.

"Evening, Minnie Louise," I said, pulling out a chair and sitting down.

"H-m-m-m," Minnie Louise answered between sips of coffee. "Sad old day this is, in this old house."

"Yes," I agreed, but smiling just a little because I sure knew how happy Miss Addie had been to see her very own papa coming for her.

Minnie Louise looked at me real sharp-like. "They say you was with her when she passed?"

"That's right. I was right here with her."

Minnie Louise was pretending to study her biscuit, but I knew she was really working up to what she wanted to ask, and finally, she said, "You see anything?"

"Just what kind of anything do you mean?"

"You know," she grumbled. "Like what you told me about when your grandmama passed."

"Oh . . . *that*. Well, now you mention it. . . ."

"*What?*" Minnie Louise whispered anxiously, her eyebrows stretching up almost into the edge of her hair.

"Something," I whispered back to her and took a big bite of the cake.

"*What?*" Minnie Louise asked in a louder voice, thumping her hand on the table.

"S-h-h! You sure you want to know?"

A cloudy look crossed her face, but she didn't say anything— just sat there looking from one of my eyes to the other, back and forth, back and forth the way she always did. Because Minnie Louise had what her mama called "dancing eyes," the way they went back and forth so fast. Always made me dizzy though.

"You visiting or working?" I asked, figuring I might as well go on and ask, while Minnie Louise was trying to make up her mind if she wanted me to tell her what Death was like when he came for Miss Addie.

A look of relief on Minnie Louise's face. I expected that's the way it would be. Because she wanted to know, but she didn't want to know—all at the same time.

"Working," she said. "Been just about going crazy trying to find somewhere to put all this food."

She waved her arm at the table and the kitchen counters, where every available inch was laden with platters and bowls. Chicken salad, deviled eggs, casseroles, pies, cakes, gelatin salads.

"Unh," I grunted in sympathy. "Sure is a lot of food. Why you reckon that is?" Because even in a house so full of sadness—as Minnie Louise had put it—I just couldn't stop myself from wondering about things.

"Why there's so much food? Why, cause folks brung it, that's why."

"I don't mean that. I mean I wonder why we do that? When somebody passes on, the very first thing we always try to figure is what to fix and take over to their house. I just wonder why that is."

Minnie Louise frowned. "Why, it's so family has plenty to offer folks, without them having to worry none about cooking at such a time."

"Maybe," I said, taking another bite of cake. "But I'll bet it's more than that. I bet it's so we can stuff ourselves, and that way we know *we're* not the ones dead and gone. Cause dead folks don't need any food to eat."

Minnie Louise didn't say a word. Just stuffed the rest of the cheese biscuit in her mouth and chewed fast.

I smiled. "Too much vanilla in the frosting," I said.

In the parlor, Wynona and Miss Cora sat and ate and whispered—like folks always do in a house where someone's lying so still. Sitting there in the room where Miss Addie's things were still around them. A lovely old room, with the soft shine of old mahogany and Miss Addie's hand-crocheted doilies on the back of every single chair. And the fireplace all clean and nice.

Miss Cora sitting in the parlor and me in the kitchen, but I expect we were remembering the very same thing: a Christmas tree in the front window. A long-ago, cold Christmas Day but the room warm from the fireplace and the glow of the lamps. Miss Addie sitting on the floor beside the tree, holding Thompson on her lap. Her so young and so sweet, sitting on that maroon oriental rug and with the flames from the fireplace shining in the red and green glass balls on the tree. In the red balls, white flames, and in the green balls, yellow. Thompson's toothless grin and wet chin and him grabbing at the ribbons and the wrappings. Miss Addie's face, so lovely above Thompson's baby face and her lifting one of his blonde ringlets and letting it spring back and saying, "Miss Cora, just look at him. Isn't he the most beautiful baby in the world? Aren't I lucky to have him?"

"Yes, Addie, he's certainly the most beautiful baby I ever saw in my life," Miss Cora said out loud—that sad day all those years later.

"What did you say?" Wynona asked.

"Nothing," Miss Cora said, and then she added, "Not enough vanilla in the frosting is all."

When Miss Cora told me about it later on, I knew exactly what she was feeling like. Because when we get to an age, it's easy to get things mixed up. The edges going all soft on us so we forget what we're supposed to remember. And sometimes, we remember what we're supposed to forget.

For Miss Cora, it was things like the great oak being gone. And now Miss Addie being gone too. For me, it was something entirely different.

First thing on my mind when I woke up the next morning was we had ourselves a funeral to get through. The next thing was I could see light around the edges of the curtains. Why, it was only the second time in my whole life sunrise ever caught me still in bed! So I threw on my clothes and rushed into the kitchen and put slices of country ham into an iron skillet that was already full of sunshine coming in through the window, and then I went to Miss Cora's room to see if she needed any help getting dressed.

But that tall old bed was empty and the covers just as smooth as if nobody had slept in it at all. I looked out on the porch, and there she sat, wearing her black crepe dress and sitting in the middle of a little cloud of mothball smell, rocking and looking at Miss Addie's house across the street.

I went out on the porch, taking a sweater to put around her shoulders. "It's too chilly out here for you," I said.

"I sure do wish it were time for Camp Meeting," Miss Cora replied, just as if I'd been there with her on the porch the whole time, and we were simply taking up a talk we'd already been having.

"We've got some time before that," I said, zipping up the back of her dress for her, putting the sweater around her shoulders, and trying to figure out how to get her to come back inside and not just sit there looking at that empty old house. "It's not even good spring yet, so we've got some time," I added.

And I was thinking: *Yes, we have time before we go back down the road again, and I'll be remembering when it wasn't even paved . . . when summer rain made that old clay road just as red as blood and that big car of Miss Anne's skittering this way and that in the slippery clay. Especially going down that last hill and feeling the tires beginning to slide sideways. And Miss Anne holding the wheel tighter and tighter and her chin set hard, and Miss Cora and one of the aunts, both in the front seat, looking so hard at the road, like they could hold that car on it just by looking.*

I'd always be in the backseat alone, me just a young girl and packed in as tight as Dick's hatband and jammed up against the window, and with all the pillows and the quilts and the hanging clothes and the brown bottle of Clorox clutched in my hands because Mama said I mustn't let it spill on anything. And that warm-cotton sunshine smell of summer quilts and the car sliding around and me stretching my neck and trying to see where the bridge railings were, and would we get across all right? Because if we didn't, we'd crash right through the railing, old black wood all soaked

71

through with rain, the car quivering and toppling down into the creek, and the sharp smell when the Clorox bottle breaks in my hands.
But we always made it.

"It would be ever so much better to be at Camp Meeting now and not have to look at Addie's empty house," Miss Cora said.

"You ever find out about Sister Betty last year?" I asked, trying to think of anything I could to get Miss Cora's mind off Miss Addie.

"No, I never did," she said. "But this year, soon as we get to Camp Meeting, I'm going to find out what happened to her. I didn't see her last year a single time, and nobody I asked knew where she was. I just wonder if she's passed on."

That sure wasn't a conversation that was going to take Miss Cora's mind off Miss Addie, not if all we talked about was somebody else who'd maybe passed on.

So I asked, "Isn't she the one used to come around every evening and shoot the devil with a water pistol?"

Miss Cora laughed a little, and I was so glad to hear it.

"Heavens, yes! And most folks got so used to it, they never even paid any attention to her anymore. We'd be sitting at supper and she'd come right in just squirting water in the corners of the room hollering, 'Get out, devil! Christ is the head of this house! You ain't got no business here!'"

"When I was real little, it used to scare me to death, because I'd never thought about the devil being there to begin with, and every time Sister Betty squirted that gun, I could imagine him jamming himself tight into the corners of the room and holding his breath, trying to be real still so she wouldn't see him." Miss Cora stopped smiling. "But she always did, and when she'd squirt that water, I thought I could hear him screaming and see him shriveling up, with his skin all smoking where the water had touched him. I used to look around at my mama and the aunts—while Sister Betty was shooting the devil—and they didn't even look up. Just went on biting into a drumstick or pouring more iced tea and being so polite, but their smiles a little tight. Or something like that."

I said, "Sister Betty came out to the kitchen one time when my mama was frying up a whole big pan of chicken. Mercy! It was so hot in that cookhouse! And Sister Betty commenced to squirting water all around, and some of it hit that hot grease, and how it did sizzle! 'Goodness, Miss Betty,' my mama said. 'I don't think there's a devil around here, for surely it's too hot near this stove, even for him!'

"Mama just meant it for a joke, but Sister Betty got real mad. Said the devil's everywhere. Then she pointed that old water gun at my mama and squirted her good!"

Miss Cora laughed. "Yes, she was sure serious about it. She sure was. And I suppose she's gone now."

"Maybe."

"Well, this time I'll find out for sure. When we get to Camp Meeting."

"That's right. We'll find out then."

"They just keep disappearing, don't they?"

"Yes'm."

But I was thinking: *No way to get around it, I suppose. Because one by one, they go. Sometimes we don't even know they're gone until we get to Camp Meeting, and they're not there. Like when we first get there and all the other people are coming in too, and I always watch when a car drives up and parks under the shade of the trees, and the children spill out of the car, laughing and whooping, and then their mamas and papas get out and look around to see where the children have run off to. And then the old ones swing their feet out and wait until somebody comes and takes the box of dishes or the baby out of their laps and pulls them up and out of the car, holding them until they're balanced over their own feet. And when they finally get straightened up—the old ones, I mean—they always look at the tent first. At the old wooden cabin they've come to every August as long as they can remember. I always see it in their eyes, how they are looking at it all over again, but through the newest layer of the seeing it, and all the Augusts before this shining through.*

And then one year, they aren't there anymore. Just like that.

Lauralee didn't go to Miss Addie's funeral with us, but then, we hadn't expected she would. In fact, we said as little as possible around Lauralee about it, because we learned a long, long time ago that Lauralee couldn't go to a funeral. Any funeral.

So we got Minnie Louise's next-door neighbor's granddaughter to come stay with Lauralee, and we went off, leaving Lauralee sitting on the porch humming to herself and the neighbor's granddaughter—skinniest little girl I ever did see—sitting on the portico steps and looking mighty uncomfortable at being left alone with Lauralee.

Miss Cora, Wynona, and I rode in Miss Cora's old Buick, driving around the corner to the Baptist Church, where the long, black hearse from Mr. Grower's funeral parlor was parked around at the side of the building, backed up so the whole rear end of it was hidden in the shade of the pine thicket, and only the front showing, that gleaming chrome bumper like a wicked smile and those tinted windows almost—but not quite—hiding Mr. Grower, who was asleep in the passenger seat. That was a sleepy old buzzard sitting in a tree, sure enough!

"I'll park around the other side," Wynona said.

Inside the church, I stood at the back until I found Minnie Louise, and I went and sat beside her on the back pew.

"You working or mourning?" I whispered.

"Both. Brought Miss Delia," Minnie Louise whispered back. "She tried to get me to drive us over here in her car 'stead of my truck, but I said, 'Goodness, Miss Delia, I ain't never drove no big old fancy car, and I'm way too old to learn how now.'"

Minnie Louise's cardboard-Jesus fan picked up its tempo.

"Don't you go getting yourself all het up about it," I whispered.

"Makes me mad as fire, that's all. Truck's good enough when we go to the grocery store all right, but not for coming to her church. If she wants somebody to drive her car, she ought to call one of them snippy granddaughters of hers. Let one of them come on over here and drive her around. That's what I say!"

Then we were quiet, with Minnie Louise fanning herself and me watching Wynona guide Miss Cora toward the front pews, where Miss Cora and Miss Addie's old friends were already gathered in the church and watching too.

"Good old Miss Cora," someone in front of me murmured. "And I do wonder how many funerals she's been to in this very church?"

"I don't know, but I'll tell you one thing: she's worn the same hat to every one of them."

"Hush now! That's a terrible thing to say about her, and her so faithful about coming to all the funerals. You watch out or she'll not come to yours. And to think that now it's Miss Addie's turn. Sweet, old Miss Addie."

"Wasn't she some kin to Miss Cora?"

"Seems to me she was. Distant though."

Self-consciously, Miss Cora touched the back of her hair, right below the net of the black hat, and tucked in a loose hairpin before she turned her head a little to the side and nodded to two elderly ladies sitting in the pew behind her.

Miss Cora, we're glad you're here, I could feel them saying.

I'm glad I'm here too, she said without speaking.

And after the silent greetings, there was nothing more to do but to sit in the big, still church, breathing the cool smell of the flowers that came out of the glass cooler in Mr. Grower's flower shop and singing "When the Roll Is Called Up Yonder" and "Shall We Gather at the River," and listening to the preacher and his words about how a good woman is more valuable than rubies. Me sitting there seeing a flowing river full of sparkling rubies that led from Miss Addie's casket right out the door and all the way down the street, right to the door of that big house. Rubies for Thompson to walk on to go to the house she worked so hard to keep for him.

All of a sudden, a sob broke out of Thompson's throat where he sat bowed and trembling in the front row and with Maude so pale and shaking beside him. It was a terrible sound that shocked us all away from the preacher's comforting voice, but only that one sob, because Thompson got ahold of himself right away and behaved in a way that would have made his mama proud of him.

Minnie Louise went through three handkerchiefs but never made a sound. And I just sat there quiet as could be, making myself remember Miss Addie's passing and almost being able to hear her papa's voice:

Addie? Baby? Papa's here.

When the service was over, we followed the casket down the steps and out into the warm sunlight, too sweet a day indeed for what we had to do. And then we got back in the car and followed Mr. Grower's hearse along the highway and through the intersection of Main Street, where the sheriff had stopped the traffic coming through from Highway 1. He stood beside the dusty patrol car, holding his hat over his heart.

And the people on their way back north from their winter in Florida—the ones who were waiting for the traffic to move on—stared from their air-conditioned cars, and they were wearing shirts with dancing oranges and blue palm leaves printed on them and watching us from behind their dark-tinted windows.

I had to smile when I thought of Minnie Louise and Miss Delia driving along in Minnie Louise's old truck, because it would be just like Miss Delia to get upset all over again on account of those strangers seeing her riding in such a beat-up old truck. That would sure enough make Minnie Louise hopping mad. But of course, Minnie Louise wouldn't say anything about it. Not to Miss Delia anyway.

Then out the Waynesboro Highway to the cemetery where the hole in the red clay was waiting.

Because that's the way it's always been.

That night, when we were sitting in the dining room, I had another spell sure enough. But this time, I didn't have to worry about Miss Cora noticing anything, because she was telling Miss Addie's story. Again.

So once more, I knew we were all together. Us and all the others too, even those who have been gone for a long time. But the one I was paying most attention to that evening was Mama Sunrise, because she sat there and stared at me for the longest kind of time, smiling, before she finally said, "It's okay to put the baby down now, Pet."

And I sure didn't know what she meant. Not back then, I didn't.

What a special blessing it was that spring came along nice and early that year, and I like to think it was because Heaven just couldn't wait another minute to start celebrating Miss Addie's getting there. Oh, I was so glad to see that lovely, surprise-spring that just crept into the yard one night in early March while we were all snuggled down under our comforters and quilts and dreaming that winter was going to be around a good long time yet.

But we waked up to air that was so tender and sweet, and the trees wearing a green haze because of all those little leaf-buds getting ready to pop out.

"Won't last," Wynona pronounced, but Miss Cora and I looked at each other and smiled. We knew it would.

So I used a nut-pick to pry out the cotton and the strips of old sheets we'd packed so tight around the parlor door, pulled them out, and swung the door open to where that room was waiting, all breathless-like and chilled, and with a gleam of sunlight coming in around the edge of the drapes and glowing on the floor like a flame on a candle.

But we'd no sooner gotten the door open than Miss Cora gazed around that old, familiar room and said, "Well, the weather's plenty warm enough now for us to go down to Brushy Creek cemetery. We'll go on Sunday; that's what we'll do."

Lord, have mercy on us!

There was nothing else we could do. So after dinner on Sunday, we helped Miss Cora down the steps of the portico and loaded her into the passenger seat of the old Buick. Wynona drove, and Lauralee and I sat in the backseat. As we were backing out of the driveway, Miss Cora said, "Maybe we should ask Addie if she'd like to ride along."

Why, we didn't know what to say!

But then Miss Cora got her mind straightened out.

"Oh . . . well, have youall heard anything about when Thompson and Maude will be moving into Addie's house?"

"Sure haven't," I answered. "Far as I know, Thompson hasn't even set foot back in his mama's house since . . . "

I stopped, because Miss Cora knew what I meant, so no need saying it. Besides, I was thinking of that sad old morning he'd gone rushing up the stairs to Miss Addie's room. But spring made me think it was time to start moving on, away from that memory and on to some new ones, so I hoped he and Maude would be moving into the house real soon and maybe even have them some babies. Miss Addie would have liked that, sure enough. And it would be so good for us to see lights on in that old house again and know that somebody loved it and would take good care of it.

"Let's take the Old Quaker Road," Miss Cora said.

And, of course, Wynona did as she asked, even though it was an unpaved road, and with the car windows open, we'd get covered in dust. It would have been nicer to go by the Waynesboro Highway, because it was a paved road. But Wynona said not a thing and drove on down the street, making a right-hand turn beyond the flour mill and going onto the old clay road that leaned into the hills. Then she cut down through the deep, red banks near the creek.

"This is Brushy Creek, north of the church," Miss Cora announced as we approached the wooden bridge—as if we didn't know where we were—and she got that faraway look like she always gets when she's remembering things. And me sitting there, watching her, and wondering how much she was going to be able to remember when the time came for me to do what Miss Addie said.

78

Miss Cora went on with the same things she always said whenever we took her down to that old cemetery.

"My papa told me how the creek starts way up in Warren County, in a little old spring that comes up from under a rock ledge way deep down in the ground. He took me up there one time to see the spring and show me where my grandpapa used to go to hunt deer. Papa said it was a law of nature made the spring bubble up and another law of nature—something he called least resistance, I think—made the water hear the Savannah River calling to it from all those eighty miles away, so that every little drop of water, the very minute it comes out from under that rock, can hear the river calling and calling, and it wants more than anything in the whole world to get there."

The bridge groaned under the weight of Miss Cora's Buick, and Wynona stepped on the gas pedal and sent us roaring on up the hill, leaving a cloud of red dust behind us that settled on the bridge and under it. Deep down in the dark and shady places where that old creek goes on and on forever and ever—rubbing against the bridge-legs like an old cat will do to you when it's wanting its supper.

We drove past fields of knee-deep winter rye just waiting to be plowed under to make the soil rich for summer corn, and at last we got to the intersection of the Old Quaker Road and the Waynesboro Highway, where Wynona turned. A mile or so farther on, she turned again and drove up alongside Brushy Creek Church, a square old building sitting solid-like against the hill and looking out over the creek. Wynona eased around the holes in the gravel drive, drove on down toward the cemetery on the other side of the church, and finally stopped in the deep shade of a hickory tree near the long, wooden tables that had been built in its shade.

Miss Cora said: "I remember coming to all-day singing and dinner-on-the-ground here, when I was just a child. I remember a big basket strapped to the back of our buggy and it all packed with fried chicken and a big pan of Dilsey's mama's wonderful, deep-dish chicken pie. My! What a crust! Flaky and light as air on top and creamy-soft underneath."

That sure made me happy, hearing Miss Cora saying such nice things about my grandmama, and it set me to thinking about

79

fixing a deep-dish chicken pie some time or other. Except Wynona would fuss about my getting the kitchen so hot, what with the oven going and all.

"Dilsey's mama followed in the wagon," Miss Cora went on. "With the stone jug that held cold tea with big chunks of crystal-clear ice floating in it. And I remember riding between Mama and Papa on the buggy seat and feeling Papa's jacket sleeve stiff and scratchy against my arm on one side and, against the other, Mama's sleeve was voile and soft. Goodness! I can even remember the smell of Papa's pipe tobacco and Mama's lemon verbena cologne, just as well as if it were only yesterday!"

"Yes'm," Wynona said. Then to me she whispered, "We have to be careful she doesn't get too hot or excited. Oh, how I wish we could find that old grave so maybe her mind could be at rest!"

"And us at rest too," I whispered.

"You needn't talk about me as if I'm not here!" Miss Cora snapped at us while we were helping her out of the seat and guiding her feet to the ground. When she could straighten up all the way, we took hold of her arms very lightly, one of us on either side and started following her around, like she was some kind of a divining rod, holding her between us and waiting for her to go nose-down at the right place and yell, "This is it!"

Miss Cora stopped walking and looked around: "I used to play down at the bottom of this hill," she said. "Because when church was over, all the children just poured out of the church and down the hill, with our hair ribbons flying and all our good manners thrown aside. We'd race down through the cemetery to the creek, to make green leaf-rafts and watch them float away and wonder how long it would take before they'd get all the way to the Savannah River. . . . Not this way," Miss Cora interrupted her own story. "Help me to find the old slave cemetery. That's how I'll be able to tell where the great oak used to stand. I'm all turned around. My! I feel like a child again, running down the hill after church, wondering why God made gnats, looking for bluebells under the shade of the trees; and I feel like a young lady too, walking around holding onto my sweetheart's arm and trying not to get grass stains on my white kid shoes."

Miss Cora's voice got a catch in it, and Wynona said, "Well, for goodness' sake, let's go look over here!" She said it kind of happy-like, trying to get Miss Cora to forget about the old times.

But I knew she wasn't going to do that. Not ever.

Finally, weaving in and out of the tombstones and guiding Miss Cora over soft spots in the ground, we came to the old slave cemetery and saw that another section of the stone wall had crumbled and fallen during the last winter, so only the one old wall was left standing.

Wynona said, "When I was a little girl, I always wondered why there was no gate in there. I'd climb up so I could see over, and it was just like it is today—nothing but weeds and bumps in the ground. One time I asked Grandmama why there weren't any tombstones and no gate even. And she said, 'Well, that's the old slave cemetery, you see. And long years ago, the folks who were slaves had no place to be buried except whatever folks who owned them decided on, and the walls were built so where slaves were buried would be separate from where white folks were buried. Because it wouldn't have been proper to bury them all together. And no tombstones, but I don't know why; maybe no one wanted to spend the money. And the cemetery has no gate in it because white folks didn't want black folks' ghosts roaming around at night. Because that's the way they did things back then.'"

Wynona looked at me and added, "I'm glad it isn't like that anymore. I read a poem one time about there being something-or-other that doesn't love a wall, and I sure don't love this one."

I didn't say anything, but I was sure thinking that maybe things hadn't changed as much as Wynona thought they had. Oh, for young people, I suppose. But not for the old ones, like me. Because I didn't know how to do things any differently. So I just looked over that wall and thought about the bones of my own Mama Sunrise, buried right there. And the bones of her papa too. He was still a slave when he died, but I know all about him and about Mama Sunrise, because my mama told me their stories.

How the very same day Mama Sunrise died, a grandbaby of hers died too, of a terrible fever no one could do a thing about. And Mama Sunrise and the baby were buried together, the baby in her arms. Somewhere in there are her bones and the bones of the little baby who could have grown up to be my aunt or maybe even my mama. Because we don't know about those things. And my mama said: "I remember all about Mama Sunrise. Only we didn't call her that because we weren't supposed to use African names. Her papa was the one who came from Africa on a slave ship to a rice plantation down near Savannah. Worked there for over twelve years before he was sold upstate. He said the slaves died like flies because of the fever and all. But he didn't die, and he was the one who built this wall with his own hands. Said he didn't mind building it at all, if it would only keep the white folks' ghosts away from him for all eternity."

"Now youall help me find that big cedar tree," Miss Cora said. "There was one that grew south of the great oak, and when we find that, I'll remember where that grave is."

But the big cedar tree was nowhere to be found either, because it had fallen over years ago. In fact, I remembered later that it was Miss Cora herself who'd hired the men to cut it up and haul it away, because that was the year she was in charge of home-coming and dinner-on-the-ground, so that kind of thing was her responsibility. But now she'd forgotten, and nobody else knew it, except for me, and I didn't say a thing. So it never really happened. Or that's the way it would get to be, as long as nobody said any different.

"Well," Miss Cora finally said, "I don't know where that grave is after all, but I'll keep thinking, and surely I'll remember it sooner or later. Maybe I'll write Aunt Frances in Dallas and see if she remembers where it is."

"Aunt *Frances?*" Wynona whispered to me. "She died years and years ago."

"That's right," I replied.

"Now walk me back to the creek one more time. I want to see it again before we go," Miss Cora ordered.

"It's getting way too hot for us to go all the way back down there," Wynona protested.

"One more time before we go," Miss Cora insisted, and as usual, she got her way.

When we got her back to the creek, she said, "You know, it's the funniest thing—when I was little, I could come all the way back up the hill, and there wasn't a single gravestone in sight until I reached the very top. But look how many there are now! They're starting to bury folks on down the hill, that's what they're doing."

"Let's us go on home now," I said, glancing at Wynona. But Miss Cora was still planted as firm as a tree and watching the creek.

"That old creek always going somewhere. I'm sure it means something, but I forget what it is!"

Her eyes filled up, and Wynona and I started trying to get her turned around and headed back toward the car, so we could start driving and get her mind on something else. But Miss Cora just kept on talking and talking about the creek.

"All that water coming up out of one little bitty old spring and finally getting to the creek and then on to the river and at last to the ocean. Along comes a cloud so thirsty, it takes the water up into it and goes along with the wind right back in this direction. So rain falls way up in Warren County and gets all drunk in by the earth, and then it bubbles up again. Starting all over. It's a law of nature my papa told me about, but I forget just what it is."

So we knew we needed to get her home and cool her off and quiet her down.

All the next day, Miss Cora worked on writing a letter to Aunt Frances, her pen scratching words onto page after page, and she'd stop once in a while to look off into the distance and smile and sometimes laugh under her breath. On Tuesday, Wynona pretended to put the letter in the mailbox. Because she'd tried to tell Miss Cora—real gentle-like—that Aunt Frances was gone, had been gone for years and years. But Miss Cora pretended that she couldn't hear a thing Wynona was saying.

Next morning, Miss Cora told me she'd dreamed she was with Aunt Frances, and the two of them were strolling through the cemetery on a hot, August afternoon—with a storm cloud just coming up over the trees behind the church, and a lot of thunder that kept on drowning out whatever it was Aunt Frances was saying to her.

"Where'd you say it is?" Miss Cora asked in her dream. But there wasn't any answer. Just thunder.

I didn't say anything, but I'd dreamed too. Of Mama Sunrise. Legs like tree trunks, big round face, and strong, white teeth shining. Smiling at me like she knew exactly who I was, sure enough, and saying "Almost white, she was."

That's what Mama Sunrise told me in my dream.

"Who?" I tried to ask.

Because I knew she was trying to tell me something very important. But no matter how hard I tried, I couldn't remember what it was, once I got awake.

And you know, that very afternoon, Miss Cora said, "Did we take Aunt Frances down to the cemetery last Sunday, like I wanted to?"

"Well, he certainly *should* be hiding his face!" Miss Cora sniffed. "I still just don't believe it! Him selling the very house his mama struggled so hard to keep for him, and her gone to Glory not even six months!"

It was late summer, and we'd been sitting on the porch all afternoon just like a bunch of statues or something, not moving a muscle while we watched Thompson loading his pickup truck with furniture he wanted from his mama's house and driving away time after time. He took rolled up carpets and oak bureaus, rocking chairs, and lamp tables, and, finally, the bed Miss Addie's papa made with his own hands. And never once that whole day did he even look in our direction.

"It must be the worst feeling in the world," Wynona ventured.

"I'm sure it is, and I hope he feels every bit of it!" Miss Cora said, and then, because our silence told her we thought she'd spoken a little too roughly, she hesitated for a few moments before she went on. "Well, I'm sure glad we don't have to worry about something like that happening, because there'll always be a member of our very own family living here in this house."

I didn't say anything, of course, but I felt like I just wanted to grab her and shake her good. *Why, Miss Cora,* I wanted to say. *You take a good look around you, you'll see how old we all are! And just who do you think is going to be left after we're gone? Just who do you think will be here? Because I loved Miss Addie with my whole heart, but I still think she's wrong about what's going to happen when I tell you about the family you do have left!*

But, of course, I didn't say anything, because I could almost feel Miss Addie's hand patting my shoulder, telling me it wasn't the right time.

Not yet. Not yet. That's exactly what I could feel her saying to me.

Yes'm.

"Look at that," Miss Cora said. "I knew he'd be careless in moving those things, because he's put Addie's lovely hobnailed lamp right there against the tailgate and with not a thing to pad it, and if he hits so much as a tiny bump, the glass will shatter, and it will be lost. What a shame! She put so much store in that lamp and told me a hundred times the story about how it belonged to her grandmother, who got it from a tinsmith who came by their farm in a wagon. She traded a dozen eggs for it, which was a terrible price back then. But her grandmother said it was certainly worth it, if only for being able to polish it and light it every evening and wonder who owned it before and how the tinsmith came by something so beautiful and fragile. And what kind of a woman would trade that lamp for something made out of tin?"

"Maybe one who didn't have anything to cook her butter beans in," I said.

"He's rushing with it because he can't stand it, you see," Miss Cora explained. "It's Maude made him sell his mama's house. How can he stand it? Addie's turning over in her grave, I'll tell you!"

We nodded, because we all knew a long, long time ago that Maude could make Thompson do anything she wanted, and we also knew it wasn't good for a man to be so crazy about a woman as Thompson was about Maude. Make him sell his mama's own house! His heritage.

But there wasn't nothing we could do about that. So we just watched him carry out all the things he wanted and load them into his truck, and at the last, he nailed a FOR SALE sign up on the porch banister, a sign that gave his phone number at the car dealership where he worked.

Then he drove off and never once even looked across the street. And he knew we were sitting there. That's when Miss Cora said what she did about him hiding his face from us. But then we saw something even worse—he'd left Miss Addie's green wicker rocking chair sitting all alone on the front porch, and that was almost more than we could bear.

Because nearly every evening, Miss Addie would come over to sit and rock and talk with us, but when she went home, sometimes we could look across the street and see her sitting in that very chair on her porch.

"I remember exactly when she got that chair," Miss Cora said. "Because the furniture store in Augusta had an advertisement in the newspaper about wicker rockers, and she just purely took it in her head that she was going to have one. Took all kinds of persuading for her to get Thompson to drive her over to Augusta so she could pick out the one she wanted and bring it home in his truck. But she finally got him to agree, and once she told me that every time she sat in it, she had to laugh to herself to think of how Thompson's chin jutted out and how he wouldn't even stop at the Dairy Queen to let her treat them to ice cream that day. He was that put out with having to miss a day of work and take her all the way to Augusta for the chair."

"You think he'll come back for it?" Wynona asked no one in particular.

"No," Miss Cora said. "I don't think he will. Don't think he'd want something around that would remind him of how short-tempered he was with his mama."

"Then I'm going over there and get it," Wynona said.

"Wynona!" Miss Cora scolded. "That's stealing!"

Wynona thought for a moment. "It's not stealing if I call Thompson and tell him we've got the chair, should he ever want it."

Miss Cora thought for a moment and then nodded. Still, just like thieves or something, we waited for dusk before Wynona and I scurried across the street and fetched home Miss Addie's chair.

"It should be yours, Pet," Wynona said when we got it up onto the porch. "You did so much for Miss Addie, and I think she'd want you to have it."

I didn't say anything, but I was thinking that what I still had to do for Miss Addie was going to be the hardest part, but I would find a way. Because of what *she* did for me. And maybe—just maybe—sitting in her chair would give me the courage I needed.

So we put Miss Addie's chair in my quiet, shaded corner near the side steps that went down to the portico, and I sat there in it that evening for the very first time, wishing I could have done even more for Miss Addie while she was still on this earth and more for Wynona and Lauralee too, back when maybe I could have made a difference in what happened later, because it's the kind of thing that stays with you, even after you've forgotten it.

And the strangest little things can bring it back, like the way the linoleum in the hallway makes popping noises under your feet in the wintertime when it's late at night and the linoleum is stiff and cold, and the smell of flowers—especially carnations—that you've smelled at funerals, but you don't remember it being exactly that, you know. Just something so hurtful, you can't hardly stand it, but you can't quite figure out what it is.

But maybe there was something about Mr. Adkins I should have noticed. Something that would have made me stop and take a harder look at him. I'm still not sure that would have changed anything, even though I've thought about it for all them years. But maybe it would have, if only . . .

I'd looked closer into his eyes. I might have been able to see something there—some little glimmer, so I could have warned Wynona and Lauralee. But I didn't look, because I was just like everybody else—all caught up in it. Like we were in a play, and somebody had already written down what all we were supposed to do and say.

Wynona said she wanted to be married at Brushy Creek Baptist Church, but Miss Anne tried to get her to use First Baptist, in town, and finally it came out that Mr. Adkins was the one wanted Brushy Creek, so Brushy Creek it would be. Miss Anne, she said right then and there Wynona should assert herself a little bit, but I guess having her papa rule over her the way he'd always done just made it easy for Wynona to start letting Mr. Adkins do the same thing.

He wanted Brushy Creek, because that was about the time he got started with the whole religion thing. Miss Anne sure didn't want to get involved in that, and too, she and the aunts were all pleased that Wynona was going to marry a man who was a merchant—a "white-collar" man, they called him. It was a far better marriage than they'd ever hoped for, and they ran around saying things like, "So all Sam's foolishness about those girls learning how to be farm wives was in vain!" And Miss Anne didn't keep on pressing Wynona to use First Baptist at all. We found out later that Mr. Adkins had already gone to see the preacher at Brushy Creek the very first thing, before we even knew there was going to be a wedding.

Back then, most small churches couldn't afford for preachers to come every single Sunday, so little churches had to share one preacher. He only came once a month for a service at Brushy Creek, and the other Sundays, he was at Zebulon Baptist, Warrenville Baptist, and Lost Trail Baptist in Zebina. Mr. Adkins had gone and talked to this preacher right away because it was his Sunday to be at Brushy Creek.

I'm not sure what happened—maybe that young preacher was just too fired up or something, and he did a good and proper job. Told Mr. Adkins right off the bat he was going to burn forever. I thought about that sometimes, you know. After it all happened.

But anyway, this young preacher told Mr. Adkins that the wedding couldn't be done in the church unless Mr. Adkins got saved and said so in public and got himself baptized.

That sure upset Mr. Adkins something terrible, and he got right frantic about it. Took to reading the Bible all the time and mostly crying while he did. I sure don't know what kind of religion it was he finally got—or thought he got—but it wasn't what it was supposed to be. And it can be very dangerous, that kind of thing. I know good and well that young preacher had the very best intentions in the whole world, but maybe he was just too innocent to recognize something truly evil when he saw it, when he was looking it right in the eyes!

Anyway, Mr. Adkins got himself baptized and "filled with the Holy Ghost." That's what he said it was. All I know is he sure got filled with something, but I don't think it was anything holy. For the day he was baptized was something Wynona told me about years and years later.

How hot and sticky it was that morning down at the bottom of the hill by the church, where the baptismal pool is, and locusts already humming away in the pine thicket, though it was only about ten o'clock in the morning, and that little congregation of good folks standing around the baptismal pool just singing to beat the band. Then here comes the preacher, and Mr.

Adkins coming behind him, wearing old trousers with no belt and a shirt with no tie and kind of just ouch-ing along because he was barefooted and his fat, old, pink feet were way too tender for those little pebbles on the path.

The preacher didn't seem to realize what a hard time Mr. Adkins was having, so he just kept on walking and smiling and nodding to folks, and he got a good deal ahead of Mr. Adkins. The people were singing "Shall We Gather at the River," and the preacher got to the baptismal pool on about the second stanza and went right on down the mossy steps and into that icy water and never even lost his smile, though it certainly tightened up a bit. And he held out his hand to lead Mr. Adkins in, but of course, Mr. Adkins wasn't there yet.

Those good people standing around the pool and singing were trying not to stare at Mr. Adkins, because he was still ouch-ing along like he was sure hurting plenty and grimacing and flinging out his arms this way and that, just like an old scarecrow blowing in the wind. And the people still singing and looking at the ground.

But that wasn't the worst part. Not by a far sight. Because when Mr. Adkins finally got to the baptismal pool and took the preacher's hand and stepped down into that icy cold water, he jerked back like a snake had bitten him and bellowed out, "JUUUUDDDAAASSSS!"

And the singing stopped. Just like somebody had pulled the plug on a record player.

All those years later, when Wynona told me about Mr. Adkins' baptism and what happened, we looked at each other for a long time before she added, "I guess I should have paid more attention to that."

But of course, she didn't. And then it was too late.

Well, regardless of all that, at least Mr. Adkins realized he'd done something very wrong. He turned fire-red, and so did that young preacher, but Mr. Adkins went down the steps and never flinched or said a word. But someone said later they thought the preacher held Mr. Adkins underwater for an uncommon long time.

But even that good, hard dunking must not have washed him clean, because he carried that bad temper of his around for a long time before it finally caused all the trouble. I guess he was one of those folks who thinks it's okay to do whatever you want, just so long as you keep on telling every-body about how you've been saved.

Thompson selling his mama's house was the first thing Minnie Louise started talking about when she stopped by for me on Wednesday evening so we could go to prayer meeting. Of course, Wednesday evenings were prayer meeting time over to the Baptist Church too, but Wynona and I took turns. We never went off at the same time, because we didn't want to leave Lauralee and Miss Cora all alone.

We'd been swapping Wednesday evenings since the 1960s. Until then, Wynona always assumed I'd be the one to stay home and she would be the one who got to go to church. But after everything got started about Civil Rights and all, Wynona took it into her head that we should swap off Wednesday evenings. Why, I almost dropped my teeth! I never expected to get anything out of all the overcoming stuff, because things had been done a certain way for as long as I could remember, and I really didn't have any idea of how to go about doing them any different.

But still, it was a hard time for all of us. Why, we just about had to stop watching the television set together at news time, because it was the worst thing I ever saw in my whole life—those sharp-toothed police dogs biting everybody, and big fire hoses knocking folks right off their feet!

Miss Cora and Wynona never said a word to me about it, but if it came time for the news, and I was in the room, they'd look at each other in an embarrassed kind of way, and first thing you know, they'd both find something else needed doing, and the television set would just keep on playing away, but with no one to watch it. Except Lauralee.

And once, I was watching the news and seeing those billy clubs flying all around and all kinds of folks—black and white together—lock-armed with each other and singing; then out of the corner of my eye, I caught Lauralee looking at me like she had never seen me before in her whole life.

Like to broke my heart. Her such a little shell of a person and not saying a single word. But then sometimes, you find out she can still feel things, and when it came to what was on the tele-

91

vision, I don't think she understood much about what was going on. Just saw all those folks getting done so bad.

That was about the time Wynona said she'd been thinking, and she reckoned *I* wanted to go to prayer meeting sometimes, over to my own church, so why didn't we take turns? I said I'd appreciate that, but it sure did make me feel kind of funny. All those people getting beat up and dog-bit, and the only thing I took away from that was getting to go to prayer meeting every other Wednesday.

So it was "my Wednesday" the week Thompson put up the for sale sign, and Minnie Louise pulled up in the driveway and started in to talking about it before I could even get the door to her truck open.

"I heard all about it!" she yelled at me through the window, motioning her head toward Miss Addie's house. "It's Maude's doings! Why, sometimes I just don't know what the world is coming to!" she added.

"I tell you one thing," she continued as I got in. "Did my mama ever manage to leave me a big old fine house like that, I'd never let it go. No. Not for no amount a money."

She shifted into first gear with a vicious thrust, and we rolled off down the street.

"I know," I sighed.

"And what's he gonna leave to his own children—does him and Maude ever get any, that is—that little old dinky house he built, and it not even paid for?"

Minnie Louise was working herself up into a fine head of steam, and for some reason, I felt like joining in with her. But I couldn't have said why.

"Maybe that's why he wants the money so bad from Miss Addie's house," I suggested. "Pay off the mortgage on his and Maude's."

Minnie Louise hesitated for a moment. "And pay off all that furniture too, I expect. And that newfangled hot-tub thing she made him buy."

Her words seemed to hang in the air, and we both tried to stay mad, but we couldn't, not with thinking about that. So we glanced at each other and couldn't help but smile. Then Minnie Louise went on, in a softer tone. "I'm grateful as can be for that little shotgun house on Railroad Street my sweet mama left to me; I'll say that much. Wouldn't sell it for nothing."

In my mind's eye, I could see that little house. *Petunias planted in buckets along the edge of the porch. The old-fashioned swept yard Minnie Louise tended so carefully, so not a green blade of any kind marred it. And the rusted tin roof that made such a fine sound when rain fell on it. Like it did the night after my Lizzy was born. Me waking up in the dark to the sound of it and remembering that sweet little baby tucked into the crook of my arm. And smiling and going back to sleep. Rain on that old roof and Lizzy with me. So sweet! So sweet!*

Minnie Louise inclined her head toward me, as if she could see what was right there in my mind.

"Lizzy's doing just fine," she said. And the very sound of that name made me take an extra little breath.

My Lizzy on her third birthday. The table set up under that big chinaberry tree in Minnie Louise's backyard, and with a red tablecloth on it and a high, white coconut birthday cake with three red candles.

Lizzy in a snow-white dress and her black eyes dancing when I gave her the present wrapped in paper that had red and green and blue and yellow balloons all over it and little specks of confetti colors.

"Oh! Thank you, Aunt Pet!" Her eyes meeting mine for only a precious moment before she took the present and ran to Minnie Louise.

"Mama! Look! Aunt Pet brought me a present!"

And Lizzy on all the other birthdays, her growing into a fine, strong young woman. And the gifts I gave to her—dolls at first and then dresses, and at the last, a leather-bound calendar of days she could fill in herself.

That fine, beautiful, young woman looking deep into my eyes.

"Thank you, Aunt Pet. This will help me keep all my classes and assignments straight at business school."

And then her turning, as always, to Minnie Louise.

"Look, Mama, what a lovely gift Aunt Pet has given me."

And the two of them looking at me, Lizzy with a warm, open smile. And Minnie Louise with none at all.

Then the gift for her wedding and then for the coming baby. And that was where it ended, for me.

"I'm sorry, Pet," Minnie Louise's voice intruded.

"No," I said. "It's okay. You were right in telling me."

I didn't add: *I should have asked, but I couldn't.*

By then, we were at the church, and we hurried inside so as not to be late for prayer meeting.

Later on, Miss Cora told me about how she went to bed early that night, before it was even full dark. So that after Wynona turned out the lamp, Miss Cora could still make out a rim of light around the edges of the window shades. And her knowing there was a for sale sign on Miss Addie's house across the street was almost more than she could bear.

No breeze of any kind that she could notice, but in August, breezes are pretty scarce anyway, and even if one does come along, it just stirs up hot air. But there must have been some kind of a breeze that night, just enough to carry the sound of our good singing from the AME Church all the way across town right to her bedroom window and loud enough for her to hear it above the hum of the fan.

> We're marching to Zion,
> Beautiful, beautiful Zion;
> We're marching upward to Zion,
> The beautiful city of God!

She was listening when that first wave of sleep washed over her, and she tried to rise up out of it, so she could keep on listening to our singing. Next thing was her wondering how on earth she could hear us from our church all the way across town, but she couldn't hear a single note from the church Wynona went to, right down the street.

And while she was lying there, almost asleep but still awake enough to wonder, she said she felt something or other trying to come into her mind, and she wondered what it was. Said she knew something was coming back to her—and her so old she couldn't remember what she ate for breakfast or where she put the cream pitcher. Said it was something about old voices and a hot sun shining down on dirt roads that she knew good and well got paved over more than fifty years ago and voices that seemed to whisper to her from the front porches of houses that weren't even standing now.

So that when she finally fell asleep, she went right into a dream about Camp Meeting a long time ago. A hot August sun and dry weeds and opening up the tent and hearing the popping sound of the tin roof heating up under the sun. And her mama, Miss Anne, calling to my own mama:

"Dilsey?"

"Yes'm?"

"Dilsey, you get all those windows open, and I'll start looking to see if there's any wasp nests inside."

And Wynona saying, "Grandmama, me and Pet's going down to the tabernacle."

And before anyone can say a word, Wynona and Pet hold hands and run down the grassy hill toward the tabernacle. Then Lauralee running behind them and when they hear her calling, they stop and wait for her. Then, with Lauralee between them, one of them holding each of her hands, they run along, sometimes lifting Lauralee right off her feet and making her laugh.

"Dilsey, that's going to have to stop. Pet's got to have a talking-to!"

"Yes'm. But they're just children."

"It's never too early for proper training, Dilsey. You know that. Pet's got to start learning what her place is."

"Yes'm."

Then Miss Cora said the dream disappeared, and all that was left was those voices singing far away:

> We're marching to Zion,
> Beautiful, beautiful Zion;
> We're marching upward to Zion,
> The beautiful city of God!

At breakfast the next morning, Miss Cora said, "We didn't go down to the cemetery last Sunday, did we?"

We all kind of held our breath, waiting for her to say something about Aunt Frances, but she didn't.

"We went down there the Sunday before," Wynona said. And before Miss Cora could say another thing, Wynona pushed back her chair and stood up.

"I'm going on to the grocery store while it's still cool. Anybody want to add anything else to the list?" I could tell she was trying to change the subject before Miss Cora got on a roll about that same old thing.

"How about some more Hadacol?" I suggested, tilting my head a little toward Miss Cora.

"Oh, yes," Wynona said, smiling. I guess she'd forgotten what a wonderful tonic it was, 'specially for somebody older when they started getting all upset about something or other.

After Wynona left, Miss Cora lingered over her coffee at the kitchen table, and even though she hadn't told me a thing about her dream then—didn't tell me until after everything got done happening at the end of the summer—I felt in my bones that very morning that she was getting close to remembering something or other. So I kind of kept my eye on her.

She sat there without saying a word the whole time I washed up the dishes, dried them, put them away, and then started in on the hand laundry, and when I'd gotten it done and was ready to take it out to hang on the line, I asked her, "You feeling all right this morning?"

"Oh." She seemed a little surprised to hear my voice, as if she'd forgotten I was there. "Oh, yes, I'm fine. I was just thinking."

Well, of course, that's exactly what I was worried about, but there was nothing for me to do about it, so I loaded the clothes into a basket to take them out back and hang them on the line. Miss Cora came out on the screened porch and watched me.

"Where's Lauralee?" she called.

"Front porch," I said. "Shelling butter beans."

"Oh."

Oh, Heavens! I was thinking. *How come me to say that?*

When I came back inside, Miss Cora followed me back into the kitchen.

"You want some more coffee?" I asked.

"No, thank you. That Jell-O stain come out of the tablecloth?"

"Sure did. Took some scrubbing though."

"Youall have a good service last night?"

"We sure did that!"

96

"Good crowd?"

"Right good crowd," I said, glad for the conversation to be about something happy and safe.

"I could hear the singing after I'd gone to bed."

"You could? I guess we must have done some good singing, sure enough, for you to hear it all the way across town."

"Sure did. Sounded real fine," she said. And then, without missing a beat, she said, "I was thinking about Camp Meeting last night while I was listening to the singing. Or maybe I was dreaming about it, but I don't know which."

"Well, you've sure had it on your mind, haven't you?"

"Yes, I've certainly done that. But I was thinking about a long time ago, when you and Wynona were just children. How you two loved to run down the hill toward the tabernacle. Just like little wild colts or something."

"Those were good days," I said. And I didn't add about how they were good days only until Mama said I mustn't run off and play anymore but stay and help with the work. And I just didn't understand that. Because I loved Wynona and Lauralee more than anything in the world, and just being with them was as close to Heaven as I could be. And I told that to Mama, and she said the way to show them how much I loved them was to take good care of their dresses for them and brush their hair and make it look pretty. And not go running off to play all the time.

"I think I'll go back to bed for a little while," Miss Cora said. "I had such a hard time falling asleep last night." She looked at me closely. "But I certainly will be glad when it's time for Camp Meeting," she added.

Set me to thinking, that sure did, because Camp Meeting seemed to be dying off, just like all the folks who used to enjoy it were getting old and dying. Used to be that every single tent had a big family in it, and services at the tabernacle four times a day, with a whole tribe of preachers—four or five, at least—carrying the preaching and the saving load.

But now times were changing. And folks were changing too. Didn't as many live on farms anymore but had jobs in town and couldn't leave their work so easily. And the children, once they got grown, always wanted to move away. Go someplace better.

So better than half the tents were boarded up and closed now, and I always wondered if maybe one of these days, we'd get out to the Camp Ground and be the only ones there.

Why, even the preachers weren't the same anymore. Usually just one, and him right young at that, and with his head all full of dreams about working with the young people as well as having two services a day. But it usually turned out the same. He'd wind up preaching to all the old folks, who were the only ones who ever came to Camp Meeting anymore. And by the last service, that preacher would be looking out at us with wounded eyes.

Things always changing. Always. And sometimes not for the better!

Later, Wynona told us how she was standing in the checkout line at the grocery store and noticed Miss Alma Anderson in line ahead of her.

"A *funeral parlor!* Can you imagine?" Miss Alma was saying. "Thompson and Mr. Grower signed the papers yesterday afternoon. Wonder what Miss Addie would think of that!"

Wynona was standing there with her mouth hanging open, just like a bump on a log.

The house sold. Just like that, and for a *funeral parlor!*

Wynona said she must have almost lost her mind for a little second, because all she could picture was Miss Alma down at the courthouse in Louisville where she worked every Tuesday and Thursday from nine to noon—bending over an old Olivetti typewriter in that high-ceilinged room, slowly tap-tapping the keys, correcting the mistakes with the hard, white eraser, and blowing off the residue. Typing the very paper Thompson put his name to and signed it all away.

A funeral parlor! And right across the street and staring us in the face every time we water the flowers or sit on our own front porch!

Miss Alma was still in full cry, telling everyone in line and others gathered nearby every single detail she could remember about the sale of Miss Addie's house, including how Thompson's hand was shaking when he signed, and what Mr. Grower paid for it, and why he needed to move his funeral parlor from where it had been for the last thirty years.

"Why, he has so much business, what with most of the people around here being elderly, you know, that he needed room for expansion."

Then the clerk gathered Miss Alma's groceries, and reluctantly, she followed him out the front door and into the glaring sunshine. It was only then that Wynona realized she'd forgotten to get Miss Cora's Hadacol.

I know exactly how Wynona felt when she was coming home from the store, knowing what she had to tell us.

Thinking about how everything would have been so different if only Thompson had moved his family into the house. Because then something of Miss Addie would still be there.

Wynona was thinking so hard, that she drove right on past our driveway and had to brake hard and back up until she could make the turn. But she never once looked at Miss Addie's house, and when she drove up under the portico and saw Lauralee sitting alone in Miss Addie's chair, shelling butter beans in the shaded corner of the porch, she felt a strange surge of relief, like maybe she'd been worried about Lauralee and didn't even know it.

*W*ynona didn't say a thing when she came up the steps to the porch; she just stood still for a few minutes, looking at Lauralee and with that strange feeling still holding on. Seeing Lauralee sitting there shelling beans, with the bowl resting on her knees and the light against her cheek on one side. Said she thought it was something she'd seen before. Maybe a long time ago in another kitchen with windows that looked out over a field and all the way to the edge of that field where the trees started. And beyond that, seemed to her there was a ravine that went down to a creek. But she said she couldn't for the life of her remember where it was she'd seen such a thing.

Thank the good Lord, whatever Wynona had been close to remembering slipped right on past her before she could get hold of it, so she shook her head a little and said, "Mr. Grower's bought Miss Addie's house, and he's going to turn it into his new funeral parlor."

Lauralee must have understood what Wynona was saying, because immediately, she glanced across the street, as if there would be a big, black hearse already sitting in Miss Addie's driveway, like it was sitting there when we all got to Mr. Adkins' funeral all those years ago, with the back of it filled to bursting with that shiny casket and flowers packed around it, and sitting in the sun with the flowers all mashed against that hot glass. Because it was August dog days. And maybe . . . just maybe, Lauralee was remembering the flowers and wondering if among all the pinks and yellows, she'd see a face. Or what was left of it.

Oh, they both came too close that day, to remembering!

"You heard me right," Wynona told Lauralee. "A funeral parlor. And right across the street from us!"

With that, she came inside and brought the bag of groceries on in to the kitchen where I was chipping ice for the tea. When she put the bag down on the table, she gave out with a whooshing sound—as if all the air was gone out of her. Her standing there and staring at me with eyes that looked like they were burned into her face.

"Mr. Grower's bought Miss Addie's house and he's going to make it into a funeral parlor!" she said in what sounded like her last breath.

Even with the shock of it, I caught myself and hesitated for only a moment before I went right back to chipping ice and putting it into the glasses. And besides, that way I didn't have to look at Wynona, and she couldn't look at me.

"You want some tea?" I asked.

"Pet, didn't you hear what I said?"

"I heard."

"And . . . ?"

"And nothing. It's Mr. Thompson's house now, and I guess he can sell it to anybody he wants to. You remember to get the Hadacol?"

"No."

Lauralee had come into the house through the cool living room where the drapes were shut against the summer sun and fans were humming; she stopped in the kitchen doorway, still holding the bowl of half-shelled butter beans.

"Never mind," I said. "I'll go get it this afternoon." Then I went back to chipping ice as if that was the only thing in this world that mattered. Because I sure didn't want to think about what

101

it might bring, this shocking thing that was going to be happening right across the street from us.

Wynona stood silently for a few moments and then turned and went back toward the porch with Lauralee following her. I guess it surprised her, me not seeming to care much about there being a funeral parlor right across the street from our very own house.

But I sure did care! I just wasn't going to show it in front of Wynona and Lauralee, is all. So I stood at the sink and chipped enough ice to fix a dozen glasses of tea, and oh, I was so afraid. Felt like I was looking down into a deep old well and seeing a tiny circle way down there, but knowing good and well that what I was seeing was only the reflection of the circle I was leaning into the middle of. Way up high above the water. A little bitty me looking up from a circle of light I know isn't really there. Way down in the cool and dark and all walled around by old stones with moss growing on them.

I stayed at the sink until I felt a little steadier; then I poured the amber tea over the ice, put the glasses onto a tray, and started for the front porch. For some strange reason, I was thinking about Wynona forgetting the Hadacol and how we were all getting so old and forgetful. But how forgetful really? And right across the street was gonna be a reminder of everything I hoped they'd forgotten about forever.

And the other thing I was thinking about was that we knew now for sure that Thompson was selling Miss Addie's house, and after all, his children would never know what it meant to walk where their grandmother walked and their great-grandmother before her. Because all the people and all the things that happened before you, get to be who you are. Or something like that.

When Miss Cora got up from her rest, Wynona went right in her room and helped straighten her hair and put on her shoes, and of course, she told her about what she'd heard in the grocery store. But Miss Cora's eyes were sleepy and cloudy, like she couldn't seem to get all the way awake from her rest.

Almost like my mama's eyes when she got of an age and I tried to talk to her about something or other that was important. I remember one day when she was putting in the tomato plants, and I went out to the kitchen garden where she was bending over tying the plants to their stakes. And that was the very first time I saw that her shoulders were rounded. And her eyes, when she finally looked at me, were just like Miss Cora's that day. Sleepy and somehow so soft, you knew that any word you'd say would just get lost in all the clouds.

Almost the way it was when Wynona and Lauralee were just children coming here in the summertimes. Sometimes, I'd see Wynona pass by the bedroom and look in and see that someone—me or Mama—had just finished plumping up the featherbed until it was like a giant marshmallow and had smoothed the crisp, snowy-white sheet over it.

Something would always take hold of her, and she'd race into the room at full speed, leaping into the air and landing smack in the middle of the plumped-up bed and then feel that wonderful slow-sinking of the feathers and the cool smoothness of the sheet. She did it a lot, so I guess she figured it was worth the scolding she'd get if Miss Anne or the aunts caught her at it. But if it was me or Mama, we knew that there are some things a child just has to do. And we'd plump back up the feathers before anyone else found out about it. And it would be our secret—mine and Mama's and Wynona's.

I don't know why that reminds me of what Miss Cora's eyes looked like that day when Wynona tried to tell her about Miss Addie's house, but it did, sure enough. Maybe it's like when Wynona tried to tell her, someone just came along and plumped up the feathers again and it was like she'd never said it at all.

And come to think of it, that's the way we've pretty much always done things in this family—pretend we don't hear anything anybody says, or else pretend we don't understand. And it will all go away. Turn out to be a dream or something.

I could tell that Wynona was waiting and waiting for somebody to say something or other about what she'd heard in the grocery store, but nobody did. Maybe we were all waiting for somebody else to say something, but nobody wanted to be first. And besides, it couldn't be said anyway.

When we did start talking, it was about the weather and how hot it had been—because the summer heat had settled in, with that old sun just like a blast furnace and always overhead. And besides, weather was something we could talk about that was safe, you see.

So that's what we talked about when we sat out on the porch and fanned ourselves and watched Miss Addie's house. Me thinking about how it looked almost just the same as it always had. Except for something I couldn't quite figure out. An empty look, like all empty houses get to them. Like Miss Addie's house was holding its breath, waiting for the footsteps across the dining room or the echo of a voice.

On Friday of that next week, the heat wave broke at last, and that very change in the weather made us feel ever so much better. Because in the evening, the air was cool and somehow very fresh, because of the thunderstorm that came up that afternoon. I had seen it from the kitchen window and called out to no one in particular, "Bad cloud coming up fast! Better get the clothes in off the line!"

Lauralee got the big wicker basket and went outside to where those old black clouds were just boiling around in the sky, and hot gusts of wind lifted her apron and mussed her hair. I watched from the window as she took down the cotton bloomers and flowered aprons and dishcloths and two sheets that had grown all crisp and sweet-smelling in the sunshine. And just as she came back inside the back porch and closed the screened door behind her, the first deep growl of thunder came.

She dropped the basket right onto the porch and ran into the living room, to find Wynona.

It was sure some storm—with thunder and lightning and the coolingest wind. Then it settled into a good, drenching rain and finally cleared completely around eight o'clock. That was good, because then there wasn't enough daylight left for the sun to come back out and steam everything up.

All during the storm, Miss Cora stayed out on the porch, and Wynona said Miss Cora was gonna get struck by lightning one of these days, for sure. That's the way it always was between Miss Cora and Wynona when a storm came. Because Wynona was always one to run around and close every last window as soon as she heard that thunder, but Miss Cora wanted to leave the windows open so the cool air could flush the heat out of the house.

But Wynona always got her way about the windows, and I knew why.

Because when she and Lauralee were just children, living with their mama and papa in that old shanty house on Mr. Bondurant's land, they were scared to death of thunderstorms. Why, Mr. Sam, he would be out in the fields plowing, and sometimes Miss Emma got caught in the barn where she was milking. So Wynona and Lauralee were in the house alone, and Wynona kept looking and looking through the window to see if her papa or mama was coming. But they never did.

Mr. Sam didn't even quit his plowing unless the lightning got real bad, and then he'd head for the barn, because it was closer than the house. I guess nobody knew how scared Wynona and Lauralee really were.

Wynona would run through the house with Lauralee crying and hanging onto her waist and close every window, even while the thunder was rattling the panes of glass, and the lightning crackled and struck at the trees on the hill. Then they'd jump into their bed and pull the covers up over them, making kind of a tent out of it, so they could see each other. Wynona said that Lauralee always had her eyebrows drawn way down and looked at her so hard. Like something bad might happen if she lost her hold on looking at Wynona's face. And they never changed. Not one little bit.

But Miss Cora always went right out to the front porch the minute she heard thunder and stayed there the whole time it stormed, sitting in the porch swing, with the wind blowing her hair and the rain spattering her dress.

After the storm was over, we all sat out on that cool, damp porch, and Miss Cora started in on her storm story.

"Once, when I was just a child, I went with my papa to Savannah, to visit with Uncle Joseph. And while we were there, the weather turned real funny. So sticky and hot, and that was because a hurricane was coming. Right up the coast. Why, Papa and Uncle Joe had to push the upright piano against the door to keep it closed, that wind got so strong. It blew and blew for the longest kind of time.

"And I loved it more than anything in the whole world.

"Right after midnight, when I'd fallen asleep on the foldaway bed Uncle Joe had set up in the living room for me, Papa touched my shoulder, and I sprang awake right away—because Papa had said that we should be ready to run if the house started to blow apart. That's why Papa and Uncle Joe were sitting there watching the storm while I slept.

"But when Papa touched my shoulder, I knew right away that we wouldn't have to run from the storm. Because the storm was gone!

"Such a silence there was. Like I've never heard before. And Papa said for me to come with him because he wanted to show me something called the eye of the storm. So he and Uncle Joseph pushed the piano away from the door, and Papa took me up into his arms and carried me out onto the front porch steps.

"And there, in the blackest sky I've ever seen, were millions of stars winking. I'll never forget it. That black sky and the stars so close, I thought my hair would get tangled in them. Papa's shoulder so strong under my hands.

"He said the reason we could see all the stars there were in heaven was because the clouds were gone. Not even a little wisp to hide the stars, and the air so clean and clear and yet somehow so still, it almost pulled my breath away. Those big old palm trees standing there dripping and without a quiver, without a breath of wind to stir them.

"I wanted to go out into the yard, but Papa said we had to go back inside and get ready for more big winds. Because the hurricane would come back, and the wind would be from the other direction. He was right. Just as we got settled back inside, the wind smashed against the house, and how it did whistle and scream! And the whole house shuddered with it. And Papa and Uncle Joe had to push the piano through the kitchen and against the back door, to keep it closed.

"I could never forget what it was like, going out into the eye of the storm with my papa's strong arms holding me. And that's why I love the wind and the rain. Because maybe someday—but only if I'm very lucky—I'll get to be there again. That's why I'm not afraid of any storm in the whole world. Because I know that in the very middle of it there's something so beautiful, you can't even imagine it!

"A deep, peaceful place where you can see everything there is in the whole universe and where you can reach up and put your hands into the stars."

I thought about that a great deal, you see—what Miss Cora
said about being in the eye of the storm. Because that's
exactly what it was like for me, right then—a calm place in
between finding out about Thompson selling his mama's house
and whatever Mr. Grower would be doing to it. And in between
my promise to Miss Addie and what was gonna happen when
I kept my word.

Goodness!

But the first part of that calm didn't last very long, because one
day a truck from Wilson's Lumberyard pulled right up onto Miss
Addie's lawn. I don't know why it couldn't have used the driveway, but it didn't. Hurt me plenty, seeing that old truck driving on
the grass Miss Addie worked so hard to keep all pretty and green.

Two men got out and stood around with their hands in their
back pockets for awhile before they nodded their heads to each
other and started unloading lumber and drywall onto the porch
and some big boxes marked "equipment" and two kegs of nails.
We watched from behind the parlor curtains until they drove away.

"I wonder what kind of equipment it is," Wynona said. And
I sure don't think she meant to say that out loud. Just to think
it, was all. Miss Cora must not have heard her, and I just ignored
it, but Lauralee turned and walked toward the kitchen at the
back of the house.

Wynona looked at me and shrugged her shoulders. So it wasn't close to Wynona, but I knew it was to Lauralee. Almost coming up behind her and breathing on the back of her neck. Or worse, jumping out all of a sudden right in front of her eyes, like little white pebbles caught in the tread of rubber tires.

But maybe if she went in the kitchen and lifted the lid on the pot of peas and stood there stirring them or looking at the red geranium in the window over the sink, it would keep the memory away from her. So that whatever came too close would never find its way through the steam from the peas and the leaves of the geranium in the window and the dish towels and the coffeepot and the pitcher we used for making iced tea every single day of our lives.

Same kind of things Miss Emma worked so hard every day of her life to keep clean and pretty in that little old house. Because even though Miss Emma and Mr. Sam were both good, God-fearing people, Miss Emma wasn't interested in much of anything anymore, except cleaning and cooking, and Mr. Sam, why he didn't put any stock in church-going, and especially the religions that said the "going under" type of getting baptized was the only one any good.

Mr. Sam was a hard man in many ways, and he certainly had a notion about what it meant to be God-fearing, and he made the girls read the Bible, of course. But something must've happened to him somewhere down the road, because one time he said too many people talked about religion all the time, but that's all they did—talk about it—and most of them, those he knew of anyway, just hung up their religion with their Sunday pants and turned right around and cheated you on Monday morning. So he wasn't one to go to any church, though he'd been raised a Presbyterian.

When Mr. Adkins got such a bee in his bonnet about religion, he started coming by on Sunday mornings—when it was Brushy Creek's turn for the preacher—so Wynona could go to church with him, and Mr. Sam didn't mind.

"She's going to be his wife," he said. "And if church-going's what he wants, I guess she'd better get used to it right now." After awhile, Lauralee got to where she went along to church with them too, because as I've said, those girls were so used to doing everything together. So the three of them went to church once a month, and the other Sundays, they sat on the porch most of the afternoon, and Mr. Adkins read the Bible out

109

loud and told them exactly what it meant, word for word. Lauralee would slip away after an hour or so, but Wynona sat right there and listened to Mr. Adkins talking about what miserable sinners we all are and how every single one of us deserves nothing better than burning forever and ever.

One day Wynona let it slip that Lauralee hadn't ever been dunked—only sprinkled. Now Wynona herself had been baptized at First Baptist, because one of the aunts insisted on it, but that aunt had passed on right before Lauralee was born. Miss Emma took a long time to get her strength back and didn't seem to care about much of anything, but Mr. Sam took that baby right on over to a little church near Waynesboro and got her sprinkled.

Well, Mr. Adkins tried to stir everybody up about that, telling them it was dunking and only dunking that did the trick. But all his carrying on never came to anything, because nobody really listened to him anyway, except Wynona. Finally, Mr. Adkins went to the preacher about it, and pretty soon, the preacher came to call one Sunday afternoon, trying to get Mr. Sam to make Lauralee come and get dunked. Mr. Sam didn't bother to tell him Lauralee had already been sprinkled, and I'm sure Mr. Adkins didn't tell him either. If he'd known, I don't think he'd have come around, bothering them about it. Because a baptizing is a baptizing. Period.

But from what I've heard, when Mr. Sam heard what it was the preacher wanted, he just got up out of his chair and went to the barn and started doing the milking. Of course, that was Miss Emma's job, the milking was, but Mr. Sam did it that day, and Wynona said he almost pulled that poor old cow to pieces, he milked her so hard.

So nothing ever came of it, except that some folks clucked their tongues and said when a man like Mr. Adkins thinks he's got religion, things can get pretty miserable for everybody else.

That's why I say maybe if I'd looked deep in his eyes, I might have seen something there—something I could have warned Wynona and Lauralee about. But I didn't look. Because, like I said before, I was all caught up in the plans for the wedding.

Oh, I never did see Wynona and Lauralee have such a good time. Of course, they didn't have any money for buying fancy things, but it was all a lot simpler back in those days, and nobody ever heard of paying a florist, not when there were plenty of flowers all around for the picking. And nobody'd heard of using what you call a caterer, because there were always plenty of womenfolk who'd get together and plan everything out and help me and Mama fix the food. And too, back in those days, girls sewed their own dresses. So money wasn't really very important.

Of course, Miss Anne and the aunts did everything they could to help. Bought fabric for the wedding dress and the maid-of-honor dress—that was for Lauralee, of course. And they did most of the hand-sewing them-selves, but Wynona and Lauralee spent many days here in this very house, sewing on those dresses and on Wynona's trousseau.

What a wonderful time that was, with those yards and yards of taffeta spread out in the dining room and Miss Cora bending over the old trea-dle sewing machine and all of them doing hand-sewing and laughing together every now and then. And there were so many straight pins in the rug, I thought we'd never get 'em all out.

When time came around for the wedding, we took all kinds of flow-ers to the church to make it look pretty. Apple blossoms and peach blos-soms and some narcissus, and too, we had big bushes of baby's breath and bridal wreath in the yard and we pretty well stripped them old bushes bare. But the church sure looked pretty. Like all springtime had gotten gathered up and put in one place.

And I've always kind of wondered about that—flowers, that is. Because we load up a church with them for a wedding, and we do the same thing for a funeral. And two such different things they are. Maybe.

Of course, people in town knew about the plans for the wedding, and there was some talk about a man of Mr. Adkins' age marrying a young woman in her twenties. But mostly, folks also thought—and probably they were right—that no other caller would've come along for Wynona, so maybe it was a blessing for a girl who would've been a spinster for sure. Nobody was worried about Lauralee getting married, because she was just getting prettier and prettier every single day of her life, and boys was already trying to talk to her, and her not even fifteen years old yet.

Mr. Adkins was a very private man, so nobody knew much about his business, except, of course, for when he got religion. After that, if any-body tried to talk to him, he'd just come out with something like, "Repent!" And folks were pretty uncomfortable with that, 'specially when it got around town that he said that to anybody from First Baptist who came into his store. Maybe he was trying to drum up business for Brushy Creek Church and get new members so they could get a regular preacher for every single Sunday. Still, he seemed to be right honest in his business;

he never charged too much for anything—and he could have, seeing as how he owned the only hardware store in town—so he had a good business just about guaranteed. That is, if you could get in, buy what you needed, and get out—without him getting all revved up about religion.

The wedding itself was lovely. Not too many people because it was a small, private wedding—Miss Emma and Mr. Sam and Miss Anne, Miss Cora, and the aunts. And Lauralee and also the girls' Aunt Fairleigh, from Mr. Sam's side of the family, who drove over from Augusta for the wedding. And me. Mama was invited, of course, but she said she'd better stay home and make sure everything was ready for the party afterward.

Mr. Adkins hadn't any family in these parts, but his nephew came up from Swainsboro to be the best man. He was thin and pale and had a real bad complexion and wore a Sunday suit that smelled to the high Heavens of mothballs. But the wedding was pretty anyway.

Wynona was lovely, just like all brides, and Lauralee wore a pale pink dress and flowers in her hair. The only thing that seemed the least bit strange was that Wynona had asked Miss Anne if she could borrow our banquet-sized lace tablecloth, and of course, Miss Anne said yes, thinking it would be for some table or other in the church. But lo and behold, when Wynona started down the aisle, she had that tablecloth on her head like a veil, and it was way too heavy for something like that. Just for an instant, when I first saw her coming down the aisle, I almost laughed because she looked like one of those Saturday suppers my mama used to leave on the sideboard all covered up with a cloth. I could see one side of Miss Anne's face from where I was sitting at the back of the church, and she was fire-red with embarrassment.

If we'd only known Wynona wanted a lace veil, we could've fixed up something that would've been better than a tablecloth for goodness sake. But we didn't know. They were very proud people, you see, and didn't like asking for things. Still, Miss Anne said later that Miss Emma certainly knew better than that, and she should never have let Wynona walk down the aisle with a tablecloth thrown over her head for Heaven's sake! And I thought so too, but, of course, it wasn't my place to say anything.

When the wedding was over, everybody came back to this good house for a reception, and we had us a cake with sugar frosting on it that took me and Mama two whole days to make and put together, and all kinds of the best things to eat you could ever think of, like little bitty sandwiches

112

with the crust cut off the bread. And the cake and sandwiches were served on the fine crystal plates, and them with little fancy cut-out papers on them. Why, I'd never before in my whole life seen those crystal dishes outside the china cabinet. And we had us little silver dishes full of mints and even one of candied almonds, and a fruit punch with ginger ale in it.

Mama and me stayed busy, what with making sure everybody had plenty to eat, but we could pretty much watch everything that was going on in the parlor. Mr. Adkins hadn't said much of anything, and we really didn't think he would. This was a woman thing, you see, and somehow or other, it pleased us the way he kind of stood around and didn't seem to know what to do with his hands. I don't know why that was. Maybe, sometimes, women like to see a man feeling helpless, you know, and it isn't anything unkind. Just maybe our way of having all the answers for once. Still, everybody was nice to him, of course, and he was right pleasant, and he sure looked nice in his new suit.

All of us was having the best time, and once, when I was bringing out more little sandwiches, I saw Wynona looking at herself in the dining room mirror, and it was one of those things you remember forever and ever. She was so pretty that day, and she knew it, and that was just fine. I guess it's only on a woman's wedding day she gets to look and feel just like a queen or something, and she doesn't have to pretend to be humble.

But, you know, when folks was just about ready to go around the table a second time to have more good food, Mr. Adkins heaved a deep sigh and looked at Wynona, and I thought maybe he was going to make a toast to her. Because he still had a cup of fruit punch in his hand, and everybody stopped talking and looked at him and smiled. But he just put his cup on the mantelpiece and said to Wynona, "It's time to go home."

I still don't know what there was about it seemed so blunt-like, but it was, and it stopped everything. Thinking back on it, I suppose there was some sort of a clock ticking away inside us that told us about how long a party should last, and it was just like he was cutting everything off right in the middle.

Like he was in a hurry.

That was the first time I believed maybe Miss Anne and the aunts were wrong about thinking he was a gentleman. It sure takes more than a white collar to make a man that.

The way Wynona looked up at him, I could tell her heart had gone right into her throat, and she was just now realizing—after all the planning and

113

the excitement and the wedding and the party, that she had to leave with him. Go home with her husband. Leave Lauralee for the first time in her life and her mama and papa too and go to Mr. Adkins' house and start a new life. Too, she was a very proper young woman of course, and she didn't know anything about being with a man. Not in the way a wife would be with a husband.

Years later, Wynona told me that when she went into the room to put on her going-away suit, Miss Emma followed her, and Wynona figured her mama would say something to her about being a wife, but she didn't really want to hear it. Because she was already scared to death, without hearing anything about that. So she hurried up changing her clothes and fixing her hair, and Miss Emma sat right there on the bed, running her hand back and forth, back and forth over the bedspread.

Finally, Miss Emma spoke, but she didn't look at Wynona, and Wynona didn't look at her mama.

"Whatever he wants to do, you let him do it."

That's what Miss Emma said to Wynona, and that's what Wynona did. Or, at least, that's what she tried to do.

Right up until the very day we killed him.

*O*h, the things that were going through my mind! Remembering and feeling all the terrible hurt of it—just as hurtful as when it really happened, all those long years ago.

And I knew full well that what was still to come was gonna be the worst of all.

So I guess I got myself into a little bit of a mood. I just didn't feel like talking. Felt like I needed to curl up inside myself and rest for a good long time—get ready for it. And that's pretty much what I did.

Nobody seemed to notice, except for Wynona. She cornered me in the pantry one day and whispered, "Are you feeling all right, Pet? You aren't getting ready to have another spell, are you?" There was nothing I could answer to that, so I shook my head and prayed to the sweet Lord Jesus that I was telling the truth!

Mostly, we went about our business during the days and sat together on the porch nearly every evening, and I was happy when Miss Cora got into a mood to tell us her stories all over again— every last one of them. The great oak story, and the one about Hezekiah Longwood, the unmarked grave, and about the eye of the storm. All the while her voice droned on, I sort of rested myself against those comfortable, old words and watched the piles of lumber and the boxes sitting so still and quiet on Miss Addie's porch.

I really wasn't surprised when one twilight evening, a strange, black car came down the street so slowly and turned into Miss Addie's driveway. Two men got out, and there was just enough light left for us to see that one was Mr. Grower and the other a stranger. They went inside, and we watched the lights go on and then off in every room, one by one. After a while, the two men came out on Miss Addie's porch and stood there talking for the longest kind of time. The stranger moved closer to Miss Addie's porch light and wrote things on a little notepad and showed them to Mr. Grower, who nodded his head.

When they finally went back across the yard to the car, Mr. Grower hesitated for a moment, looked across the street toward our porch, tipped his hat, and said, "Evening, ladies."

Early the next morning, I was running the carpet sweeper in the parlor when I saw the man who'd been with Mr. Grower the evening before come driving back up in Miss Addie's driveway in the same black car, followed by a truckload of shirtless, sun-tanned young men who all needed haircuts and were carrying big hammers and one a crowbar.

I called to Wynona to come see, and we watched from behind the curtains while the men—just like a swarm of ants—carried the lumber and the drywall and the kegs of nails indoors. In a while, we could hear all kinds of banging and tearing up of things, and then the men started bringing out stacks of ripped-up boards and big barrels of trash and throwing it all into the back of the truck they'd parked in the shade of the big pecan tree.

At noontime, the men ate their lunch on Miss Addie's front porch, with their big work boots propped up on the banisters, and then, one by one, they stood and stretched and scratched themselves and grumbled and went back inside and started again with the sawing and the hammering and the ripping out of goodness-knows-what.

Seems like all we could hear that whole day was hammering and sawing and wood splintering and plaster falling, and once in a while, a man's voice hollering, "Hold it, Tiny! It's done come loose on this end." Late in the afternoon, one of the men took a big sledgehammer and went around in the back of Miss Addie's house and commenced to knocking out the very back wall of her lovely old carriage house. Wynona was the one who figured out it had to be enlarged if Mr. Grower was going to get his hearse into it. So all the noise continued until five o'clock, when the men loaded themselves into the truck and drove away, leaving Miss Addie's house looking exhausted.

"Oh, I hate to see things change," Miss Cora announced that evening, when we were sitting on the porch. And it didn't seem to be the kind of thing she expected anyone to answer—just something she needed to say out loud. Because what kind of an answer could anybody give to that? Nobody likes changes, I guess. We get used to things a certain way, and we want them to stay like that. And when—as it always happens—something changes that we don't like, we kinda step backwards in time and try to keep a little place in us where the old ways can walk around in a circle like a tired old dog and then settle down and stay forever.

"Makes me feel just like I did one time when a traveling circus came to town, and my mama and papa took me and Emma to it," Miss Cora said, and we all perked up at that, because we never heard that one before. At least, not that we remembered.

"There was something called a freak show that Mama and Papa wouldn't let us go see, because the sign out in front of the tent said there was a real, honest-to-goodness 'Reptile Lady' inside, and the picture on the sign showed her limbs almost to her knees, something Mama said was shameful!

"But I wanted to see that reptile lady so bad, because the man out front was hollering to everyone about how the reptile lady's mama had been scared by a terrible snake, and that's why her baby was born with real snakeskin all over her and also a split-in-two tongue. And sure enough, her legs—what we could see of them on the picture—were covered in shiny, green-gold scales!

"But Papa said no. And I'd never in all my life disobeyed him, but my wanting to see that reptile lady was too strong for me to fight against. So when Mama and Emma were busy laughing and watching Papa try to win a kewpie doll for Emma by knocking over some milk bottles with a little ball, I sneaked away from them and went right back to the reptile lady tent.

"No one was out front, so I just lifted up a little flap in the canvas and went right in. So dark in there I could hardly see and the smell of sawdust and wooden benches and cigar smoke. And the whole place was filled with men and they were clapping their hands and whistling.

"The stage was all lit up just like daylight, and that reptile lady was sitting there on a little stool, wearing hardly anything at all. She was all purple and green on her skin and covered with shiny scales like sequins or something, and her split-in-two, purple tongue was hanging out of her mouth. And with its little split ends just twitching around!

"I stood there as if I were rooted to the ground, and all of a sudden, something grabbed my arm—liked to have scared me half to death! It was my papa come after me. He took me out and never said a word to me about it, but when we got back home, he told Mama to put me to bed without any supper."

I was sitting there thinking how much I'd enjoyed that little story but wondering what on earth it had to do with anything. And then, as if Miss Cora could tell what I was wondering about, she added: "That's the very same feeling I have right now about Addie's house. I hate it, and I'm so scared of it, and whatever is in there is so terrible, I have to see it. Only this time, my papa won't be there to take me out."

We all sat silently for a long time, and then Miss Cora added, "I wonder if any of those workmen know anything about carving gravestones . . . and did we go down to Brushy Creek Cemetery last Sunday?"

"Yes, ma'am," Wynona and I chorused. "We went!"

Because what we had finally decided to do was tell Miss Cora we'd gone down there, and maybe she would think she'd just forgotten it. And we were right.

"Oh, that's right," she admitted reluctantly. "I remember now. And I wrote to Frances. She sure is taking her time answering my letter!"

I glanced at Wynona and lifted my eyebrows as if to ask, *Well, what now?*

But Miss Cora didn't say anything else.

For the next two weeks, the men came back every single day except Sundays to work on Miss Addie's house, and then one day they drove away and didn't come back at all. Just like that. About that same time, Wynona went out to our carriage house and brought in some of the boxes we would use to pack things in to take with us out to Mount Horeb Camp Ground in August.

"Awful early for that, isn't it?" I asked.

"A little," Wynona admitted. "But I just can't wait to go somewhere else so we won't have to be so close to whatever they've done to Miss Addie's house. Getting ready for Camp Meeting will give us something else to think about, at least."

"Won't stop what's happening over there," I reminded her.

"I know. But I'm just so weary of it."

So we busied ourselves for Camp Meeting, spending more time than we needed to and looking for ways to draw out the preparations. But I kept wondering if this would be the year when we'd be the only ones there. Why, even Miss Delia was getting on in years and couldn't stay out there the whole time. So maybe this time the lone, young preacher would be the most wounded of all— and he'd have to deliver his sermons to long rows of empty pews.

Still, we got ready, just as if it was all those long years ago and practically everyone we knew was going there. Wynona even drove us over to Waynesboro, just to buy a new oilcloth for the table, though we could probably have found one right there in town. But we sure had ourselves some fun. We looked through one interesting store after another and, when lunchtime came, we stopped at a grocery store and bought picnic fixings and found us a roadside park where there was a table in the shade of a big oak tree, and we made our sandwiches and ate them and had a good time.

Later, on three Saturday mornings in a row, Wynona and Miss Cora went shopping to find exactly the kind of new sheets they wanted for Camp Meeting, even though the ones we already had were perfectly fine. They went to lunch at the Dairy Queen every time they shopped for new sheets, and one day they even brought home an embroidery kit for Lauralee. Wynona spent many long afternoons teaching her how to make all the stitches. The hardest one was a French knot, but Lauralee was real sweet and patient about taking out the tangled stitches over and over again. And when the day finally came that she drew the needle through and discovered a perfect French knot on the front, she looked up at Wynona with her eyes shining. And, I declare, I think she almost smiled.

And that's how it came at long last—time for Camp Meeting. The third Friday morning in August, we packed up everything we would need and called the icehouse to deliver the ice out there on Friday afternoon so the icebox would be ready for us to use right away. Wynona went and got Minnie Louise so she could go with us out to Mount Horeb to help with the cleaning.

All morning, Wynona, Minnie Louise, and I loaded the car with boxes of new sheets and towels and canned goods, two electric fans, the spare bed pillows, and a cardboard box full of Miss Cora's things—tonic, liniment, ace bandages for her knees, and a lavender plastic box of lilac-scent bath powder that was mixed with cornstarch for her heat rash. Then Wynona drove me and Minnie Louise out to Mount Horeb.

The ice truck was already waiting for us, so I wiped out the icebox on the back porch first thing, and when the huge block of ice was settled in it, there was something in the cold, musty smell of that box that reminded me of all those ice slivers I'd snitched as a child.

"You sure you and Minnie Louise will be all right out here alone tonight?" Wynona asked, after the ice truck left and we had unloaded the boxes from the car and propped open all the windows and looked under the bed frames to make sure no snakes were hiding there.

"We'll be fine," I said. "I see there's a right big wasp nest under the eaves around to the side, so be sure to leave me some matches and a good piece of newspaper."

"Kitchen matches are in the grocery box," Wynona said. "And I didn't bring any newspapers, but we covered the mattresses with them when we left last summer, so you can use those. Just don't burn the place down."

"Been burning wasp nests all my life," I protested. "Haven't burned anything down yet."

Minnie Louise rolled her eyes at Wynona as if to say, *Don't get her started,* and somewhat reluctantly, Wynona went back toward the car.

She called back to us, "Some of the Pattersons moved in today down at the end, and I saw someone sweeping out the Public Tent, so if youall need anything, just remember they're here. And there's a phone at the Public Tent."

"All we need," I said, "is for you to go on so we can get started." But I was glad to hear there were other folks already at the Camp Ground. So at least this wouldn't be the year when we were the only ones who still came for that grand old family tradition.

"We'll see you tomorrow then!" Wynona hollered from the car, and when the Buick pulled away, it left behind a red dust cloud that floated away toward the cemetery and broke up among all the white stones.

I pulled some of the old sheets of newspaper off the bed in the front room and rolled them into a long taper. "Let's get those wasps out of here first off," I said to Minnie Louise.

The nest was a good-sized one, nearly as big as a lunch plate and with about fifty full-grown wasps crawling around on it. Evil-looking black things, with their tails arched in a terrible curl, like all they had on their minds was stinging somebody.

Minnie Louise and I stood there in the grass, listening to the sound of crickets from across the road and the low hum of the wasps fanning the nest with their wings. For a little minute, it seemed almost sad, me getting ready to destroy something so complicated as that nest. But then, wasps and people don't get along too well, and I knew that one of these days, there wouldn't be any more folks coming out to Mount Horeb anymore, and the wasps could do anything they wanted, with nobody to bother them.

"You got any tobacco on you, case I get stung?" I asked Minnie Louise as I lit the end of the newspaper taper.

"Got cigarettes, should you need them," Minnie Louise replied, taking a few steps backwards. "You be sure you get them good the first time," she warned. "Else we'll be eat up!"

The flame caught on that old dry paper and flared up as I held it. I pulled the collar of my dress up tight around my neck and before the wasps could get the least little bit suspicious, I pushed that fire up against the nest and hunched my shoulders up over my ears. The wings burned away so fast, and wasps started falling all around me. Not a one had gotten away before the fire had done its work. When the last one fell, I dropped the burning paper on the ground, and Minnie Louise and I danced around on it, stomping the ashes and the wingless wasps.

"Any in my hair?" I asked, shivering a little.

"Not a one, and I sure would be able to see 'em," she laughed. "Your hair's just as white as cotton!"

"Well, you're not any spring chicken yourself," I retorted, and Minnie Louise jutted out her bottom lip in protest. We stood for a few moments, looking at each other, and I guess maybe we hadn't taken such a good and meaningful look at each other in a long time.

"We're gettin' old, Pet," Minnie Louise finally said. "And so much we haven't never taken care of."

Well, I sure didn't want to hear about that, so I said, "I want that nest," and started swinging at it with the broom. Minnie Louise backed up and I finally hit it a good blow and snapped that stem where it was anchored under the eaves. "I been wanting to do some good fishing, and here's my bait," I added.

I picked up the nest and turned it in my hands to study that piece of work—tiny chambers, each fire-singed but still I could see through the covers to where the black eyes of the bulging white grubs looked back at me.

"That's amazing," I whispered. "Wonder how on earth they know to build it so?"

"You was always one for wondering about things," Minnie Louise said. "You always had to know why things was the way they was. Almost drove your mama crazy, what with all your wondering."

"But don't you wonder?" I asked.

"No," Minnie Louise answered. "And don't you start wondering why I don't wonder. Now let's get busy or we'll never get it all done before dark."

So I put the wasp nest in an old bread wrapper, set it in the cool icebox where the grubs would keep for fishing bait, and the rest of the afternoon, we worked almost without a word, dragging the straw mattresses out to air in the sweet grass, cleaning the wood cook stove, getting an old mouse nest out of the dresser drawer, and putting fresh paper on the shelves in the cabinet beside the stove.

At suppertime, we sat at the long table and ate canned peaches, johnny cakes, and cheese. And washed it all down with cold RC colas.

Right out of the blue, Minnie Louise said, "Ain't you even gonna ask about Lizzy? And Samantha? You don't even want to see Lizzy's letters anymore, you know that?"

"I know that." And I also knew she'd had something or other on her mind all day long, especially after what she'd said about us getting so old so fast and with so much we hadn't taken care of.

"Well, I don't know what all you've had on your mind this whole summer, but it ain't right—you not reading Lizzy's letters."

"I know," I repeated.

"I try so hard to be patient with you," Minnie Louise said, her voice rising a little, so I knew she had quite a flood of words all saved up. "But I'm near about the end of my rope!"

She groped around in her apron pocket and pulled out an envelope. "So here's the letter I got this week, and it says some things you need to hear." When I made no move to take the letter, she said, "I'm gonna read it to you then. And you just sit right there and listen to it, whether you want to or not."

Minnie Louise took the letter from the envelope and unfolded it onto the tablecloth, smoothing it with her hands and watching me with her hawklike gaze.

"Dear Mama," Minnie Louise read and then stopped and frowned at me. "And you never even took care of that! Said a long time ago you'd tell her. But you never did. That isn't right, Pet. Lizzy still calling me Mama, after all this time!"

Minnie Louise's nostrils flared out and her chin jutted. But still, I said not a word. She snorted and then went back to reading the letter in a voice that broke each word into separate sounds. Like bricks she was gonna use to build a wall or something.

"I am writing this letter to you on my new typewriter. I have been made a manager in this office, and that means I get a new typewriter—an electric one—and a raise, as well. I have much more responsibility now and haven't had time to write to you in quite a while. I'm sorry about that. Everything has been happening so fast around here, I have been running to keep up with it. As if my being made manager wasn't good news enough, we just got a letter yesterday saying Samantha won a scholarship to the University of Georgia. Can you imagine? My baby girl going to college? So in spite of my longer hours at work, I'm going to try and find time to do some sewing before classes start. I want her to have nice clothes like the other girls. So if you and Aunt Pet get a hankering to do some sewing, Samantha would appreciate it, I know. She said the other day she wanted to have a skirt of black watch plaid. I can help pay for the fabric, if you and Aunt Pet could please do the sewing. Oh, Mama! Can you imagine! Our Samantha going to college!

"I'll write again next week and tell you more. Hope you are being faithful about taking that new arthritis medicine the doctor recommended. Is it doing any good for you? Write and let me know. Give my love to Aunt Pet. Love, Lizzy."

"College?" I asked.

"College," Minnie Louise answered. "Your granddaughter's going to college."

"Well, I never! Little Samantha?"

"Samantha ain't little no more," Minnie Louise growled.

"Little Samantha?" I was stuck on the words. They were the only things I could say.

"I *said* she ain't little no more!" Minnie Louise was almost shouting, but for the life of me, I couldn't imagine why she was upset. "Just do you think and see how long it's been," she added.

I tried my best to think, but *little Samantha?* was all I could find.

"How long's it been since you looked in a mirror, Pet?" Minnie Louise asked, but I sure couldn't see what on earth mirrors had to do with anything. "I done told you your hair's white," she added. "Whatsa matter? You think time's standing still?"

"What's that about my hair?" Somehow, I was feeling all confused, thinking that certainly, it had been only a few months ago when Lizzy held the newborn Samantha out to me. "Here, Aunt Pet," she had said. "Would you like to hold the baby?"

"Pet?" Minnie Louise yelled, but I studied the pattern in the tablecloth for a long minute before I finally responded.

"What?"

"I'm worried about you. And I want you to tell me what's wrong with you."

Me sitting there still studying the tablecloth and thinking that yes, maybe I could tell Minnie Louise, and I looked up at her and opened my mouth to say it, to let it all come out to somebody else, so I wouldn't have to carry it by myself ever again. But my mouth opened and closed a few times, and nothing came out, because *what* could I tell her? Why, I didn't even understand, myself, what it was I was hurting so bad about.

"Miss Addie . . ." I started out, though I didn't know where on earth I was going from there.

"Miss Addie?" Minnie Louise prompted, drawing down her eyebrows. "What about Miss Addie?"

"I promised . . ." I tried again, and Minnie Louise was patient for only a second or two before she snorted, "Well, I sure ain't seen you worried about no promises before!"

Now, Minnie Louise was a very good person and mostly full of real good intentions, but it was just like her to lead you on with a show of genuine concern and then turn right around and blast you with whatever you were trying to say. So I smiled and shook my head while she flung at me all the words that had been threatening to spill over all afternoon.

"I sure don't see you worrying about no promise you made to me!" she huffed. "Promised me a long time ago you'd take care of telling Lizzy, and you never done it, not to this very day! You never done it, Pet!"

I said not a word, because she was right, of course. But I sat there wondering why I had taken my promise to Miss Addie so seriously. Because it was almost what you could call a death-wish. Was that it? Would the day of Minnie Louise's death have to come before I would be able to keep my word to *her?* It was a terrible thought.

125

But Minnie Louise wasn't gonna wait for anything else from me. She went roaring along, in typical Minnie Louise fashion: "Well, all I can say is, thank the good Lord Lizzy and Samantha ain't like you, and they didn't have to do like you done."

"They could've done worse," I said, waking up a little and wondering what I would see, did I ever decide to look in a mirror. How old was I really getting?

"But they did better," Minnie Louise countered. "In spite of you, they did better."

"Of course, I wanted them to do better than me," I raised my voice and entered into a conversation I had no real way to understand. Still, that seemed better than just sitting there trying to weather Minnie Louise's anger. "What else do you think I left Lizzy with you for?"

"You left her because you said you couldn't take her back to Miss Cora's, and I never did understand that. Why, your very own mama raised you right there in that very house, and it worked out just fine."

"I couldn't," I said. "And I can't tell you why."

"Have anything to do with Wynona's little baby?"

"Maybe."

"Well, I don't think that was it," Minnie Louise said. "I think it's just that you were scared of Lizzy, right from the time she was a little bitty baby. Because she wasn't like you. You couldn't stand to be around her because you knew Lizzy was strong, and she wouldn't never learn to bow and scrape and grin like a chessy cat all the time. Like you did." Then she added, "Like you still do."

"She got that honest, sure enough," I mused. "Her daddy was a man who never did learn how to stay safe."

All of a sudden, I remembered what he looked like, all those long years ago. Tall and straight and with beautiful, mahogany skin. How he showed up in town, and we fell head-over-heels in love, and even though Miss Cora tried to warn me, I went with him to the church and we got married. I knew he wouldn't last long, and I was right. It was only a week or so before the sheriff got him. That's how arrogant he was. But that was long enough for me to remember him forever. And to get Lizzy.

"You mean he never learned how a black man had to do, to get along," Minnie Louise said.

"I guess that's right."

"Well, you know good and well that ain't where she got it."

I sat as still as a statue, scared of the words I knew were coming.

"It was her granddaddy gave it to her, and you know that as good as I do!" Minnie Louise said, and she got up and wiped the johnny cake crumbs off the table with the palm of her hand.

"And now Samantha's going to college, and she's smart, and she's beautiful, and you don't even care about her."

She stormed out, and I heard her running water into the dishpan.

"I care," I said to the red-checkered tablecloth.

By dusk, we'd brought the sun-freshened straw mattresses back indoors and put clean sheets on all the beds. The dishes were washed, dried, and stacked on shelves covered in fresh paper. Minnie Louise latched the screen door and we sat down at the table where the lamp put a yellow glow over the tablecloth. Behind us, in the graveyard and in the deep woods, tree frogs pumped out their singing and the locusts chirped in the tall grass near the kitchen.

"Tell me more about Samantha," I said.

"Whatcha wanna know?"

"How come she's going to college."

"I already told you. 'Cause she ain't like you. And her mama ain't like you neither."

"I guess you're right."

"I know I'm right."

I didn't say anything, and Minnie Louise continued.

"Makes a body sick to see you bowing and scraping like you do. How come you still doing that?"

I didn't try to answer her, because I knew Minnie Louise would never understand the way it had been for me. The way it still was. Because everything changed too fast. Rosa Parks and what she did. And I knew Miss Cora and Wynona were watching me and wondering if I'd rise up some morning singing "We Shall Overcome!" and tell them to fix their own doggoned breakfast.

It was terrible, the waiting they did. The waiting I did.

And while we waited, we were so very polite to each other.

"Pet, may I please have some more coffee?" Wynona said. And "Of course," I said. And "Thank you," she said. And "You're welcome," I said.

And it never happened, my rising up. Because I wanted us all to forget about it so we could just go back to being with each other.

But Lizzy rose up. And then Samantha rose up too, higher than any of us had ever gone before! And I never lifted a finger to help either one of them.

I sure enough didn't say that to Minnie Louise.

"Sure is quiet out here." Minnie Louise's voice broke into my thoughts, and I smiled because I could tell by her eyes she was worried she'd hurt my feelings.

"Hard to believe it's time for Camp Meeting again so soon," I said. "Seems like only yesterday we were here. But it's been a whole year. A whole year and it feeling like it was only yesterday."

"Time gets away from us," Minnie Louise said.

"Sure does," I answered and I looked through the screen door to where I could see the white tombstones glowing in the darkness.

We went to bed in the smallest bedroom, the only one near the kitchen. The cook's room, it had been, years and years ago, and the room where my mama slept during Camp Meeting, and her mama before her. And maybe even Mama Sunrise. Maybe.

As I drifted off, all of them came and gathered around the bed so quiet-like that Minnie Louise never heard a thing. And I fell asleep to the sound of my mama's voice, telling me once again about Mama Sunrise: "Great big woman, not fat, mind you, but plenty big. Her wearing real African clothes too, like I saw one time in a book. Blood-red rag wrapped around and around her head, just piled all up layer after layer, until it looked just like a big red crown. And her face big and broad and always smiling. Goodness! Could she ever smile. Shiny white teeth and a

128

pretty gap right in front and her smiling so big, you'd think she'd just explode or something and shower gold sparkles all over the place. And she was strong, yes, Lord! Chopped wood like a man, and carried a baby on her back while she did it. And if she'd known about your papa, little Pet . . . I think she would have been real surprised, but she would have been pleased. Because he was the finest man who ever drew breath on the face of this old earth. And when you were born, I was just praying the whole time you wouldn't look like him. Or if you did, that they wouldn't notice. Because then, I'd have had to send you away. Like you had to do with your baby. Because it all, or most of it anyway, waited for her. Because when it came time to . . ."

"I LOOKED OVER JORDAN AND WHAT'D I SEE-E-E?" A deep, strong voice that crowded in over my mama's voice. And Mama looked up, surprised.

"COMIN' FOR TO CARRY ME HO-O-O-ME . . ."

Mama Sunrise?

And then I finally got awake, and I heard the voice reach out for the high note and hold it just like a big dog howling, and the crickets stopped and so did Minnie Louise's snoring, and she sat up. "What in the name of Heaven is that?"

"A BA-A-ND OF AN-GELS, COMIN' AFTER ME-E, COMIN' FOR T'CARRY ME HO-O-O-ME."

When I got up, the old bed springs squeaked, and the voice stopped, but it had been there; I was sure of that. Couldn't have been a dream I was having, not if it waked up Minnie Louise as well.

"Somebody out in the yard. Singing," I whispered.

"What on earth!" Minnie Louise whispered back, sounding half scared and half angry.

We tiptoed to the window and looked out, and there, in faint light from the moon, we could see a woman squatting on the ground under the window. A big woman, and old. And when she saw us, she bellowed, "Well, it's about time you come. 'Cause I be hongry!"

An old, old woman. A gray woman. Gray hair and black skin long ago turned to the color of old ashes. And eyes so deep and black, but somehow flat, and almost like an animal's eyes at night along the highway, when car lights shine back from them.

"Who're you?" Minnie Louise hollered.

"ME!" the old woman shouted happily, showing her toothless gums. "Hongry!"

"Who are you?" I asked again, after we'd gotten her inside and made her sit down at the table. We gave her a johnny cake and an RC cola, and she chomped and slurped as if she was starved half to death.

"Don' know," she said after awhile. "Don' rightly remember. Don' make no nebber mind."

"Whatchu doing out here in the middle of the night?" Minnie Louise grumbled, and the woman looked at us intently. She seemed to be reaching deep down and far away to find an answer. Her eyes moved from Minnie Louise to me and back again, without a speck of understanding.

"Something bad wrong with her," Minnie Louise whispered to me, with the whites showing around her eyes.

"Looking for my mama," the old woman finally muttered.

"Your *mama?*" we chorused, for if that old woman had a mama who was still alive, she'd be older than anybody who ever lived.

"Mama," the woman repeated. "She know where the Sin-eater be."

"Lord, have mercy on us!" Minnie Louise breathed. "Sin-eater? What's that?"

"Never heard of such a thing," I said. "Sounds terrible."

"Sin-eater," the woman insisted. "He gotta come now. Mama'll know. Mama'll hep me find him." And she fell silent again.

I watched her for a few moments.

"Well, there's no use sitting here all night trying to figure out this foolishness. Let's us go to bed, and we'll see about it in the morning," I said.

Minnie Louise stared at me in horror. "You gonna let her sleep *here*? What'll we do if she cuts our throats in the night?"

"Look at her real good, Minnie Louise. She ain't up to doing anything, much less cut somebody's throat."

The old woman was falling asleep right where she sat, hands resting palms up on the table, and the skin on her arms like thin parchment or one of those old fall leaves, all dried up and ready to fall apart. Her chin drooped down, a slow folding-in and drifting away.

We made her a bed on the settee, because Minnie Louise wasn't about to put her in a real bed. "No tellin' what kind of bugs she's got, and I'm not washing those sheets again!" she insisted. Then we got one of us on either side and led her to the settee where she settled down, grumbled a little until she got the pillow just right, and fell asleep.

Minnie Louise and I slept very lightly, if at all. Still, near dawn, I thought I heard a noise, but I forgot to wonder about it, and when daylight came, I got up and found the screen door unlatched and the woman gone. I went outside and looked all around, but she wasn't anywhere to be seen. Nothing to do but wait until Wynona came and tell her about it.

But I didn't want to go back inside right away, because the Camp Ground was all still and gray in the morning light, with a little mist gathered in the hollow where the tabernacle sat. Made it look like that big old tin roof was rising up out of a dream or something.

Such a sad, sweet feeling came over me then, and it took me a while to realize what it was—just that the early morning like that put me so much in mind of that year we came out here, and I'd just found out I had Lizzy in me, and her so small, she was still a secret to everybody but me. How I just went around humming in tune with everything that summer. Leaves on the trees and the rise of the land behind the cemetery and clear water running through that little branch down in the ravine behind the tabernacle, just so soft and light but enough to keep rubbing all the pretty stones smooth.

A long-ago summer when I first felt Mama Sunrise with me so strong.

How I had smiled all the time for the way it was, for me going along with it all just the way God Almighty made it to be, the birds singing and me singing too, for the double heartbeat in me. And I heard Wynona and Miss Cora saying to each other, "What on earth is Pet so happy about?" when they thought I couldn't hear them. Why, I couldn't stop smiling to save my life, but I didn't tell them anything, because every time I thought I was ready to say it, I remembered about Hope.

That long-ago year, there was a lot of morning mist too, like me and the earth had something we better keep still about.

Around eleven that morning, Miss Cora's old Buick pulled up under the big pecan tree behind the kitchen, and the minute I saw Wynona, I knew she and Miss Cora must have had some kind of a fuss.

"She fumed and fussed the whole way out here because she says we didn't stop and pick up Aunt Frances," Wynona said to me as she carried an armload of Miss Cora's dresses inside.

"Back on that again, huh?" I asked. Wynona nodded and rolled her eyes Heavenward. I took some of the dresses out of Wynona's arms and followed her into the bedroom. Out front, Minnie Louise was sweeping out some cobwebs we'd missed in the corner of the porch.

"We had a visitor last night," I told Wynona. "An old woman sitting out in the yard and singing. We brought her inside and put her to bed on the settee, but she got up and left sometime during the night."

"Good Heavens," Wynona said. "Where'd she go?"

We could hear Lauralee and Miss Cora coming in the back door and Minnie Louise saying, "No, ma'am, Miss Cora, I don't think there's no Aunt Frances of yours around here. Not that I've seen, anyway."

"I don't know," I said. "But she sure was some kind of crazy person. Said she was looking for her mama to help her find something called a Sin-eater or some such thing."

"A what?"

"Sin-eater. You ever hear tell of such a thing?"

"No. I never did. Maybe we ought to call the sheriff and tell him about her. It can't be good for an old woman to be wandering around in the dark. Especially if she's confused like that. Was she white?"

"Colored. And you're probably right. We better call the sheriff."

But about that time, we heard Miss Cora calling, "Frances? Frances? Are you here?"

"Oh, Good Heavens!" Wynona moaned.

Now that everyone had come, there were all the dresses to hang up, and underthings and stockings to put into the freshly cleaned dresser drawers, and dinner to fix, and all such things as that. Wynona and I ran around, getting everything all settled, and then she tried to hand me the car keys so I could drive Minnie Louise home. I guess she forgot for a little minute that I'd never driven a car in my life. Don't know how come her to forget that, all of a sudden.

So Wynona took Minnie Louise home, and I started frying chicken and forgot about the old woman.

That evening, Miss Cora was still mad at us, because she was sure we'd forgotten to bring Aunt Frances to Camp Meeting, and no matter how we tried to tell her that Aunt Frances had passed on a long, long time ago, Miss Cora wouldn't listen. So that when we were at supper, she said, "I'm not going to eat one bite until you all go back and get her!"

But just at that moment, and from right under the window, came a raspy voice singing, "I LOOKED OVER JOR-DAN AND WHAT'D I S-E-E-E . . ."

Lauralee dropped her fork, and Miss Cora and Wynona and I stared at each other. I went outside and brought the old woman in once again, and after taking one startled glance at her, Wynona said she was going down to the Public Tent to call the sheriff.

But Miss Cora got up from the table, went straight to the old woman, and hugged her. "Frances! Where *have* you been?" And the old woman took one look at Miss Cora and cried, "Mama!"

"Frances, what on earth are you talking about?" Miss Cora led the woman over to the table, and they sat down together across from Lauralee, who was watching the whole affair as if it made sense.

"And, dear," Miss Cora said in a very slow and patient voice. "I'm not your mama. She's been gone a long time. You must try to remember."

"Mama," the old woman persisted, "I come get you to hep me find the Sin-eater. He gotta come." The massive jaw quivered.

"The what?" Miss Cora asked.

"Sin-eater, Mama. Please?"

"I declare, you sound just like Jackson when he would get all confused. Do you remember how he kept saying things none of us could figure out?"

"I 'member," the woman said.

"Well now, dear, you certainly get it honest, this crazy talk. It was Great-Uncle Raymond first brought that into the family, and Papa says it had to have been Great-Uncle Raymond's daddy's people, because no one in the whole family was ever like that before."

"Great-Unca Raymond?" the old woman repeated. "He be the Sin-eater?"

"Oh, no. We don't have a Sin-eater, whatever that is. We have a devil-shooter, though," Miss Cora offered hopefully.

"Nome. Don' wont no devil-shooter. Wont the Sin-eater."

"Now listen, Frances," Miss Cora went on. "Before I forget about it, there's something I have to ask you. Do you remember where that unmarked grave is, down at Brushy Creek?"

"Brushy Creek?"

"You remember. It was my sweet Bix's grave, and I can't find it. Think, Frances. Surely you remember."

"Is that where the Sin-eater be?"

Miss Cora sighed and started in on the full story of the unmarked grave.

By the time Wynona came back, Miss Cora and the old woman were holding hands on the red-checkered tablecloth, and Miss Cora was talking up a storm.

Wynona took me aside. "The sheriff said she's probably a woman named Maggie Brown, who's supposed to be over at Twilight Hills Home in Keysville. She walked away yesterday morning, and they've been looking all over creation for her. And what's going on here?" She motioned toward the table.

"They're confused," I told her. "Miss Cora thinks she's Aunt Frances, and the old woman thinks Miss Cora's her mama."

"Give me strength," Wynona said, more of a moan than a prayer. "Well, the sheriff asked me if we'd please take her back to Twilight Hills. But I told him I didn't like to drive in the dark, so we'll have to let her sleep here tonight, if you think she won't cause any trouble. We can take her back first thing in the morning."

It was nearly 9:30 when we got Miss Cora to stop telling "Aunt Frances" about the unmarked grave and go to bed. We put Maggie Brown to sleep on the settee again. And this time, I took a hairpin and twisted it around the latch on the screen door so she wouldn't walk away again into the dark.

Then we all went to bed and never heard another sound out of Miss Cora or old Maggie the whole night.

Not even the low whispers right before dawn.

Or the door opening.

Or the old Buick starting up.

I didn't know the whole story until a long time afterwards, and even then, Miss Cora had a hard time making up her mind about whether she could tell even me about it. She was awful funny about not wanting any of us to think she was getting old and crazy or anything like that, you see. But I guess she finally figured out it was safe to tell me, because, after all, Minnie Louise told her a long time ago about how I could see Death whenever he came around. So maybe Miss Cora thought I was already old and crazy myself. For whatever reason, she finally told me about it.

How it was still dark outside when she woke Aunt Frances up and they finally got the screen door open. Right hard time they had, getting off that hairpin I'd put around the latch. But I'd thought that would stop old Maggie—didn't know it was Miss Cora I had to worry about.

And Miss Cora said she even remembered to open the door just wide enough so they could squeeze through, and that way the bottom of the door wouldn't scrape against the floor and wake everybody up.

How they went across the dark yard and got into the car, and Miss Cora told Maggie, "Be real quiet, and whatever you do, don't slam the car door. Not until we get down the road a piece."

Maggie grunted and grumbled about it, but she got in the car. And she remembered not to slam the door. But she said, "This seat don't want nobody setting on it. Got no springs left what's any good."

"Shhh!" Miss Cora shooshed her and clicked the key into the ignition. And she was saying to herself—*Now push in the clutch and turn the key and step on the gas pedal. No second chances. Turn it again, and it'll skreek loud enough to wake the dead!*

But the engine sprang to life on the first try, and she shifted into gear and let out on the clutch. They went so slowly and quietly out along the dirt road, with the engine purring and the little pebbles on the road crunching under the tires. When they were far enough away, she switched on the headlights.

Just ahead, she could see the turnoff to the Waynesboro Highway, and she stopped before they reached the paved road.

"Shut your door now, good and hard," she told Maggie, and they both slammed good and hard and sat there looking at each other.

"Well, we've gotten this far," Miss Cora said.

"Long way to go though," Maggie sighed. "Awful long way."

"Maybe not as long as you think," Miss Cora said.

Behind them in the darkness, we went on sleeping. I turned on my side and pulled the sheet up over my shoulder against the cool air from the fan. And for just a little minute, I dreamed about a car starting up. But that only fluttered a little against that warm old wall of sleep, and I went right back into a sure-enough dream, where I was looking out through a window in Miss Cora's house. A warm midnight so long ago, and some kind of perfume coming through the open window. Tea olive.

And long curtains that lifted out into the room like white arms. There was a white dress on an ironing board and with tiny pearl buttons. The hot iron against the damp fabric and the hiss of steam.

Mahogany-colored hair curled and still shining in the china hair receiver, and the perfume of all the years so sweet against the old lid.

And dust under the chifforobe in the far corner of an empty room. And I knew whose dust it was.

So none of us knew what had happened until we heard someone banging hard on the back screen door when it wasn't even good daylight.

"WAKE UP INSIDE!" a voice hollered. "I SAY, WAKE UP IN THERE! WYNONA? PET?"

I stumbled to the door just as Wynona came out of her bedroom, tying the belt of her robe.

Together, we stared through the rusted screen where Mrs. Rander's face peered anxiously into the dim hallway. She was wearing a green chenille robe, and the hem of it was wet from the dew in the tall grass along the path to the Public Tent.

"Wynona! Thank goodness! I just had a phone call from town, and you better go quick! Miss Cora and some real old colored woman are eating breakfast at Sarah's coffee shop in the Gulf station, and Sarah said she almost fainted when she saw them drive up, because she knew Miss Cora hadn't driven a car in—must be—twenty years or so. And she says Miss Cora almost ran over one of the gas pumps, and Sarah says who on earth is that colored woman, and is Miss Cora maybe being kidnapped, for Heaven's sake?"

"They're gone!" Wynona yelped. "And they took the car! Listen, Miz Rander, please call Sarah back and tell her to keep them there. Whatever she does, tell her not to let them leave! And then call Thompson and get him to drive out here and get us quick!"

"Youall could take my car," Mrs. Rander said. "'Cept Gilda had to go back to town last night." Then the anxious face on the other side of the screen disappeared, and Mrs. Rander went running off toward the Public Tent, still hollering back to us all the details about Gilda and her important errand.

We got dressed and started waiting. Waiting for there to have been enough time for Thompson to get the call and drive out to Mount Horeb for us. But he didn't come and didn't come. Finally, Wynona sent me to the Public Tent to see if Mrs. Rander made the call.

But I met her halfway along, on her way back to us. "I called Thompson," she said. "But Maude said he's gone fishing over to Louisville. So I called Minnie Louise to come get youall. She's on her way."

Twenty minutes or so later, Minnie Louise drove up so fast in her pickup that she threw up a cloud of dust.

"Come on. Let's go!" she hollered.

Wynona turned to Lauralee. "You stay here, in case they come back," she said.

Lauralee nodded her head and went back inside.

"I forgot to make coffee for her," I said as we got in the truck, and Wynona called back to Lauralee, "Can you make your coffee?"

Lauralee nodded.

I didn't say anything, of course, but I wondered why Wynona had forgotten how Lauralee could sure enough make the coffee. But she couldn't pour it. Hasn't poured a cup since that day so long ago. Because that's what she was doing when Mr. Adkins called her a harlot. But I didn't say anything to Wynona because I thought maybe it was the kindest thing if she'd forgotten all about it. Sure wish I could.

We spoke not a word on the way, and I guess we were all thinking the same thing—the old Buick and Miss Cora and Maggie Brown riding along in it in the early darkness, and them all confused and laughing and talking and calling each other "Mama"

139

and "Aunt Frances" and acting like nothing bad could ever happen to them.

And those deep ditches on either side of the road yawning open like fresh-dug graves.

Cora!

Miss Cora had stopped at Sarah's for some breakfast, and she just sat there, watching Maggie sop her biscuit in the egg yolks and stuff it into her mouth. Then she slurped her coffee real loud.

"Dear," Miss Cora finally said to her. "People are staring at us! You're acting like you haven't eaten in days!"

"Hongry!" Maggie said.

"And don't you have a napkin?" Miss Cora asked her, looking down at Maggie's crumb-littered lap.

"Got one. Rat-chere." Maggie pounded her fist on top of the napkin, still folded by her plate.

From across the room, Sarah came back to their table. But she had a nervous-looking smile on her face. At a table near the window, two men stirred their coffee, and Miss Cora could tell they were watching her and Maggie very closely.

Maggie thrust her mug at Sarah, who filled it slowly.

"Miss Cora," Sarah began carefully. "Who's your . . . uh . . . guest this morning?"

"Oh," Miss Cora said. "This is Aunt Frances from faraway Texas come to visit me and help me find . . . something I've been looking for."

"Texas," Maggie grunted.

"*Your* Aunt Frances?" Sarah asked.

"That's right," Miss Cora said. "And I'd like another pat of butter for my toast, if you please."

"Yes, ma'am."

At the table by the window, the men spoke in voices so low that Miss Cora could make out only a little of what they were saying. But it was something like—"Knew there'd be trouble. Knew it soon as Doris told me that help of theirs sits right on the front porch with them."

Miss Cora thought it was just Maggie's bad table manners that had attracted their attention, but now she could feel their disapproval going across the back of her neck just like a cold draft.

Sarah came with the butter and offered them more coffee.

"Take your time. Don't go rushing off," she said.

And that's the very minute when Miss Cora knew for sure that we were coming after them.

When Minnie Louise's truck pulled up in front of the coffee shop, Miss Sarah herself came out, so we knew she'd been standing at the window, waiting for us. And even though her hands were dry, she was wiping them on her apron, as if she'd just finished washing the dishes.

"They're gone!" she wailed. "I did everything I could to keep them, short of knocking them in the head and tying them up!"

"Good Heavens," Wynona muttered. Then, "Which way'd they go?"

"Toward Louisville. I couldn't do a thing with them! Miss Cora sure is headstrong, I'll say. And who on earth is that old colored woman she says is her aunt?"

"I'll explain later," Wynona said. And to Minnie Louise, "Let's go on down the highway real quick. Maybe we can catch them."

But Miss Cora was too sharp for us. Soon as Sarah tried to get them to take their time, Miss Cora had it figured out how someone must have called us. Said she figured what would happen is that we'd come running after them and treat them like bad children, when all Miss Cora wanted to do was take care of what needed doing, and without any of us hovering around, telling Miss Cora what all she was too old to do anymore, and trying to make her believe that folks were dead and gone when she knew good and well they were sitting right there talking to her just last night.

Miss Cora knew they shouldn't have stopped, especially at Sarah's—but Maggie was so hungry and fretful and just as mean as a snake. Said her aunt Frances took after her own mama that way, and they both got it from somebody she never even knew but she'd heard about all her life, and that was her great-great-

141

great-grandmother, who was famous for getting to be just about the meanest woman alive when she was hungry.

So when they left Sarah's, Miss Cora knew she had to fool us. Get to where she needed to go and in a way we wouldn't know about. So she headed south on Highway 1, figuring Sarah would think they were going to Louisville. And only a few miles down the highway, she turned off onto a country road that used to come out just south of the railroad crossing at Zebina. Or at least, that's where it came out fifteen or twenty years ago. It had been a long time since Miss Cora had been on it.

When she made the turn, she saw that the road was freshly scraped, so she figured it would still go all the way through.

And she knew that Wynona would never, ever think to turn there.

When Minnie Louise's truck roared past a Stuckey's a few miles south of town, we came out of a deep curve over the edge of a hill and up to where we could see a good two or three miles of highway ahead of us. And not a car in sight.

"Brushy Creek Cemetery!" I yelled suddenly. "I bet you anything that's where they're headed! 'Cause of Miss Cora's being all confused and thinking that old woman was Aunt Frances!"

Wynona nodded: "Yes! That's got to be it!"

So Minnie Louise braked hard, turned the truck around, and we started back. And a little way back down the highway, Wynona noticed that there was some dust hanging in the air near a dirt road, and she suddenly remembered a fine spring afternoon maybe ten or fifteen years before and Miss Cora laughing and saying, "Heavens above! How my mama used to love to drive on this old road, especially after a good rain, and how that car did slip and slide around so much, you'd think your heart was going to stop."

"Turn here!" Wynona yelled to Minnie Louise. Just in time.

Now the next part of Miss Cora's story was something even harder for her to tell me about, and when she finally did, she kept glancing at me the whole time. I guess she was trying to see if I thought she'd lost her mind. But I was one who had been on the receiving end of that kind of thinking, so I wasn't gonna judge her. *Judge not,* I kept saying to myself.

"Frances and I were probably only a mile or so along where we had turned off when I saw a fork in the road coming up, and those two different ways seemed to waver in front of my eyes just like feelers on some kind of a giant bug! I didn't know which one to take. One was rutted, twisted off toward the north, and seemed to disappear in deep woods. The other, just as rutted, turned to the southeast and disappeared around a curve that seemed to go downward. I could see where the road scraper had turned around right there at the fork, so I knew that neither road had been scraped smooth in a long time.

"I sat there for a good two or three minutes while I tried to remember something—anything—that would tell me which road would be the one to lead us through to Zebina. And of course, Frances was no help at all, because she had fallen sound asleep and was snoring to beat the band!

"Then I seemed to remember one time when I was just a child, sitting in the back of the buggy and Papa driving the glistening horses. I could almost see his high, stiff collar and the side of his face where his jaw showed through the whiskers. He was talking about the unmarked grave.

"'We really should find it, you know,' I heard him say. 'Because one of these days, there won't be anyone left who knows where it is. And it's our duty to take care of it.'

"I shook my head to try and clear it. Goodness knows, it was no time for me to be having dreams! But then, just for a moment, I thought I saw my mama—when she was young, I mean—walking across the field and toward the woods. She was wearing a pale blue dress that was nipped in at the waist, and she was holding the dress out at the sides, almost like she was doing a dance of some kind, swaying a little from side to side with every step. The way a beautiful young woman would do on a fine spring day.

"'Find him, Mama,' Frances said in her sleep about that time.

"'I'll find him,' I promised Frances. 'But that still won't tell us whether he was a Longwood or a Bixley.'

"I must have been confused, but I really thought that if Mama could just show me where to find the creek, I'd know exactly where I was. Because water flows to the south, trying to find the river. Then I'd be able to get to the cemetery, and Frances could finally help me find that old grave.

"And because I believed I had seen my own sweet mama walking in the field to the left and that she was trying to lead me, I turned down that fork in the road.

"I drove around most of the deep ruts and avoided the edges where heavy rains had washed away the clay, while the road tilted up and then curved toward the northwest, getting even narrower as we went along.

"'Maybe I better find us a place to turn around,' I said to Frances. 'This must be the wrong way, or we would have come to the creek by now.' But Frances just kept on snoring.

"The road bent downhill again, and it had gotten so narrow, I couldn't keep the wheels on the road any longer. Then the right front tire slipped on the edge, and the car started sliding toward the ditch, all the while moving forward just like it had a mind of its own!

144

"I held onto the wheel just as tight as I could, but finally, it jerked itself free of my grip, and the car just rolled down into the ditch real easy-like, until the right front bumper nosed into the bank of earth on the other side and the car stopped—but at a sharp, sideways angle that leaned me practically on top of Frances, who was pressed against the passenger side door. She woke up then, sure enough, and struggled to pull her left arm free, where I was leaning so hard against it.

"'You all right, Frances?' I mouthed into the side of her neck.

"'I'm all right,' she answered. 'But how we get outta here?'

"'Open your door, but be careful to . . .'

"Before I could finish, Frances pulled the handle, and that heavy door swung open, dragging her out of the car and me along with her!

"She tumbled out and landed down in the ditch, and I flopped out right on top of her. Made me think how when I was a child, I loved flopping down in the middle of a plumped-up feather bed.

"'Well, that's one way to do it, I guess,' I said, trying to get off of Frances without jabbing her with elbows or knees. Surprisingly, once I stood up, I felt strangely excited and not the least bit hurt or shaken up. Frances got on her hands and knees and started chuckling before she even got to her feet.

"'Us like two old bugs in a hole!' she laughed.

"Why, I thought that was the funniest thing I'd ever heard in my whole life, and we stood there in that ditch, laughing and laughing until we were almost crying.

"'Missy! I done wet my britches!' Frances howled in distress, and we laughed even harder. But after a while, we both sobered a little bit and began trying to figure out how to get ourselves out of the mess we'd gotten ourselves into.

"'Maybe we can back the car out,' I suggested.

"'Oh, no! I ain't getting back on that bucking horse!' Frances was emphatic. 'Let's get ourselves out from this ditch; then we'll figure what to do.'

"So we walked along in the ditch toward the rear of the car, and Frances was the first to scramble up onto the road, with me pushing her from behind. Then she planted her feet in the hard clay and pulled me up like I didn't weigh a thing.

"'I guess we can't back out from this one,' I said, looking at the high angle of the car's back end and the left rear tire that was spinning slowly about six inches off the road.

"'Best we can do is walk on down this road a piece. Maybe find a house and somebody with a tractor can pull us out,' I said.

"And that's what we did. But we didn't have to walk far—only a few hundred yards or so—and there the road narrowed even more, to where it was hardly more than a path that curved around a little rise in the land. We went on around the curve, and sure enough, there was an old house set back from the path and surrounded by chinaberry trees."

"Well, they sure aren't here, Pet," Wynona said, as Minnie Louise drove for the third time around Brushy Creek Church and out along the dirt road that skirted the edge of the cemetery, right down to the edge of the creek.

But once, just for a moment, I thought I saw Miss Cora, and before I could yell, "I see her!" I realized it was that Sunday afternoon I was remembering, when we came out looking for the grave, with me on one side of Miss Cora and Wynona on the other.

Lord, have mercy!

"They sure ain't here," Minnie Louise agreed.

"We better go on to Minnie Louise's house and use her phone to call the sheriff," Wynona said. "Needs to be more than just us looking for them now."

Miss Cora said, "That old house at the end of the path was deserted. Had been for a long time, from the looks of it. We stood in the weeds, wondering if the leaning front steps would hold our weight, for even though there were no signs of life whatsoever, I knew I could never leave there without looking through the windows, just in case.

"'You go around back and look,' I told Frances. 'But be careful where you step in these high weeds. Liable to be snakes.'

"I watched Frances go on along the side of the house and turn the corner, and I was glad to see that she was stepping very carefully and watching where her feet were going. But as soon as she was out of my sight, I suddenly got to feeling short of breath, and I almost called to her to come back. But it was more than being out of breath—almost like somebody had just turned a page when I wasn't done reading yet. Or something like that. The old house standing there before me and that smell empty old houses always seem to have—of dust, but cool, like very old dust.

"Seemed as if that house was so familiar-looking, just the way the paint was peeling off the banisters and the screen door was leaning off its top hinges.

"What's that? I was thinking. *Somebody calling to me?*

"I held onto the leaning banister and went up one step at a time. Those old planks groaned a little, but they held. The porch floor was in better shape than the steps, but still, I was careful to walk only where I could see the nails, for that was where the wood joists were, under the porch.

"And the closer I got to the window, the stranger I felt! But I cupped my hands around my eyes and peered in.

"Inside the shadow made by my own head, I could make out an empty room—an almost empty room. Wide, plank floors bleached gray by years and years of being scrubbed with lye soap, and in the middle of the side wall, a smutty, brick fireplace with ashes in it and them still holding something of the shape of the log that had last burned there. On the windowsill inside, just half an inch from my nose pressed against the glass, three dead flies, upside down. And my own face in the dark shadow.

"Against the other wall, an old-fashioned baby crib and one side let down, as if whoever lived there had just now picked up the baby and walked into the next room. And when I saw it, something crowded in on me, and I stepped back.

"'Where's the baby?'

"That's what I heard someone say, just as clear as day. I even looked around to see if it was Frances. But she was nowhere to be seen. Why, I was so dizzy, I stepped backward, felt the porch railing against me, turned, and held the old wood as tight as I could while I felt the whole world tilting beneath my feet.

"What was it about that crib? Or another crib? Not iron, but white wood. Not chipped, but satin-smooth. And an eyelet ruffle on a tiny pillow for the head. For us reborn. For Mama's pretty blue eyes and Jackson's earlobes, and Papa's chin, and all the faces out of the living and the loving together, above one new jawbone and topped with a little wisp of blonde curls.

"'Where's the baby?'

"'Wynona? Do you have the baby?'

"'Pet has her. Out on the porch.'

"That's what I heard, and it seemed as if my hands weren't holding the rail of that old porch at all but the side of a crib. That sweet, warm-milk smell of a sleeping baby and tiny blonde ringlets at the edge of the pastel blanket and the curve of the full, pink cheek so sweet.

"But when I reached out my hand to touch it, not a crib any longer, but a cardboard box and a baby with dark hair and a curly sweep of black lashes against the curve of a full, brown cheek.

"Lizzy?"

I knew, of course, what it was trying to crowd into Miss Cora's mind, but I didn't say anything. Because she told me all of this only after I'd made her remember about Hope anyway. So there was never a need for us to talk further about it.

But when that was all going on after Miss Cora and Maggie ran off like that, she hadn't yet remembered everything. But it was surely knocking on the door!

Miss Cora said: "Well, I got to feeling a little better, though I sure didn't know what was happening in my head. I went down the steps and around back, to see if I could find Frances and tell her about the baby.

"In the back part of the house, the porch had fallen apart, and there were rough-hewn railings in the yard, some of them crossed over upon themselves when they fell. Gave me a funny feeling, it did, like maybe the house had held itself together as long as it could, waiting and waiting for someone to come back. And finally it couldn't wait any longer and just let it all go. Let the railings fall into the dark grass with a clunk like a hammer blow, so that the crickets stopped chirping.

"I stood staring down at those crossed boards before me on the ground, and I could almost hear singing: *On a hill far away, stood an old rugged cross . . .*

"That old hymn and those earnest voices, the high note something the singers stretched their necks out for, and they nearly got it. They nearly did, this time.

"But I'll cherish . . .

"'Mama! Where ARE you?'

"The voice came from somewhere behind me, somewhere close to the edge of the woods where dry weeds fringed the shade under the trees. Pine trees, scraggly but glowing in the early morning sun, and little beads of dew on the pine needles, like pearls strung out just so and all lined up. And the strangest thing was that in the center of each drop, I could see myself. But so very small.

"It made me feel so strange! Like it was a dream I was having, only I knew good and well that I wasn't asleep. But I had to find Frances, tell her about the baby I saw in the house, so I walked into the woods.

"Watch where you're stepping. There's liable to be snakes, I heard my own words, and I lifted the hem of my dress and watched the ground. One step at a time I moved into the woods. Pine needles beneath my feet, brown-black old twigs and leaves. Scurrying sounds under a dogwood tree, and a honeysuckle vine winding around an old oak, with one green tendril that had moved upward and held on and now was reaching up to the light.

"Then there was a tilting down to the ground, and my feet slipped a little in the pine straw. Sent me to skating, I tell you! And sliding toward the tall grass where there could be needle teeth and smooth scales, some wicked green thing poised to sting.

"But at the bottom of my sliding, no stinging at all, just a small spring, crystal-clear and smelling so cool. I held onto a scraggly branch of a tree and stopped and looked around me.

"'Mama?' The voice again, yet not from a place I could find but from everywhere at one time so that . . . I don't know what happened, except that there was a little breeze high up in the pine trees. I looked up into the green of it with sunlight slant-

149

ing through it like yellow rays and it holding my eyes so that I would never want to look at anything else again as long as I lived! And as if that wasn't strange enough, I felt myself beginning to turn in a little circle, so the leaves and the light swung around me, green and yellow-red and silver, around and around until the edges of things blurred, and it was all one something. And I knew that if I could only find a way to just let go of things, turn loose of it all, I could be it when I fell."

When Miss Cora told me about this much later, her eyes filled up, and she clutched my arm and had a look in her eyes like my arm was all that kept her holding onto the face of the earth! She went on in a choked voice: "If that happened, I knew I'd open up just like a pod and put down milky-white roots that would go down under old grass and the dark leaves and take hold good and strong and then sprout me upwards like a young tree!

"But right at that moment, I heard Frances calling to me again: 'Mama! Where on earth ARE you?'

"'Frances?' I called back, but just about that time, all that turning around I was doing got me dizzy and sick-feeling and I didn't know what happened until . . .

"'Here. Drink this.'

"Frances was kneeling by me, her hands cupped, and cold, clear water from the spring resting in a pool against her palms. Hands coming closer and the hand tilting and a little cold water going down my throat.

"And a ringing . . . no, a singing in my ears: 'The Lord is in His holy temple. Let all the earth keep silence . . .'

"'Whatchu doing way down here?' Frances asked. But I couldn't say a word. I could only think that I didn't know what on earth I'd do if something happened to her. Because she's flesh of my flesh and bone of my bone, and the only one left I can look at and see my papa's pretty blue eyes.

"'Come on,' Frances said. 'There's nobody lives in that house no more. We better go on and find somebody to hep us.'

"'Frances,' I said. 'Listen to me just a little minute. I thought I saw a baby in the house. A little newborn colored baby asleep in a cardboard box. Why, it was so real, I could smell the milk

150

on it and I wanted so bad to kiss the very back of its neck, where that sweet dimple goes up into the edge of the hair. Right below the jutting-out part of the head—the white skull under the black hair and the soft, pink folds of what we remember!'

"'Huh?' Frances asked. 'What's that you say 'bout a skull?'

"And I took a deep breath and said, 'I guess it was just my mind playing tricks on me.'

"So we walked on and on, first trudging back up the hill past the house and then following what looked like an old tractor path that went around an empty field and along a line of trees, until the ground bent down again.

"I knew that if we kept on going down, we were obliged to find the creek, although we would be on the wrong side of it for getting to the cemetery. But if we could get that far, I'd find a way to get us across.

"Finally, we certainly did come to the creek, but the water was deep and dark and faster moving than I remembered. So we walked along the bank, helping each other over fallen branches and through vines and over old rotten stumps of big trees that had fallen a long time ago. As we walked, the sun was getting hotter and hotter, and we were soaked through to the skin. And so thirsty!

"Around a deep curve, we came to a higher embankment and it bare of weeds. Below, there was a wide, deep place in the creek, a swimming hole maybe, and the bank worn smooth by the feet of boys who would jump toward the black water, their legs spraddled and arms flailing.

"'We ain't getting nowhere, you know,' Frances puffed. 'Seems to me like we're just going further and further away from . . . where was we going, anyway?'

"'Cemetery,' I said, wearily.

"'What? No! I ain't going to no cemetery. Not me! Unh-unh!' Frances turned and started walking off into the woods that backed up along the creek bank. But she stopped dead still, and I looked to see what had stopped her right in her tracks. It was an old, ramshackle place, nearly completely covered with kudzu so that we could have missed seeing it in just the blink of an eye.

"'Look! That's our house!' she yelled. 'I ain't never forgot it. Never.' And before I could stop her, she headed for the vine-covered shack.

"'Be careful of snakes!' I yelled at her back and started after her.

"But there were no snakes, and when I finally caught up with Frances, we ducked down and went in through the open doorway, to where the air was cool and the dim light inside tinted green from the sun shining on kudzu leaves growing over the windows. Inside, I sat right down on the floor and tried to get over my feeling faint, while Frances walked around the room, running her hand over the old newsprint tacked up on the leaning walls.

"'Sure enough. Sure enough,' she chanted. 'Your house, Mama. And over here,' she gestured at the far wall, 'the bed where I was born. Remember? And here, your chair where you sit and rock in the evenings and all of us in the bed and listening to you singing. Remember?'

"'Frances, you're all confused,' I said, feeling a little alarmed that I suddenly could see myself sitting in a rocking chair right there in that tiny room a long time ago. 'And you're getting me confused too!'

"Frances came and sat down beside me and put her arm around my shoulders.

"'Don't worry none,' she crooned. 'You'll remember it all.'

"'Well, we're supposed to be looking for the cemetery, and we can't even find that. Can't get across the creek even if we could find it,' I said.

"'It's not so bad,' Frances countered. 'Plenty of times we been through worse. Like when we didn't have nothing to eat. Now them was hard times.'

"'We didn't?'

"'Thas right. And you working all day every day in that white lady's kitchen, and her not letting you bring home a thing. Not even an old biscuit out of the trash can. And her not thinking a thing about your babies going hongry. Or not caring.'

"'Why, that's terrible!'

"'I know it! But we're all right now. I'm here now, and I'll fix everything right for you.'

"I was weeping openly by then, but if anyone had asked me why, I couldn't have said. Somehow, it had something to do with the arm around my shoulder and the hand still patting me.

"Why, it was just terrible, that's what it was. That old falling-down shack, and little babies hungry, and us not being able to find the grave.

"Then we heard the sounds of heavy footsteps—twigs snapping—and saw a man's face peering in at us through the old doorway.

"'Well, Miss Cora. We've been looking all over creation for you. Are you all right?' The deputy ducked his head and came inside to where Frances and I were sitting together on the floor of the green-lit shack, hugging each other."

"Miss Cora," I said, when the deputy brought her back. "Please, ma'am, don't you never do anything like that again. 'Most scared us to death!"

The deputy took off his hat as Wynona came out to where he and Miss Cora and me were standing by the patrol car.

"Thank the good Lord," Wynona said, taking Miss Cora's hand and holding it in both of hers and close to her heart. To the deputy she said, "I can't tell you how relieved I was when I got the call that you'd found them, and they were all right. Thank you ever so much!"

"Yes, ma'am," he said, replacing his hat and touching his finger to the brim in a polite salute. "I sent a wrecker to get your car out of the ditch, and it'll probably be at the Gulf station now. No damage at all, not even a scratch as far as I could tell. Guess it just slipped off the road real easy-like."

"Nobody was hurt. That's all that matters," Wynona said. "Thank you for taking care of the car." Then she added, "Where's that old woman? What was her name?"

"Maggie Brown. I took her back to Twilight Hills before me and Miss Cora come on back here."

Miss Cora pulled her hand away from Wynona. "I do wish you could have seen where Frances lives now. Big old pretty house and two maids in clean blue dresses to help her get inside.

153

But, listen. I'm really worried about some hungry children down at that old shack by the creek."

Wynona glanced at the deputy, who was shaking his head at Wynona and smiling a little to say, *Ain't no children down there.*

"I'll be glad to give you a ride back to town, ma'am," he said to Wynona. "So's you can get your car."

"Yes. Thank you."

And when the deputy and Wynona had driven away, I took Miss Cora inside and bathed off her face and hands and put her to bed just as the tabernacle bell began ringing for the three o'clock service.

"Pet?"

"Yes'm?" I smoothed the pillow and turned on the fan.

"There was something in that house. The first one we went to. A baby crib. And not another piece of furniture, mind you. Not a living soul around. And I saw something, but I don't know what it was."

"Yes'm. Don't you worry yourself about it."

"Well, anyway, I'm glad Frances is living in such a grand house. And has someone to help take care of her. But I just wish I could make her understand that her mama's gone."

"Yes'm."

"But she's just like Great-Uncle Raymond that way. All confused and . . ."

"Yes'm. You get some rest now. You can tell me all about it later."

"But what about the babies?"

"I'll see to the babies. You just rest."

And I didn't add: *Because I always see to the babies, and there's no babies down there wherever you and Maggie Brown went. Only babies around here is what we remember. And they aren't nothing except whatever we say they were!*

When Miss Cora woke up, she seemed a little surprised to find that we were out at the Camp Ground, but she didn't say anything. After she had eaten a good, big supper, she got interested in Camp Meeting and finding out who all was there this year. And she didn't mention "Aunt Frances" again. Or say another word about babies. But for the next several afternoons, she sat out on the porch, rocking and talking about who all used to come to Camp Meeting, and she claimed that every last one of them was her relation somehow or other, even down to "Papa's third cousin, twice removed," and "Papa's uncle's second wife's first cousin."

On another day, she gave Wynona and me another scare, because she said she was going to her room to take a nap, but instead, she slipped away and went down the lane to the Public Tent and was interviewing perfect strangers to find out "who they were," which meant, of course, how they were related to her.

After we found her and brought her home, she wrote in the Family Book the names of all the people she had talked to, and she also wrote that Frances was getting to be just like Great-Uncle Raymond.

"What a mess she's made of it," Wynona whispered to me.

"Doesn't matter," I answered. "Keeps her happy anyway."

But Wynona shook her head. "I'm not so sure it does."

On Monday, Miss Cora remembered about Sister Betty, and when she asked old Miss Delia Patterson about it that afternoon, Miss Delia said, "My, yes. She's gone, poor thing. And I sure do miss her, even though everybody was always laughing at her."

"I miss her too," Miss Cora said. "How'd it happen?"

"Oh, I don't know," Miss Delia sighed. "Only we drove out here one Sunday afternoon last February, and I saw her grave-stone in the Rogers plot. Never knew her middle name before. Emily. Isn't that pretty?"

That evening, Miss Cora made a new entry into the Family Book:

"Sister Betty Emily Rogers, fourth cousin of Cora Alderson Bixley. Died in 1971. Buried in Mount Horeb Cemetery, near the town of Morgan, Georgia. Sister Betty Emily dedicated her life to fighting against the Forces of Darkness."

J'll be right glad when it's time to go on back home," Miss
Cora said about halfway through Camp Meeting. And I
think it had finally come home to her that only five of the family tents had folks staying in them, and the Public Tent, which
had always been for folks who didn't have a family tent of their
own, had only four folks from a church in Augusta staying in
it. Things sure had changed, but the preacher was a good one
that year—young and fired up, preaching real good to whatever
folks showed up for services and giving them his best. Didn't
seem to bother him one little bit that the tabernacle wasn't full
and that there weren't any young folks to work with.

Miss Cora went on, "I love it out here, but by the time it's nearly
over, I'm ready to go home and see to things. And I want to find
out what's going on across the street."

Wynona glanced over at me, because we knew. Because when
Wynona had driven the car back from the Gulf station, she stopped
by home to get us some fresh tomatoes from Mrs. Downs next
door. And when she came back, she whispered to me that Mr.
Grower had put a big blue and white GROWER'S FUNERAL
HOME sign in the front yard of Miss Addie's house. And worse,
he'd cut down Miss Addie's big pecan tree and put in a gravel
parking lot, right where the front yard used to be.

And I remembered the old funeral parlor and how it had room for only three or four cars at the most, and them parked every which way beneath the big oak tree in the front yard, and going there together when Miss Emma passed on.

Because Mr. Sam still didn't set much store in churches, and he sure as anything didn't trust preachers. So he had Mr. Grower do the funeral right from the old funeral parlor.

It was only a couple of years after Wynona married Mr. Adkins that Miss Emma and Mr. Sam both passed on. Miss Emma first, after she had been sick for a long time and just never did get well. And the day she was buried, Mr. Sam came to the funeral all confused and wearing an old shirt that needed ironing and with tobacco stains all over it, and even with his fly unzipped. Somebody said later he smelled of strong wine. I wish I'd known that, because that wasn't like him. Because he never, ever had touched wine or strong spirits.

But nobody told me, and the night after the funeral, Mr. Sam put the muzzle of a shotgun in his mouth and pulled the trigger with his toe.

Oh, it was terrible! But I guess he just couldn't go on without her.

I think about Mr. Sam and Mr. Adkins sometimes. Mr. Adkins talked about having religion all the time, but he didn't have it. Not really. He was just a devil-man who dressed himself up in a angel-suit, to fool everybody. And Mr. Sam, why he turned down the Everlasting Arms that he could have leaned on when he was hurting so bad. So I guess one was just as sad as the other—except that Mr. Sam never hurt a living soul but himself. And Lauralee, I guess, but he didn't mean to hurt her. Just that she was left all alone, and her still so young. So I guess Mr. Sam could've thought of her, but he didn't. Didn't even care that she waked up because of the terrible sound of that shotgun blast and ran into the kitchen to find him there. And her so torn up about it all, she couldn't even go to the funeral.

After he was gone, Lauralee couldn't stay on in Mr. Bondurant's house, of course; and even if she could, it wouldn't have been proper for a girl her age to live alone. Miss Anne and Miss Cora and I begged her to come live here with us, and, as I heard, the girls' Aunt Fairleigh, Mr. Sam's sister who lived in Augusta, wanted Lauralee to come live with her too. But what we didn't know was that Lauralee already knew where she wanted to live, and that was with her sister.

So she moved in with Wynona and Mr. Adkins. They'd always been so close, those two girls, and I can sure see why they both would've wanted it that way. Still, knowing what we know now—well, we didn't know, that's all. We just didn't know.

I had a notion that something wasn't right between Wynona and Mr. Adkins, even before Lauralee came to live with them, but it wasn't something I could have said. Little things, like how Wynona looked at him, and even though she never said a word to me against him, she'd sometimes let out a sigh and didn't even know she was doing it, and so I thought maybe something wasn't right.

Anyway, Lauralee moved in with them and the first thing Mr. Adkins did was have her baptized—dunked, good and proper. Of course, that was up to him because, after all, it was going to be his roof over her head, so if he wanted her baptized like that, it was his right, I guess. She was still just a child. But I always thought he must not have told the preacher that Lauralee had already been sprinkled. Otherwise, that preacher would have called up the "one baptism" rule, sure enough.

So no matter how Mr. Adkins got it done, it was the very first thing on the very first Sunday Lauralee was with them. Wynona invited me to come to the baptism particularly, but she didn't say anything about it to Miss Anne. Still, I guess she wanted somebody in her family to come, and so I went, the way I would've done just about anything in this world Wynona asked me to do. Wynona knew about Lauralee having been christened as well, but I guess she didn't say anything.

I went to the church that Sunday morning and on down the hill to stand a little ways back from all the folks gathered around the old baptismal pool, and then Lauralee came down the hill just as quiet and sweet as you please. I'll never forget seeing her standing barefoot beside the baptismal pool at the bottom of that hill at Brushy Creek Church. She'd already begun getting a woman's figure, but she was still just a little girl in her way of thinking, and just as pretty as a picture, what with the way her skin was so lovely and pale and that pretty blonde hair just curling all by itself. Looked like an angel, and the sunlight that morning behind her head, like a golden halo.

Mr. Adkins had made her unbraid her hair and take out all the hairpins too, so there wasn't a chance that any spot on her head would not get wet, and she was wearing an old choir robe with not a stitch of clothes under it, because he said she had to get wet all over to be baptized good and proper. Made me mighty glad that I'd been baptized long ago when

folks weren't so picky about it. Because in my church, when we have bap-
tizings, we all go singing down the road to Brushy Creek where it curves
around the side of town near to the church and wade out into the water
behind the preacher, still singing, who dunks us under one at a time, and
we come up to all that shouting and singing. That's sure something!

But Mr. Adkins, of course, wanted it all done "good and proper"—so he
said—and he seemed to know exactly how God Himself wanted it done.

Lauralee stood there with her hands folded in front of her and her
head bowed and with sunlight in her hair, while the preacher prayed
about John the Baptist and how he baptized the Lord Jesus. The preacher
was already in the pool, standing in that cold, cold water up to his waist,
and with his long white robe floating around him.

Us all standing around, me and Wynona and Mr. Adkins, and all kinds of
people from the church, and I guess we were all thinking about how sweet
Lauralee looked. Such a pretty morning too. In August, I remember, and just
one of those old tender-sweet mornings that stays on your skin forever.

The preacher got done praying and held out his hand, and Lauralee
reached out and took it and started down those slimy cold steps into that
icy water, and I heard her catch her breath, but she didn't stop or say a
word. And when she stepped down like that, I saw that the sunlight com-
ing through that old choir robe just showed her whole figure in a shadow
under the gown, and the preacher turned his face away a little so he
wouldn't be staring at her.

Wynona saw it, though, and she looked over at some of the church
women, but they still had their eyes closed. Then she looked at Mr. Adkins,
and his face was red as fire. So of course, he'd seen, all right.

After Lauralee had been good and proper baptized, she came back
up the steps, streaming with water and smiling, and Wynona was wait-
ing right there with a clean, old quilt to wrap around her, and they went
right on up the hill and into the back room of the church so that Lauralee
could get dressed.

It was long years later that Wynona told me what happened after they
got home. How Mr. Adkins took Lauralee into the bedroom and pulled
off his belt, and shook it in her face and said if she ever showed her fig-
ure again, he'd whip her.

I think that was probably the first time Wynona ever hated him, but it
wasn't the last.

No! Not the last by a long shot.

But he didn't say anything else about it, and Wynona said later that everything seemed to be all right. But when she looked back on it, maybe there were little things all along that seemed kind of funny, from the very day Lauralee moved in with them. They'd cleared out a little room—a plunder room, we used to call it, really a big closet but with a window in it so it was almost like a small room—and that was Lauralee's room. But when Lauralee would take a basin of water into her room for bathing, Mr. Adkins would wait until she shut the door, and then he'd go into her room. Without knocking. And shut the door behind him. That was one of the things Wynona said later on that just didn't seem quite right.

Once, on an April evening, the same thing happened. Wynona was sitting in the living room and sewing by the lamp when Mr. Adkins opened Lauralee's door without knocking, and Wynona could see Lauralee sitting on the side of her bed. She had her dress down to her waist and was bathing her arms, but when she saw Mr. Adkins, she covered herself as best she could. Then he went on in and shut the door, but Wynona said that for the rest of her life she would be able to see Lauralee just before she looked up and saw him in the doorway.

Wynona did a lot of arguing with herself about it all, and she thought that what with Lauralee being only a child, Mr. Adkins must have felt like a father to her, so that he could go in her room when he liked and without knocking. It was his house.

Sometimes at night, Wynona would wake up and he'd be gone from the bed, but she'd tell herself that maybe he'd heard something out in the yard and went out to see what it was. Because that's what she wanted to believe, I guess.

Like I said, we just didn't know. But we sure found out.

Because Lauralee came to me in secret about it. But I knew it even before she came.

They were all at the dinner table one noontime, almost a year after Lauralee moved in with them. That was right after Miss Anne passed on, so nobody was left in this house but me and Miss Cora. The last of the aunts had gone on to her reward not too long after Wynona's wedding.

I'd been missing Wynona and Lauralee so much, what with there being only Miss Cora and me left, and too, I was worried about Wynona, but I couldn't have said why. Just seemed to me like she was all buried somewhere inside herself. Like whatever was really her was all pulled in and scrunched up in a little ball, the way it is when the weather is so cold, and you hunch your shoulders up. Because deep, deep in the middle of her, in her very center, there was a tiny little something that was warm and very much alive, but maybe asleep. And too, she'd made herself stop feeling things. I don't know why to this very day. She never said. But maybe it was because if she felt anything at all, she'd have to feel everything. Whatever that was. And then the little curled-up thing, the only thing that was really alive, would just die right then and there. Uncurl, and then the cold would get it. And it would die. That's what it seemed like for her.

And I'd thought maybe Wynona would've been a little happier now that her very own sister was there with her. But like I said, we just didn't know. Not then.

Anyway, they were having their dinner, and Lauralee had just poured another cup of coffee for Mr. Adkins. She walked around the table to put the coffeepot back on the stove, and just as she did, he glanced up at her and just kept looking and looking at her for the longest kind of time. Wynona said later that she was looking at Mr. Adkins, and he was looking at Lauralee, and then Wynona looked at Lauralee to see what Mr. Adkins was looking at, but Lauralee was just wiping off the stove and didn't notice what was going on. Just about the time Wynona was going to ask Mr. Adkins what he was looking at Lauralee so hard for, she heard him speak, or thought she heard him speak.

"Harlot."

The word was said so low that Wynona wasn't sure she heard it right. Mr. Adkins still staring at Lauralee, and Wynona said it was like thinking you hear one of those rolls of thunder that's so soft and far away, you can't be sure it's thunder at all. So you turn down the radio, and maybe you go and look through the curtains and see big, black clouds coming up over the trees at the edge of the field and hear another rumble, and then you know for sure there's a storm bearing down on you.

She said it was just like being in a photograph, the way the three of them were frozen in place, and she felt like she was somewhere else, floating up at the ceiling of the kitchen and looking down at the three of them so she could even see steam from the coffeepot rising up toward her. Everything just stopped, even their breathing.

That same low voice was the thing that finally broke the spell they were in, and words rolled out and fell on the table just as Mr. Adkins thrust his chair backwards so hard it fell over.

161

"Get yourself taken care of, you harlot. You know what I mean."

He was standing there glaring at Lauralee with his fists all balled up, and her just standing there with a look on her face Wynona would never forget. The same look she'd had just before the baptism, and so inno-cent, like wondering what it was all about. And Wynona stood up too, but she said it was like moving in slow motion, trying to stand up so she could fend off whatever was coming, put herself in between Lauralee and him. For Wynona didn't know what on earth was going on, but she knew enough to tell that Mr. Adkins was close to something very dangerous, something that could happen at any moment.

But he didn't move. Just stood there, still staring, and growing paler and paler, and you could almost see him marching around in his mind and finding something so vague, maybe just the faintest little echo of something, and he looked down at his fists, took his eyes off Lauralee for the first time in what seemed like hours, and just curled his hands up toward his face as if he was seeing them for the first time. Then he turned and left without a word.

Lauralee, pale as a ghost, looked at Wynona, who was still standing there at the table, and Wynona told me there was something or other she'd never seen in Lauralee's face before. Not anything any less pretty than what'd always been there, but something more than what had been before and beautiful too, but in a strange, frightening, sort of way. Lau-ralee slowly just put her arm across her waist and held it there, almost like a picture of a dancer Wynona saw once in a magazine, with the arm curved so soft and the hand palm up in the gentlest sort of way, like wait-ing for some strange and beautiful flower to drop into it.

They heard the car engine start up and Mr. Adkins driving away, spin-ning the tires in the dirt and scattering the squawking old hens that had been scratching around in the leaves under the pecan tree. When the car was gone and the silence all around them, still they stayed right where they had been when he went out the door.

Wynona was the one to speak first, though she said she felt so light-headed she could hardly form the words.

"What on earth?"

Lauralee stood by the stove, looking at Wynona with kind of a calm look and for the longest kind of time before she said, "I'm going to have a baby." Said it just as matter-of-factly as if she was telling Wynona that it looked like rain.

Wynona couldn't even understand those words, and for some reason, probably because she had to do something, she reached over and got the bowl of butter beans she'd been shelling when Mr. Adkins came home for his dinner, and she sat down in the chair and went back to shelling those beans. Because she didn't know what else to do, and she had to do something. Then Lauralee got her bowl of butter beans to shell and sat down too, and that's what they did for a long time, without saying a single word.

Wynona said it must have been truly strange, for them to sit there working away, just as if nothing unusual had happened, but that's exactly what they did, because neither one of them knew what to say. Or what to do.

Then Wynona looked at the brown earthenware bowl resting on Lauralee's knees and beyond it too, at the aproned lap where deep and underneath was something so mysterious that Wynona could only guess at what it was. Because back in those days, women—nice women, that is—didn't know about those things, sometimes not even married women until they'd had a baby of their own. So she couldn't figure out how Lauralee would know something like that.

"How do you know?" Wynona finally asked.

"I asked Pet, and she told me that's what it is."

"Why didn't you ask me?"

"I figured you didn't know any more about it than I did. And besides…" Her voice trailed away.

A silence then, a stillness broken only by the sound of butter bean hulls snapping open and the hum of the water simmering in the iron kettle.

"What'd Pet say?"

"She asked me how I thought I could get a baby when I wasn't a married lady, and I said I didn't know. And she asked a lot of questions and I answered them."

"What did she ask you?"

"She asked me if I'd been with a man, but I didn't know what she meant, so I asked her, and she told me some of the strangest things. Well, you know. Said somebody ought to shoot him. Said she wished there were some menfolk left in our family so they could fix him good. And then she said, 'God works in mysterious ways.' And also that I should tell you I was going to have a little baby."

"Who is 'him'?"

"I didn't know that's how women get babies, but Pet says it is. And she said that's what got me a baby. I mean, got US a baby. You and me, I mean. Not him."

Wynona didn't know exactly when she realized that her own husband was the "him," but it just came to her gradually. And other things came into her head, one right after the other, the first one being that she'd kill him. Because he'd hurt Lauralee. But the next thing was that there was going to be a baby. An honest-to-goodness baby. And they needed to get out before Mr. Adkins came home again.

Wynona couldn't let Lauralee stay where he was, because she knew he'd hurt Lauralee or the baby, or both. And Wynona had to get out too, for she wasn't going to stay with any man who had bothered her very own sister. I think there were some other things too. But she never told me what they were.

"Why didn't you tell me?" Wynona asked.

"I was ashamed. And I was scared you'd be mad at me." Lauralee's voice dropped to hardly more than a whisper. "I didn't want it to happen."

"I know," Wynona said without hesitation. "It wasn't your fault. I thought maybe something was wrong, but I didn't know what it was, and I never thought of that. Him always quoting the Bible and telling me all the time how sinful I am, and him after my own sister and you hardly more than a child yourself. I think Pet's right. Somebody ought to shoot him."

"Maybe," Lauralee said. "But I don't think he always knows what he's doing. Like he's sick or something. But let's not think about that—let's think about the baby."

So they sat for another long time, splitting open the hulls and plopping the beans against the sides of the bowl. But they were both thinking. About the baby.

Wynona said she could tell that Lauralee was starting to smile, and she tried not to look at Lauralee, because she didn't think this was something they should be smiling about, and she was already beginning to think they'd better stop this foolishness of shelling beans that were never going to get cooked and get out of there while the getting was good. And while she was thinking so hard about what to do, Lauralee's smile just started to feel like the sun shining right there between the two of them, and finally she had to smile too, even though she tried so hard not to.

Because this was a very serious thing, and Wynona knew that. But even when the idea of a baby coming was so new and shocking, and they were both so afraid, somehow, it just couldn't be completely bad. It just couldn't. Not something that nice, and she said she didn't even really know what she meant by that, but she knew it was true.

Wynona thought about what Miss Anne and the aunts would have said—that only women who are trash and who come from trashy families have babies without having husbands. But Miss Anne didn't know what Mr. Adkins was really like; maybe Miss Anne had lived her whole life not knowing there were men in this world like Mr. Adkins. So no matter what Miss Anne would have said, Wynona just couldn't make it stick that what Mr. Adkins had done was her fault or Lauralee's at all. Or worse, that the baby was bad too. Because of the way it had gotten started.

But Wynona was the older sister and the married lady, so it was her responsibility to take care of Lauralee, and she hadn't been able to do that. I guess she couldn't even take care of herself when it came to Mr. Adkins, so she sure as Heaven couldn't take care of Lauralee too. But still, they hadn't done anything wrong, and maybe what was happening to them was surprising, but it sure wasn't something they should be ashamed about. It wasn't their doing at all, either of them.

So Wynona and Lauralee kept on smiling, because they couldn't seem to stop. And I guess they were both thinking pretty much the same things. They know those things now that they're old, but they didn't know them then, and it would be years and years before they found them out.

And what they know now is that, in the long run, we can't go back and change one single thing, not a single thing we've done or thought or said, or anything that's been done to us either. And when it's all over, those things just don't matter anymore. All those things we think we can't stand will wind up like everything winds up . . . under some old tombstone nobody can read the writing on. Planted in the hillside above the creek and being run over every Sunday morning by the feet of all those children on their way to the creek at the bottom of the hill. And the dreamy feet of lovers who walk along together after church, holding hands.

Resting in the Bosom of the Lamb.

But way back then, when it all happened, Wynona started thinking about what Mr. Adkins said when he told Lauralee to get herself "taken care of."

He meant that she should do something about the baby. Take that long, long walk over to where a woman lived who knew what to do about babies that weren't wanted. That's exactly what he meant to have Lauralee do.

"Go pack your bag," Wynona said. "We're going home."

She called me on the telephone and said could me and Miss Cora come and get them right away? I didn't ask a single question about it because something in her voice said HURRY! Though she never said the word itself.

Miss Cora dropped her tatting, and I turned off the heat under the big pot of green beans I was cooking, and we went straight out there. We knew something terrible must've happened, and when we got there, Wynona was standing on the porch waiting for us, and we went and sat down at the kitchen table where Lauralee was still shelling beans, and Wynona told us. Lauralee never said a word, and the only thing was that her ears turned red when Wynona told us that Lauralee was expecting a child. Lauralee glanced up at us, to see if we were gonna condemn her, I guess. But of course, we didn't. It was Mr. Adkins' fault, not Lauralee's. Why, she was hardly more than a child herself. And him a grown man. And her sister's husband!

"We need to come home," Wynona said when she had finished telling us all about it.

"Of course," Miss Cora said. "You get your things and let's go." And then she added, "Somebody ought to shoot him."

But before we could gather up a few clothes and things and get into the car and drive away, Mr. Adkins came back. We heard the front door slam real loud, and we knew it had to be him, and we just froze right where we were sitting, and sure enough, he came through the kitchen doorway. And he was carrying a shotgun.

I never did know quite how things happened after that, or what on earth he had in mind to come rushing into the kitchen with that big old gun in his hands. Maybe he was going to go hunting or something. Or maybe . . . But that doesn't matter now.

What happened was that somehow or other there was a lot of shouting and someone screaming, and Miss Cora jumped up out of her chair and stood a little to the side of the sink, just like a statue or something, and then the rest of us jumped up too, and grabbed at the gun, Wynona grabbing at it, my hands on it too, pulling it away from him, the butt end of the gun somehow swinging down and against Wynona, and the barrel heaving up in the air. And all of a sudden I could see those two triggers right there, and the barrel up and away from . . . Lord, have mercy! Away from . . .

Oh, that terrible explosion! That flash of unholy light filling the room and the sound of it more than sound, more than ears can hear and it all falling in on us, and the smoke, so much smoke, and right in the very middle of it, them down on the floor, and Lauralee's mouth open against the linoleum and her hands over her ears. I guess they didn't even have time to think about going down, it happened so fast, and Wynona flying backwards against the door because the butt of the gun had kicked so hard, just like a mule and right square in her stomach. And me the only one standing.

167

A silence then, like I never heard before—or since. Silence that came from inside my ears and not outside of them, and white-blue smoke swirling and then gathering in a layer just about even with the stove top, and them on the floor with not even an intake of breath among us yet, and my head ringing like somebody had jammed me up inside a big church bell and pulled the rope.

It felt like some sort of a terrible trick somebody had played, and any minute we'd all take a deep breath and laugh and talk about how foolish we'd been to be so scared. But that didn't happen. Even though it felt like something that was supposed to be.

Because the first thing I could hear, but like I was hearing it through some kind of cotton stuffed in my ears, was Wynona crying and vomiting, and it must have taken her all that time to get a breath, because she'd been hit so hard by the kicking back of that big gun, and she was on the floor and the gun beside her. I went to her, but it was like I was walking through a cloud, and her all curled up and holding her stomach and the gun beside her, and I kicked it out of the way, and that was when it came to my mind. WHERE'S MR. ADKINS?

I looked over at Lauralee, and she was sitting up against the wall, and Miss Cora was hugging her and crying and looking over toward the stove, and her face told me what she saw.

His feet were crossed over each other, because he'd been taking a step forward, when the blast took him right square in the face.

And—God forgive me!—the only thing that came to my mind was this: He ain't gonna hurt nobody. Never again.

What happened next just happened all by itself—that's the only way to describe it. Of course, it didn't seem to be real, right then, anyway, for I guess there wasn't nothing that seemed real that terrible day.

But I knew we had to do something, and we had to do it quick. And to this very day, I don't know whether what we did was right or wrong. Maybe I won't never know. Still, it's what we did, and we didn't talk about it or plan any of it. It just happened.

We stayed where we were for the longest kind of time. Wynona had finally gotten her breath back, but she still looked awful gray, and Lauralee had turned bright red and begun to cry. And Miss Cora sitting there beside her and looking at me so strange.

Like she hadn't never seen me before.

168

Me standing there, shaking like a leaf and looking at that mess that used to be Mr. Adkins, and it seemed to me that I was the one who was going to have to say something or do something or we would all just stay there forever and ever.

So I went into the bedroom and pulled the quilt right off the bed and brought it to the kitchen and covered Mr. Adkins with it. And just in the time it took me to get the quilt, blood had started creeping across the kitchen floor and moving ever so slowly toward Lauralee. She saw it about the same time I did, and I never heard nobody scream like that! Never!

Miss Cora and I took ahold of Lauralee on either side and somehow managed to get her to her feet and out of the kitchen and into the bedroom and her still screaming. And finally, I slapped her.

To this day, the memory of that slap hurts me deep in my very bones, but something had to be done, and I did it. She looked so shocked, but she stopped screaming. And I was so angry I couldn't hardly stand it, but I didn't even know what I was so angry about.

"Do you get ahold of yourself or you'll be hurting that baby!" I yelled at her. "And I don't care what I have to do to you, I'll not stand here and see you scream until you lose it. There's been enough tragedy here. I won't see no more. You hear me?"

She quieted right down, and we tucked her into bed.

But I was still mad as fire, and I told Miss Cora and Wynona to get into the kitchen and help me. And the way I said it, so rough-like, they looked at me like I'd lost my mind. But they did as I said.

"What're we going to do?" Wynona was whispering, like that poor old piece of garbage on the floor could still hear us. Like he still had ears or something.

"We're gonna take care of him so nobody in this house goes to jail," I said. And we worked together, tying twine around and around the quilt we had wrapped him in and making it as good and tight as we could get it. And then sliding him across the floor and out to the back porch, and Wynona going to get the Buick from around front and pulling it as close to the back porch steps as she could, and us dragging him out the door and bumping him down the steps and heaving and grunting and pulling and pushing and finally getting him into the backseat. And then closing the door to the car and going back inside.

Lauralee had come out of the bedroom and was standing in the kitchen door, pale as a ghost and still crying just a little. And the mark of my hand *still on her cheek. She watched while we got the mop and all the old rags we could find and started in to cleaning the kitchen. It was a terrible job, I tell you. And one I wouldn't never want to have to take care of again. After a few minutes, I told Lauralee to go back and lie down on the bed, and she did, and Miss Cora and Wynona and me used rags to wipe down the wall, and we threw them right into the trash can we had brought in off the porch, because we couldn't stand to rinse them out in the sink. Because it was so terrible. Little pieces of . . . I don't know what all it was. Just awful.*

We wiped and mopped and wiped some more, and by the time we got done, we were dripping with sweat, but the kitchen looked pretty much as it had before it all happened. The smoke and the smell of the blast were still hanging in the air, but I figured a fan in the window would draw all that right off pretty well.

When I went into the bedroom to see about Lauralee, she'd fallen asleep, and that was good. For there wasn't nothing more important to me than taking care of that baby. It was the most important thing in the whole world. Like everything that was me was curling up around that baby. Like me all wrapped around it, though it was surely in Lauralee.

Then with Miss Cora driving the car, we went bumping down the field road toward the creek behind the house. When we couldn't go any farther, we drug the body out of the car and rolled it all the way down the hill and to the edge of the creek. And we took off the quilt and gathered up all the twine and put it in the trunk.

I stood there for a little while, thinking harder than I've ever thought in my whole life, and then I sent Wynona back to the house to bring Mr. Adkins' shotgun down to the creek, and she did that, and me and Miss Cora standing there over his body and waiting for Wynona to come back, and me looking up at all those green leaves, like I'd never seen leaves before. Because nothing was going to be the same. Ever again. And I knew it. Then Wynona came back down the hill holding that big, heavy gun as far out from her as she could, and I put the gun on the ground beside him, with the stock of it near his hand, and we went back to the house and got Lauralee and some things for her and Wynona, like clothes and such, and we emptied the trash can right into the trunk of Miss Cora's Buick and slammed it shut. We all got in the car and came home.

Never said a word about it, not even amongst ourselves. Just came back to this good house and never said a thing. Not a word. I went into the kitchen and put the heat back under the green beans and started fix-

170

ing some nice tomato sandwiches for us and iced tea, and somehow or other we just made it through those first hours and then sometime or other, someone said something like, "Maybe I should water the geraniums." And that made it start being all right again.

That night, I made one of those deep-dish chicken pies my grandmama always made so well, and we had it with the good green beans and more sliced, fresh tomatoes. When we were sitting on the porch later on, Lauralee came over to me and sat in my lap like she was a little child, and I rocked her and rocked her for the longest kind of time.

It was awful hard for all of us, knowing what was down there by the creek and all. The way I know how it was for Wynona was that the only thing she said that whole time was that she wondered if somebody was feeding the chickens. And maybe that meant she'd shut all the rest of it away somewhere. And Lauralee was good about getting plenty of rest like we wanted her to do, and she seemed to have a little more color in her cheeks.

It was two whole days before the sheriff came knocking on the door, and when I answered it, he asked to see Mrs. Adkins. I almost didn't know who it was he meant. The two of them went into the living room, and I could hear his voice, but so low I couldn't hear the words. And then I heard Wynona crying. The sheriff came out of the room, and he put his hand on my shoulder and looked right into my eyes, and my heart almost stopped beating because I thought for sure he'd say I was going to jail. But he didn't say nothing like that. "There's been a hunting accident, and Mr. Adkins is dead," he said. "You better go on in there and take care of Mrs. Adkins." That was all he said. That was all he ever said.

Over the years, I've thought of all kinds of things he could've asked but didn't. Like why Mr. Adkins would've worn a suit and tie if he was going hunting, and why there wasn't any dirt on his shoes, and why there wasn't much blood. And why weren't Wynona and Lauralee living in their own home? Those were the things he didn't ask. He'd told Wynona that Mr. Adkins' body was over to Mr. Grower's, and we should go over and make the arrangements we wanted. But I knew they couldn't do that, so I never said a thing—just went and took care of everything myself. Like I'd done when I buried that old quilt and those bloody rags too, out behind the carriage house.

The funeral was three days later, and it was a hard thing for us to get through, knowing what we knew, but we did it. And Mr. Adkins' nephew came, and he wore the same suit he had worn as best man at the wedding.

*A*lmost before we knew it, the last day of Camp Meeting came around. We'd already started getting things together to take back home and saving our newspapers again for spreading across the beds until next year.

I think it's one of the saddest things in the whole world, when Camp Meeting's over, even though we're always ready to go home and get back into the routine of things. But this time, Wynona and I knew about that big funeral parlor sign that would be glaring at us from across the street and about Miss Addie's big pecan tree being gone. So we were worried about what Miss Cora was going to think about that.

Still, the last day of Camp Meeting is always a strange one for me. Something about knowing that, all the other weeks of the year, Miss Cora's old family tent is standing right there, not even five miles away from us, just waiting for the next August to come. Oh, we drive down every month or so, just to make sure everything's all right, but it's still a strange feeling. Almost like I get when we close off the parlor in the winter, and I know good and well what's in the parlor, and that, needs be, we could open the door. But we usually don't, and the things that are shut away from us, by doors or by miles or even by years, make for some mighty strange feelings.

It's something like the way I feel when Miss Cora gestures with her hands exactly the way Miss Anne used to do; or the way I sometimes find myself heaving a little sigh that sounds just like the ones my mama used to heave, especially when the weather was hot, and she was standing in the kitchen over a sizzling skillet full of fried chicken, with the sweat just pouring off her.

The final service started at seven o'clock, and we all went to it, out of respect for that young minister who had tried so hard for those two long weeks to give us good enough sermons to carry us through for a whole year. I guess everybody who was at Camp Meeting that summer came to the service, but they still filled only the first three pews.

So that last night, we all walked down the grassy hill toward where the light came out from under the tabernacle roof, Wynona and me on either side of Miss Cora, to steady her over the uneven ground, and Lauralee behind us, marching along—almost exactly that formal step-halt walking she did when she came down the aisle at Wynona's wedding. She even had her hands held together in front of her and was looking down at them, as if she was carrying a bouquet.

When we got to the tabernacle, was I ever surprised to see Minnie Louise sitting there on the back row. I slid in beside her, while Wynona and Miss Cora and Lauralee went on down to the first few rows.

"Whatchu doing back out here?" I asked. Because Minnie Louise didn't like Camp Meeting one little bit. "Don't like leaving my home," she used to say. "Somebody's liable to go in there and mess with my things . . . with my mama's things!"

"Oh, Miss Delia's snippy, little granddaughter decided yesterday afternoon that she had to go on back to Macon, and tell the truth, I think Miss Delia was right glad to see her go. Those children about drove her crazy!"

"I know."

"Miss Delia couldn't stay out here all by herself, and the granddaughter left so fast, Miss Delia didn't have time to get packed up and move back home. So she called me, and I said I'd come out and stay with her tonight and help her move back home tomorrow morning."

"That was good of you," I said, but Minnie Louise only snorted. And about that time, the first hymn started up and that blessed young preacher led the singing, striding across the platform in time to the music, smiling as if he was getting ready to preach at the biggest Baptist church in the whole South, and singing heartily, as if that was the most important hymn in the whole world.

> Standing on the promises of Christ my King,
> Thru eternal ages let His praises ring;
> Glory in the highest I will shout and sing,
> Standing on the promises of God.
>
> Standing, standing,
> Standing on the promises of God my Savior;
> Standing, standing,
> I'm standing on the promises of God.

And it was important, in lots of ways. Good to be standing there, singing the old, familiar words beside Minnie Louise and looking over all the empty pews between us, and Miss Cora and Wynona and Lauralee sitting beside Miss Delia way up at the front, and them singing too. Something of such comfort in it. But on the other hand, I have to say that those words, "standing on the promises" was extra special to me that night. Because that's what I was gonna be doing soon. Standing on *those* good promises and on the one I made to Miss Addie.

That good old singing ringing out from under that tabernacle roof like it's done for more years than any of us have been alive. Now that's really something to think about!

"Bless his heart," Minnie Louise whispered to me, nodding her head toward that young preacher.

Bless his heart indeed! I was thinking. Such a young man—probably still in seminary—and him given a job out of a past so long ago, when whole families really came to Camp Meeting and stayed the whole time and filled every single seat in the tabernacle. But then, things always change on us. Most of the time, when we least expect it.

But the singing was real good that night, and the sermon was even better. And when it was over, folks went up and shook that young preacher's hand, and he was as mannerly as could be. *Bless his heart.*

Minnie Louise went up the sawdust-covered aisle to meet Miss Delia, but Miss Delia and Miss Cora were already arm-in-arm, moving along toward our tent.

"Minnie Louise, you go along and finish up with our packing, if you please," Miss Delia said. "I'm going to go sit with Miss Cora and them a little while."

"How you gonna get home?" Minnie Louise asked, for the little dirt path that skirted along the backs of the tents was uneven and very dark.

Miss Cora looked at me. "Will you walk her home in a while, Pet?" she asked.

"Yes'm, I'll be glad to."

Now Miss Delia was pretty stout, and by the time we got to our front porch, she was just about out of breath. We motioned her right to a rocking chair, and she sat down with a little grunt, and there she stayed, wheezing a little before she could speak.

I fixed everybody some iced tea, and Miss Delia drank almost all of hers while we waited politely for her to catch her breath, not staring at her, of course, but merely glancing from time to time while she fanned herself with her cardboard-Jesus fan and drank the rest of her tea. I went and chipped more ice and fixed her another glass, which she took most gratefully.

"I declare, Cora," she started in, "I just don't understand these young people at all."

Miss Cora nodded her head a little, to let Miss Delia know she agreed with her, even though she wasn't yet sure of what Miss Delia was going to say.

"I was so glad when my granddaughter wanted to come to Camp Meeting and bring the children along. Goodness! I was thinking, maybe some of these modern folks are really still interested in the old ways of doing things."

Miss Cora nodded again.

"But I declare, I've never seen such children in my whole life! Always complaining about being too hot or about the gnats bothering them or missing their cartoons on television or nobody

175

brought the kind of soft drinks they like. And I do wonder what will become of those children? Because they don't know and they won't listen—just want their television shows and their soft drinks and don't care a thing about what really matters."

"That's the truth," Miss Cora agreed. But we didn't have any answers about it either.

"Well, Camp Meeting's over for another year," Miss Delia said at last. "And I don't think I'll see another one."

"Hush your mouth," Miss Cora said, because Miss Cora was the only one of us older than Miss Delia, and so the only one who could tell her—even in a joking, light-hearted way—to hush her mouth.

"Lord willing, you'll be here for many more, Miss Delia," Wynona said.

And I added an enthusiastic "Amen to that."

"Well, I'll tell you," Miss Delia said, "I came here for the very first time in August of 1912, and I was only thirteen years old. Because my mama and papa lived in Charleston before that, but my papa moved us to here that June, when he opened up the new mill, and so we came to Camp Meeting with my grandmama in August."

"Why, I don't even remember the first time I came," Miss Cora said. "Seems to me I remember walking around in the back part of this place with Dilsey's mama holding my hand, and I was just a little thing. That would have been your grandmama, Pet," she added, unnecessarily.

I didn't say anything, but I sure enough remembered Camp Meeting when I was little, as well, especially that summer when everything changed. *When it was the first time my mama wouldn't let me go out and play with Wynona, the way we had always done before. She said it wouldn't look right, and I should stay near the kitchen and help her all the time. And that meant even when she didn't have anything for me to do.*

"I sure enough could never forget my first time here," Miss Delia repeated. "Because there was a terrible scandal that year!"

She paused, leaving the words hanging in the air, and she looked from one of us to another, just to make sure we were all primed and interested and ready for her story. "Because my friend's sister ran away with a boy from the youth group—a boy she had just met that very evening."

Well, even the old locusts seemed to stop chirping when Miss Delia said that, and Wynona and I glanced at each other and smiled, because Miss Delia was truly in the mood to tell a good story, and she was known far and wide for the best stories anyone ever heard, except, of course, for Miss Cora.

So we all settled back in our chairs and waited, and Miss Cora smiled and nodded her head and closed her eyes, as if maybe she could imagine Miss Delia's story better that way.

"I never did learn what happened to her, and I never saw my friend again either," Miss Delia sighed. "But I was young, and I got another friend right away. It was all a long, long time ago.

"She was some kind of a strange one all right—the sister, I mean. And maybe I wouldn't think so now, but it was a long time ago, and we were all so young and just didn't know any better is all.

"My friend's name was Molly, and she and her mama and papa and one sister all lived over to the other side of Blythe. Molly's sister was a strange one, all right. Read the Bible all the time and cried and hollered and held her hands up toward Heaven. And I do mean *all* the time.

"Every summer, the sister would pester her mama and papa until they let her go to a Camp Meeting, usually here at Mount Horeb, because this Camp Ground had a Public Tent for people whose families didn't have their own tents, you know. And because it was pretty close. And they made Molly come along, to take care of her sister. Because I think there was a little something wrong with her, but we never did know what it was. More than just her reading and crying and hollering all the time. Definitely more than that."

Here, Miss Delia paused, fanned herself a little, and took another long drink of iced tea.

"There were little things, you know, and we made fun of her, I'm sorry to say. But it was Molly herself who always set us off about it. Like at the services, because the sister always sat right on the very front row, and when she'd sing, she'd bob her head around so much—she wore her hair pulled straight back and into a tight little knot—that knot of hair would begin to slip, like a poor wounded little thing, until it was hanging and swaying. I don't really remember why it was so funny, but it was.

"It was always Molly who nudged me with her elbow and pointed it out and started giggling behind her hand, and of course, that would set us off, sure enough. Terrible thing to have snickers all caught in your throat and nowhere for them to go."

Wynona glanced at me.

"Sure is, Miss Delia," she said.

Miss Delia nodded and continued with her story: "The worst thing was that every single afternoon, Molly's sister would go to the cemetery and sit out there and cry and pray. And when she did that, she always sat on one of the children's graves. Why, I can see her right now, just as plain as day, sitting on one of those little marble slabs like a funny old hen setting on an egg.

"Now, none of the rest of us would go near any of the children's graves, because, as I told you, we were still children ourselves, and passing away was something we thought only old people did. Not children. And even if that wasn't true, we didn't want to know about it.

"Sometimes, though, we'd go close enough to read the inscriptions on the tombstones: Little Angel, Gone So Soon, Resting in the Bosom of the Lamb."

Here, Miss Delia paused for a moment, like maybe she was a little tired or had forgotten what she was going to say. She glanced around at us. And then she went on:

"Molly knew her sister was kind of strange, of course, but still, the rest of us tried not to talk about her when Molly was around. Still, sometimes Molly would say things about her sister, and when she did, the rest of us would pretend kind of a polite disinterest, but all the while, we exchanged glances and hung onto every word she said so that later, when Molly was gone back to the Public Tent, we could go over it again and again.

"That's partly why everything went so wrong and got so confusing that summer. Because on the last Sunday, there were lots of visitors, strangers who came just for that one service, and among them was a group of young men who had come over from Augusta. My! They were sure dandy-looking!"

178

Miss Delia laughed and her eyes glittered and she blushed just a little, as if she was still a young girl, giggling about those dandified city boys. Miss Cora and I looked at each other and smiled. Because we knew Miss Delia was really enjoying herself with her story. And that made us enjoy it, as well.

Then she went on, "Of course, the call to the altar at the last service was always a long, drawn-out, very emotional thing, and we were all watching Molly's sister because she always got saved. Every single service. The piano wouldn't get out more than the first two or three notes of 'Just As I Am,' and she'd be headed for the altar, crying and hollering. Always crying. Always hollering. And when she'd get there, she'd fall down on her knees in the sawdust and just—flop!—over the railing she'd go!

"I'm sorry to say we laughed at her for it. We were very young. And perhaps very cruel. But we just didn't know any better.

"Sure enough, that night, she did it again. But more. For right behind her came one of those stylish-looking young men, and when he got to the rail, he didn't seem one bit interested in getting saved, because he just kept looking at Molly's sister and winking his eye at her! Goodness knows, I believe to this very day that he was as insincere as could be and that he went to the altar just to be next to Molly's poor sister.

"Of course, she was still draped over the rail just like a noodle, and at first, she didn't even see that boy next to her. We all stood there in the pews, holding our breath and wondering what would happen next. But it was a long time to wait, and it seemed to us that nothing interesting was going to happen. The preachers had started at either end of the long row of folks up there, and so Molly and I went ahead and left, like we always did, but I turned and looked back, for some reason, after we'd walked almost halfway up the hill. And there was something about it, you know, looking back at the tabernacle in the clearing, and darkness all around us, only with little glimmers of lamps in the tents, and the light at the tabernacle spilling out and making a circle in the grass, and the moonlight glowing on that old tin roof. And me still wondering what was going to happen when Molly's sister realized that handsome city boy was right beside her and trying to catch her attention."

Here, Miss Delia paused, drained the last of the tea from her glass, and handed the glass to me.

"Let me get you some more tea, Miss Delia," I offered.

"No, thank you, Pet—that's aplenty."

She touched her handkerchief to her mouth and heaved a long sigh, while we all waited, almost holding our breath, for her to go on with the story. Finally, she did.

"Later, when services were over and the lights at the tabernacle turned off and Molly and me were sitting out front at the Public Tent, Molly whispered to me, 'Did you see that city boy trying to wink at my sister? I think he was *after* her!'

"Oh," Miss Delia moaned, and I felt my eyes filling up when she did. "I don't know what there was about it, but I've never felt again in my whole life as I did when she said that. Don't know what it was though. Almost like somebody died. Or something like that. Because that was a church, for goodness sake! And things like that aren't supposed to happen there! Not frightening things like that. Not *animal* things like that!"

She paused again for a good long time and finally wiped her eyes.

"But what I started out to tell youall was this: We decided to walk around the cemetery, while it was still early and the moon was high, and Molly said that pretty soon, she would walk on back down to the tabernacle and get her sister. So we were walking along that very path I'm going to walk along with Pet when I go home in a few minutes, and we saw the shiny car that had brought all those boys over from Augusta, coming along so slowly. We stepped off the path to let it pass, and Molly waved, but I couldn't. Not unless I could have known it wasn't true what Molly said she saw—that boy winking and flirting with her sister, right there in front of God and everyone else!

"And when the car went past, there through the back window we could see a familiar head with the little knot of hair on it, and we saw it at the same time.

"'Good Heavens!' Molly yelled, and she was running after the car, screaming and crying. 'Pa'll kill me for sure!'

"I never did know how it all turned out, because I never saw Molly again. But somebody said years later that her sister—now what was her name? Eliza? Emily? yes, Emily, that was it—got married to one of those city boys. And as it turned out, they weren't city boys at all but only wild farm boys who had dressed up like they were dandies—and they lived on a poor little farm over to the other side of Keysville and spent every summer at Camp Meetings all around. But I heard he was an awful mean man. Never was good to her, not one little bit. Some folks said he had the very devil in him.

"I don't know why it stayed with me forever. Never could figure it out. But we went ahead and took our walk through the cemetery, and we didn't say anything but just walked along and clucked our tongues at the children's graves."

So that was the end of Miss Delia's story, and we all sat in silence, with Miss Delia adding only an "unh! unh!" to what she'd said.

Miss Cora was the first one to speak, but that was only after long minutes while we all sat there thinking.

"We never do know, do we? We just never do know what's going to happen," she said to no one in particular. Then, "Would you like more tea, Miss Delia?"

When it was time for Miss Delia to go back to her family's tent that evening, I walked back with her, and she leaned pretty heavily on my arm as we went ever so slowly down that uneven little path, so I was thinking that maybe she was right. Maybe she wouldn't see another Camp Meeting. Poor old Miss Delia.

As we walked along, we saw lights on in every tent that had been occupied for Camp Meeting, where folks were packing up for leaving in the morning. Everyone was staying up much later than they usually did, getting ready to go. I could sure understand that, because nobody wants to be the last family to leave when Camp Meeting is over. Why, it's the saddest thing in this world—maybe like being the only one left in a whole family that's all gone to Glory.

We were the last ones to leave one time, and we were packing things into the boxes and closing all the windows good and tight to keep out the weather, and we kept hearing cars starting up every once in a while and driving away, and when we finally left, all the other tents were closed up. Something so lonesome in that, we nearly died.

But too, many of the tents we passed were still dark and boarded up, and they were lonesome-looking, I tell you. Maybe like they were just waiting and waiting for families to come back to them. But it wasn't going to happen.

Miss Delia broke into my thoughts: "Minnie Louise tells me youall had a little excitement the first day of Camp Meeting."

"Ma'am?"

"Miss Cora and that old woman from Twilight Hills?"

"Oh. Yes'm. That was some excitement all right."

"What happened?"

"Oh, Miss Cora was trying to help that old woman find her mama."

"Her mama?"

"Yes'm."

"Well," Miss Delia said after a long time. "I guess I can understand that, sure enough."

"Me too, Miss Delia," I said. "Guess we never stop wanting our mamas. And I do wonder why that is."

"Oh, probably just wanting someone to love us, no matter who we are or what we do. Just love us, no matter what."

"Maybe so."

"I guess that's how we learn to love ourselves, you know," Miss Delia added.

"How's that?"

"Our mamas loving us first. I think that's how we learn to love ourselves. 'Cause our mamas loved us."

I didn't say anything else, because I hadn't thought about it before, not just that way. So there was something that needed thinking through, sure enough. Someone who'll love us, no matter what!

Then I added, "The old woman was looking for something else too. Something she called a Sin-eater. You ever hear tell of such?"

Miss Delia and I had walked slower and slower as we talked, and now Miss Delia stopped to get her breath back.

"I sure did," she said. "Sure enough did hear about that. Because my grandmama's people came from up in the mountains, and she used to talk about a Sin-eater. Someone who came to the house when there was a death. I guess the custom was to wrap a piece of corn bread in a linen napkin and place it on the body, after it was all bathed and dressed in clean clothes, and laid out, you know. The Sin-eater would come in and say not a single word but take the corn bread out of the napkin and eat it right there in front of everybody. That way, he took away the sins of the dead person. Took them into himself."

"Well, I never!" I said.

"Oh, it's just among the mountain people. Not many other folks know anything about it."

"Well, I guess not. I wonder why that old woman's looking for him?"

"Maybe she's scared she's going to die, and no one will be there to take away her sins," Miss Delia said.

"Jesus already done that. Don't need nothing else," I sniffed.

"That's right," Miss Delia answered.

Such a simple thought, it was, but the more I mused on it, the more I believed it was something I had known for a long, long time. Only I didn't know that I knew it.

Miss Delia laughed. "You know, Pet, I've never told this to another living soul in this world, but I like to think of Jesus as being like a mama to us."

"A *mama?*"

"Yes. A mama! 'Cause He loves us, no matter what!"

"You don't think of Him being like a man?" I asked, incredulously. I didn't add, *A white man.*

"No, and I sure don't mean anything funny about that. Just that a mama's love must be the closest thing to the way the Lord loves all of us. No matter who we are and no matter what we've done."

I didn't know what to say about that, so we walked on slowly and silently for a few minutes, and then Miss Delia said, "You think I upset Wynona with the story I told? About the children's graves? I just wasn't thinking, Pet. After all, it's been such a long time."

"No'm," I assured her. "I don't think so. And you're right about it being a long time."

"Yes," she agreed. "So long, I'd forgotten about it until I was almost done with the story. And I sure hope you're right. I hope I didn't upset her. I just forgot all about that poor little baby so long ago, and I'm just as sorry as I can be."

"It's all right, Miss Delia," I assured her, patting her hand. "I guess they've all forgotten about the baby too."

"There was something else I wanted to ask you, Pet," Miss Delia said, shaking her head. "But I forget what it was."

"Doesn't matter, Miss Delia," I said. "Something that long ago."

After I walked Miss Delia all the way back to her tent and started back alone, I thought and thought about my mama: someone who loved me, no matter what. And I got to thinking about Mama Sunrise too. Feeling like she was walking along that little path with me and her as tall as a man and big as an oak, with a blood-red rag wrapped around her head and her big, white teeth shining in the dark. Her big, strong arm around my shoulders and her laughing to beat the band. A great big laugh that sounded like it could put a rainbow all the way across the face of Heaven.

And more than that. Because I knew that she was really there with me that night, and we did some talking, sure enough. About the time all those years ago *when I had to tell Miss Cora that I had a little baby going to come, and she couldn't seem to find what words she wanted to say. So I said them for her.*

"I'm gonna go live with Minnie Louise, and I'll come back when it's over."

And of course, Miss Cora didn't try to stop me. Because she knew, just like I did, that Wynona and Lauralee couldn't be around somebody going to have a baby. It just might remind them of everything. And I knew I couldn't bring my baby back with me to that house, because it would have hurt all of us too much.

So when Camp Meeting was over that year so long ago, and I knew my baby was coming soon, I packed my things and went to Minnie Louise's little house, and there I stayed.

When my sweet Lizzy was born, I didn't even have a baby bed to put her in, and Minnie Louise fixed a cardboard box for her. Like something you'd put a puppy in. But Miss Cora came to me. Drove over there all by herself, just to see my baby. And when she looked in the box at my Lizzy, she remembered.

Because my Lizzy was the spitting image of my own papa. But Miss Cora never said a thing about that. Still, she reached out and put her fingers— oh, so gently—on Lizzy's cheek, and she told me my baby was beautiful.

That's something I've never forgotten. Never.

And Mama Sunrise just listened to me talking about it, and then she stopped me from walking along, and she put those big, strong arms around me and hugged me tight and said I had done good.

And she walked all the way back to Miss Cora's tent with me.

The next morning, we got up early and set about stripping the sheets and summer quilts from the beds and covering the mattresses with sheets of newspaper. I took out the small chunk of ice that was left in the icebox and put it outside in the grass near the water pump. Then I wiped out the icebox and left its door standing open and took the wasp nest and put it in the top of the basket that held all the bed linens and tablecloths.

When everything was loaded into the car, Wynona and I went around and closed all the windows we had propped open when Camp Meeting started, so that the inside of the tent was dark and strange-feeling, just the way I always thought the parlor must be when it was sealed off during the winter. Only here, the heat of the morning sun was making the tin roof pop and crack as it expanded in the warmth high up under the dark rafters.

We walked back through the tent once more, just to make sure we hadn't forgotten anything. Then we went out and swung the door shut, and Wynona put the lock through the hasp and clicked it shut.

We all got in the car and drove back down the long road home. And me looking at the red clay banks and the green kudzu feelers trying to grow across the whole road but us running over them. Made me feel strange and sad, though I said not a thing of course. Because I didn't want Wynona to get started in with saying I was having spells again.

When we turned onto our street, Wynona and I glanced at each other and wondered what Miss Cora would say about Miss Addie's big tree being gone. But Miss Cora never said a thing about the tree, even though she was looking right at Miss Addie's yard, at the big sign that said FUNERAL HOME.

It was sure good to be home, and as soon as we had unloaded the car, I went and wiped out the rocking chairs first thing, so they would be ready for us to sit in that very evening.

After supper, when we were once more on our own porch, rocking and looking out over the banisters into the twilight, Miss Cora began laughing under her breath.

"I sure got confused, didn't I?"

"Yes'm," Wynona and I chorused.

"Who was that old woman anyway?"

"Just somebody looking for her mama," I said.

"Sure was a funny one, wasn't she?"

Yes'm.

"Almost as funny as me."

Yes'm.

"Lord, have mercy! Look over there! Addie's big tree's gone!"

Yes'm.

"Well now, that's too bad. Wonder when that happened?"

None of us answered.

"I'll bet it was the storm that did it. Wish I'd been here for it. Because my papa took me outside once, in the eye of the storm. Why, it was the most beautiful thing you could ever imagine! A peaceful, black place where you can see everything there is to see in the whole universe and where you can reach up and put your hands into the stars!"

"I'm sure glad to be back in my own bed," Miss Cora said later, while Wynona was lifting the sheet up and over Miss Cora's feet and fixing the covers just the way Miss Cora liked for them to be. She lay spare and slim, on her back, fully stretched out, and with her hands folded over her chest, just like she always slept. Sometimes she would even brag that she moved so little in her sleep, she never disturbed the covers:

"When I get out of the bed, it's already made up!" That's what she always liked to say. But I never did know why.

"Yes'm," Wynona said. "It's good to be home." She turned out the bedside lamp. "You want me to leave the bathroom door open a crack?"

"Please. So even if I don't need to get up, there's light across the foot of my bed, like a little path. Did I ever tell you how once, when I was just a child, my papa took me to see the ocean at night? And right while we stood there watching, the moon came up out of that black water way out on the horizon and sent a path of sparkles right to where we stood, so that we could have walked on it, if we'd wanted to; could have walked right out to where the moon was hanging in the sky just like a big pearl."

"Yes'm." Wynona said. "You try to get some rest now. You're awful tired."

"Put out your hand and touch it," Miss Cora said.

"Ma'am?"

"The moon, I mean."

"Ma'am? You want me to get you an aspirin?"

"No, thank you. Just make sure Pet gets the ones I bought in Charleston that time. The single strand. Not the double-strand ones that belonged to my mama."

"Yes, ma'am. You call if you need me."

In my own little room, I turned out the light and waited for my eyes to get used to the darkness. Soon, I began to be able to see by the dim glow from the yard light over the carriage house, and the edges of the chifforobe began to appear out of the darkness in the corner of the room. The oval dresser-mirror showed a reflection of the window, framing it just like a painting or something.

And I sure did wonder what to call that—how the mirror could hold that reflection of the window and the light coming in. I wished I knew what to call things like that. Because it had a name; I was sure of it. I just didn't know what it was.

"I'll bet Samantha knows," I said to myself. "I'll bet you anything Samantha knows what the name of it is."

We were late having our breakfast the next morning, partly because we had all slept so deeply, what with being back in our own familiar beds, and partly because when Wynona went in to help Miss Cora get dressed, she found her hunting through the drawers of the dresser, trying to find her mama's pearls.

"Well, I can't find them to save my life," Miss Cora said. "Double-strands and with a silver clasp that's sometimes loose."

"We'll find them," Wynona told her. "Let's go have some breakfast first, and then I'll help you find them."

Reluctantly, Miss Cora agreed.

But when we were sitting at the table, and Wynona was reading aloud to us from the *Jefferson News and Courier*—so we could catch up on the town news—Miss Cora interrupted her every few minutes.

"I'll bet Betty got them," she said.

"No'm, I don't think so," Wynona said absently and then went on with reading aloud: "Mrs. Mattie Lou Ambrey and daughters Susan and Barbara motored to Augusta Sunday afternoon to visit with Miss Mattie Lou's former schoolteacher, Miss . . ."

"Maybe they're in my glove drawer," Miss Cora said.

". . . Almira Johnson, who taught school many years ago. The occasion of their visit was Miss Johnson's eighty-first birthday and . . ."

"Did one of *you* hide them from me?"

"No, ma'am. We wouldn't do such a thing. . . . Miss Johnson's eighty-first birthday and many of her former pupils came to see her and help her celebrate."

"Well, I just don't know where they could have gone to because . . ."

"Good Heavens!" Wynona shouted suddenly. "Look at this!" Wynona handed the newspaper to me.

Right there on page three was a large advertisement, all blocked in with rows of garish stars. "Grower's Funeral Home," it said. "Over forty years of service to this community." And down at the very bottom: "You can trust us to care for your loved ones. Open

189

House on Saturday. New location on State Street. Free! Free! Balloons! Corsages! Refreshments! Come one, come all!"

"Open house?" I read aloud. "Open House for a funeral parlor? Balloons? Corsages . . . ?"

But I was really thinking: *Skeletons sitting on blue velvet chairs? Naked jaws clacking and finger-bones holding clear cups of ruby-red punch?*

"Come one? Come all?" I kept reading. "Why, that's the tackiest thing I ever heard of!"

"Well," Miss Cora said, "I always knew he was a tasteless man. A completely tasteless man! But I sure enough would like to see for myself what he's done to Addie's house. Still, I wouldn't go over there for anything in this world!"

I didn't say another word, but I was thinking: *And I wouldn't either. But maybe we better be careful when we start saying what we won't do—because things don't always work out the way we think they will.*

Like how there was a day, a long day, so long that it almost wasn't real but like something that's always been there, and it's always going to be there. More than just saying that it goes on and on. And you get tired, but you can't quit, and then, even when it ends, you keep on thinking about it over and over again, and that way, it's what you will have every single day for the rest of your life. Of course, that doesn't happen, thank the good Lord! Because you don't remember it, at least not all of it. Or sometimes you change it around every time you remember it, and after a long time, years and years, what you remember is something that never really happened.

But that long night before Mr. Adkins' funeral, I'd been awake the whole night. Because that night sure wasn't a time for sleeping. The next night would be all right, but not that one. Because the next night would be tomorrow, and the funeral would be over, and it would all be buried and gone, so tomorrow could get started changing things around; the way we would remember them, I mean.

On my mind the most was the pure and simple fact that it was all on my shoulders, all up to me to do whatever needed doing to take care of us.

That whole night long, I dreamed that Mama Sunrise hovered around me, whispering and saying exactly what I must do. Because I was the one in charge and through me, my mama too, and everyone who had come before her. And I had to be everything this family needed and find a way to take care of us all and not let anything hurt the baby.

Looking back on it, it was a strange kind of thing for me to be charged with, for I was still only a young woman, of an age with Wynona, but somehow, in a way I couldn't understand then or even explain to this very day, I was also very very old and wise, and even though I wasn't certain right then exactly what it was I had to do, I knew I wasn't all by myself in searching for the way to do it and that I'd have all the answers by the time I could make out the very first morning light turning the window into a gray patch against the darkness. That's what I was thinking the whole night.

Even Miss Cora couldn't help me much that time. For she hadn't gotten over it yet. And so it got left up to me. Every bit of it.

I was right about finding all the answers, because by dawn, I knew the very first thing I had to do was make sure nobody would notice anything about Lauralee. Her condition, I mean. Because if Mr. Adkins could tell just by looking at her, maybe somebody else could too. And set tongues to wagging.

One way to keep that from happening might have been for her not to go to the funeral. But that would have raised some eyebrows, and we didn't want that. Because protecting this family meant protecting it as far as the town is concerned and what people think about it and what kind of stories about it will be passed on down in other folks' families.

So once I knew what I had to do, I got out of bed and started looking through the dresser and the chifforobe and the trunks, and sure enough, I finally found one of Miss Cora's corsets from when she was a young woman and as slender as Lauralee. But the corset strings had been taken out of it before it'd been washed and put away in the trunk, and I couldn't find an extra corset string to save my life.

I went through every single drawer in that big dresser, and I found thimbles, and a dried corsage wrapped in a pink handkerchief, and hair combs, and a little chain-metal change purse. All the old things from so long ago—when nothing was wrong, and there was nothing to hide.

But I couldn't find a single corset string. Finally, I did find some red satin Christmas ribbons in the top right-hand drawer of the dresser.

When we started getting dressed to go to the funeral, I threaded that red ribbon into the corset, and Lauralee put it on, and I laced it as tight as I dared, praying the whole time that nothing would make the baby too uncomfortable.

While Lauralee was holding in her breath, and I was tying the ribbon, I talked to that little baby, telling it that the corset was only for a little while.

That's how I tied up Lauralee's waist as tight as a drum in those old corsets of Miss Cora's and with the red ribbons lacing back and forth through the eyelets. And the whole time, Lauralee just stood there, looking at the wall, and saying not a word.

From the first moment I laid eyes on Wynona that morning, I knew I didn't have to worry about her. She was the perfect picture of a grieving widow, her face so pale that I didn't need to tell her to put any extra powder on it, like I'd thought of doing, and her eyes so large and dark but with red around the rims and sunken-in so they looked as if she had cried all night. And I saw that her chin was set, just as solid as a piece of granite, and that was when I knew that she could be brave and strong and do what needed doing.

Made me think of that time when Miss Anne and the aunts said what they did about Lauralee's chin and it making them think of the Bixley chin. Maybe Wynona didn't look much like any of the Bixleys, but she was sure enough a Bixley on the inside, where it really mattered. And I'll never forget feeling so relieved when I saw her and knew she was strong, because I didn't have to try and be strong for her too.

But we still had a day to get through, and somehow or other, we did it. Went over to the church and sat there listening to singing about the roll being called up yonder and looking at that big, shiny casket and knowing what was left of Mr. Adkins under the heavy, sealed lid and me wondering if any of us would ever get into Heaven, after what we'd done.

I did a lot more talking to that baby during the funeral. Not out-loud talking, of course, but silent talking to it. And I said, "It's okay, little baby. Doesn't matter who your daddy was. It's your mama means the most anyway. And your sweet mama is so innocent and pure, and she looks like she's fragile as a teacup, but don't you let that fool you any! 'Cause she's from good, strong people, and so will you be good and so will you be strong. You just be patient for now, and this will soon be over."

That's how I got through the funeral. Talking to the baby.

Wynona cried some, Miss Cora looked as hollow-eyed as if she'd had a long illness, and Lauralee—well, I don't know what she was thinking. She just sat there like she was asleep. But with her eyes wide open.

Of course, we still had to get through the cemetery part of the service, but when we got down the steps of the church and were ready to get in the car to follow the hearse to the cemetery, Lauralee stopped dead in her tracks. Because the casket was already in the hearse, and Mr. Grower had begun putting in the flowers, the ones out of the church, to take out to the cemetery. And he was having to put the flowers in the back of the hearse, all around that terrible-shiny casket. Behind us, the people were coming out of the church, and I heard someone say, "What a pity! Wynona so young to be a widow, and left all alone, without even a child to comfort her!"

That's when Lauralee fainted dead away.

I'd been walking along right beside her and with her holding onto my arm a little bit, but she went down so fast, I didn't even have time to know what was happening until she was on the ground, right there beside the hearse.

Of course, lots of folks came over and helped us get her revived enough that she could walk a little, leaning on us. And helped us to get her in the car, and me and Miss Cora brought her on home. Wynona had to go on to the cemetery without us, and I was always sorry it worked out that way. But she did all right.

When Miss Cora and I got Lauralee into the house, I undid her dress right away, right there in the living room and started loosening those corset ribbons fast as I could. And when Miss Cora saw all those bright red ribbons, she said, "Lord, have mercy! What on earth is this?"

But before I could say a word, Lauralee seemed to come around from wherever she'd been and was looking at us like she'd never seen either one of us before. Such a wild look in her eyes! And when she looked down at herself, where I'd unbuttoned her dress, she saw those red Christmas ribbons crisscrossing over her middle and "BLOOD!" she shrieked, and she let out the most awful, long, horrible scream I have ever heard in my life.

It took us ever so long to get her quieted down, and after that, she stayed in bed for over two weeks, because like I told her, we had to take care of the baby that was coming. Nothing else mattered more than that.

*B*ut of course, it wasn't over. Not by a long shot. I thought of all kinds of ways we could keep things secret, like us sending Lauralee away. But there wasn't any family anywhere else to send her to, and besides, she'd still have to come home and bring a baby with her sometime or other. And then folks would know.

Maybe things are different now, but back then, if people in town had known that baby came from Mr. Adkins doing something bad to his own wife's sister, that little child would have lived under sort of a dark cloud its whole life. Even though it didn't have a thing to do with how it came into the world!

So I had to find a way to get around all that. The baby had to have the best we could give it, and that included having its father's name and being respectable and not having folks telling those kinds of stories about it. I had to find a way. Because flesh and blood is too valuable to lose.

Seemed like that baby was one of us already, and maybe some folks would argue that it was Mr. Adkins' baby too, but we didn't think of it that way at all. We've always put a lot more store in the mama than the papa. After all, it's the mama who carries the baby in her very own body for all that time and who suffers to bring it into the world. Maybe that doesn't quite explain it, but that's the way it has always been. And I think it's the way it always will be.

So this little baby was flesh of our flesh and bone of our bone and nothing else in the whole world mattered.

194

So I kept on figuring and figuring, and the whole time, I kept watching Lauralee, and I knew we were running out of time!

Then one night it came to me in a dream, right out of the blue. In my dream, Wynona and Lauralee were very young again and getting up out of the lawn chairs where they had been told to sit like ladies so long ago, and they went running side by side across the yard, holding hands and laughing just like they used to do. Except for one thing: In my dream, Lauralee was carrying a doll, and Wynona stopped their running and said, "Give it to me, Lauralee. It's my turn to be the mama." So there it was then!

The next morning, at breakfast, I took a deep breath and said, "We have to make folks think it's Wynona who's going to be the mama."

And they all looked at me with truly puzzled looks.

"That's the only thing makes sense. Because if Wynona had been going to have a baby before Mr. Adkins died, the baby would have a name. And that's what we've got to do. As far as the whole world knows, the baby is Wynona's baby."

They were looking at each other and thinking it through, and I could tell by their faces that we'd sure enough found the right way to handle things. Now, the only thing left was to figure out how to make it work, and, you know, it turned out it wasn't such a hard thing at all. Wynona and Lauralee were in mourning, as far as everybody in town was concerned, so if they never went outdoors and if they stayed in their room when anyone came by to visit, no one would ever know the difference. Just us. Oh, talk would go around, sure enough, but it would be that Wynona was expecting. And I knew just the few folks to tell, so it would be sure to get all over town real fast.

Besides, back in those days, a woman who was going to have a baby didn't go out in public. It just wasn't done. And if you add on top of that a good and respectful period of mourning—a year, at least—then maybe not a single soul would think a thing about not seeing Wynona and Lauralee all that time.

So that's exactly what we did. For all those long months, Wynona and Lauralee stayed in the house, and if anyone knocked on the door, they went out the hall door from the kitchen and into their rooms. The only time anything difficult happened was once when their Aunt Fairleigh dropped in on a Sunday afternoon unannounced. She and a lady friend had driven out from Augusta, come to visit with Wynona, to see how "the poor little thing" was getting along, and wasn't it just terrible for her to be left a grieving widow and with a child coming and all? Of course, soon as we'd hatched our plan, Miss Cora had written to her about "Wynona's baby."

I showed them into the parlor and asked them to wait, and I went to the back of the house just as calm as could be. And what we did was this: Lauralee tiptoed back down the hall and went into my room and stayed there, and I put Wynona in the bed, lying on her side. I tucked a pillow under the blanket so Wynona would look as if she were with child, then I pulled all the shades down and closed the curtains so the room would be in dim light and brought Wynona's Aunt Fairleigh and her friend in for their visit.

Those two old ladies sat by Wynona's bed for the better part of an hour, questioning her as to her health and all. Of course, Wynona knew exactly how Lauralee was feeling along about this time in the process, you know, so she said her back hurt her just a little, and she was having some swelling in her ankles, and that's why she was staying in the bed as much as possible.

Finally, finally, they went away, after telling Wynona to be sure and let them know if they could do anything for her and to tell them when the baby came.

That's pretty much the way we did things for all those months.

The only soul who knew about it—except for us—was Miss Addie. Because there wasn't a way in this world we could have kept it from her, not seeing as how she lived right across the street and came over so often. And besides, we all knew we could trust her. I was the one who told her about it, and she looked a little surprised, but she didn't ask any questions, and she never said a single word about any of it to a living soul on the face of this earth.

Looking back on it, it wasn't all that hard, and maybe it was even good in some ways. Not that it was fun, exactly. It wasn't ever that. But it was good in a very special way.

Because we'd pretty well gotten over what happened to Mr. Adkins. Shut it away someplace where it didn't hurt us any, and all those months while we waited for the baby, this good house wrapped itself all around us so we were all dry and warm and safe. Kind of like sitting in your mama's lap when it's dark outside.

Lauralee was quiet, and I guess we never did hear her laugh again, but she seemed right contented, and she sure enjoyed good health the whole time we were waiting for the baby. We did lots of nice things together while we waited. Played rummy and spoons and worked some real pretty puzzles, and sewed and crocheted things for the baby while that wet, gray old winter waited outside the windows, and the ground was dark with rain, and the trees looked like old ghost-sticks in the dim light.

And I liked it. Because having it all gray and dismal outside made the yellow light inside the house seem all warm and safe. The baby all wrapped up in Lauralee and us all around the two of them, taking care of them in every way. And the house around us, keeping out the night.

When the spring began coming that year, it took us a little by surprise, for it just sauntered into the yard one afternoon when we least expected it. The day before had been a raw, late February kind of day, but the next afternoon, spring was in the air sure enough, and something or other in the light and the way it came in through the windows. Even the old bare bushes had tiny little buds on them that we hadn't noticed until that very day.

And what was coming for us in the spring was so sweet!

Toward the end of April, the baby started coming. I was asleep when Wynona's hand shook my shoulder.

"Pet? Pet? You better wake up. The baby's coming."

I've never felt quite like I did that moment, and when Wynona went on back to stay with Lauralee, I had to sit still on the side of the bed just for a few minutes. To get ahold of it all somehow. Even to this very day, I can't say it just right.

It was being there in that house, with all the things around us that we do day after day and year after year. And more. Maybe like when I was just a child and on Christmas morning, before Miss Anne would let any of the family come downstairs, she'd light up the Christmas tree in the dark room, and you knew it wasn't night but morning. She always came to this room where me and Mama were asleep and tapped on the door. And we'd get up and go to see the tree before the family came down.

That big tree towering in the big room, and lights shaped like candles, but with colored water and tiny bubbles in them going up and up. Me standing in the room and Mama behind me, and the magic thing was this: the room that was always there in the early hours of other days, but we never saw it at such an early time. And the Christmas tree more than just a tree with lights on it.

Much more. Like something so entirely different from anything else in the world that the cold air we breathed had cinnamon or something sweet in it and very lovely.

I never cared anything about the presents. They weren't for Mama and me anyway. But the tree! The tree! And the magic of Christmas!

That's exactly how it felt that morning Wynona waked me up and told me the baby was coming.

Christmas on a warm April morning.

Oh, Lauralee was such a good and brave lady, but the day went on and on, and still the baby didn't come. I'd put a pair of scissors under the bed, to "cut the pain," Mama always said. But it just got worse and worse, and Lauralee was going all pale and tight around her mouth and just about wore out. Night was coming, and still the baby wasn't born. Finally, when we'd done everything we knew to do, Miss Cora told me to go get the doctor.

Of course, he knew all the town news, and he was going to be expecting to see Wynona having the baby. When he came into the room and saw Lauralee, he looked a little surprised. But he was a doctor, and so he was bound by a solemn oath not to tell anything he knew. So we weren't really worried.

Only an hour or so after the doctor came, that sweet little baby girl came into this world. Little Miss Hope, and the spitting image of her mama. And she was worth every bit of it—worth the secret and the hiding and the pain.

The doctor never said a thing, but when he made out the birth certificate, he left it blank where the mama's name went and signed the paper and left it on the table in the hall. Of course, the doctor was also the county coroner, so maybe he was the one who said Mr. Adkins' death was an accident. Maybe he'd put two and two together and wasn't as surprised as he seemed to be. But we'll never know. He's been dead and gone now all these years anyway, and he never said a thing.

So we took the paper and filled in Wynona's name as Hope's mama and tried as hard as we could to make what we wrote look exactly like the doctor's writing. But I guess if anybody had looked at it real close, they'd probably have seen that the handwriting wasn't the same. Still, and to this day, no one ever looked at it that I know of. And now, I don't even know where that paper is.

Far as anyone else knew, it was Wynona's baby that had been born, and I guess we all just finally believed ourselves that it was hers. Lauralee never really paid that much attention to the baby, so I guess she'd already made up her mind that the baby was Wynona's, because of our plan and all.

Having made up our minds like that, it got to be the truth to us, just like Mr. Adkins' hunting accident. So much so that I nearly forgot the way those things really happened.

Oh, what a wonderful time we had with that beautiful little girl. We fussed about which one of us was gonna get to give her a bath, and when she had hiccups for the first time, you'd have thought she'd done something no one had ever done before. Miss Cora and Wynona and I just looked and looked at her, and every time she'd go "hic," we'd ooh and aah and laugh about it.

And I'll bet that baby wasn't more than two weeks old when I came through the parlor one day and heard Miss Cora telling her the story of Hezekiah Longwood. Miss Cora was rocking and looking down into little Miss Hope's face as if that tiny baby could understand every word she said. Hope was looking back at Miss Cora and cooing once in awhile, and when she'd do that, Miss Cora would say "That's right!" just as if she could understand exactly what that little sound meant.

But . . . it all came to nothing.

All those great hopes and that wonderful happiness. That's why I say things don't always work out the way we think they will.

Because when Hope was only about four months old—just old enough that she was starting to smile at us real big and wriggle all over when she was happy—she got a fever. She'd been fussy the night before, and that afternoon I was sitting out on the porch behind the trellis, rocking her so Wynona could have a nap. Because Wynona had been up almost all night long, trying to comfort her.

I was sitting there, just rocking away and looking at that little face and seeing all the familiar bone-shape to it and remembering how happy I was when I'd gotten to hold Lauralee when she was a baby, and I got to loving Hope so much that I tilted her up and kissed her on the forehead.

"Why, Hope!" I said to her. "You're hot! Do you have a fever?"

Just as I said it, I heard a noise down in the portico, where . . .

At first, I thought it was the most beautiful creature I'd ever seen in my whole life. An angel, it was—I was sure of it—and the whole portico lit up with its light. I just sat there and stared and stared at it. Why, you never saw such a face in your life, and the sweetest smile and softest eyes just shining out some kind of glow and . . .

But then I knew! Oh, it all came together at once! About Hope being so hot and that shining creature in the portico!

I jumped up and saw that just that fast, it had already come up the steps and was looking so sad and holding out its arms for . . .

"NO!" I screamed, and Miss Cora came running out onto the porch, and she was just as white as a bed sheet, and me still standing there doing nothing in this world but screaming that same word again and again and again.

"NO! NO! NO!"

"Where's the baby?" Wynona yelled from inside the house.

I almost knocked Miss Cora down there on the porch, because I slammed right into her and shoved her aside so rough-like, so I could get inside the house with the baby, and I did the same thing to Wynona, when she tried to come at me across the parlor, to take the baby out of my arms.

"Pet! What's wrong?" she screamed at me, but I was already running down that long hallway and one of my shoes came off, and I thought I saw Lauralee standing down at the end of the hall and behind her, that same angel. Why, he'd come in the back door! Just that fast!

Lauralee holding out her arms.

"Give me the baby, Pet," she said. "She's my baby. Give her to me."

I couldn't say a word or move a single muscle in my whole body. And while I stood there like a frozen person, Lauralee lifted Hope right out of my arms.

Just as I fainted dead away.

Scarlet fever. That's what took Hope, and I'm the one gave it to her. Took that sweet little baby so fast, and for days, I begged and begged it to take me too. But it shook its head no. In between all my beggings, I had terrible dreams, so that I waked myself up screaming and didn't know whether it was day or night or what was happening. And Miss Cora always there by my bed when I waked up a little bit and her face as gray as ashes and eyes all red and burned looking.

Sometimes I waked up with a terrible jerk because I thought I was holding Hope in my arms and I'd fallen asleep and was so scared I was going to drop her.

I don't know exactly how or when things began to make more sense to me or when I began to add it all up and know that terrible truth about Hope, but when I did, all I wanted was to go back to sleep and never wake up again. Never.

Oh, Lord, have mercy on us all! What things I could hear when I waked up in the middle of the dark nights—all the crying!

Looking back, I know there wasn't nothing in all creation that could have prepared us for losing that baby. Not a thing. And when it happened, the whole world had gone wrong, and there wasn't never going to be another spring. Corn wasn't never going to grow in the fields again, and the sun wasn't never going to heave itself up over the horizon. Never again.

I don't even know how I found out there was a funeral to get through, but I did know that they whispered about it when they thought I was asleep, and I wasn't supposed to know anything about it, much less go to it. Because the doctor said I was to stay in bed for a long time.

But somehow or other, I knew exactly when that funeral was coming. I knew it better than I had ever known anything else in my whole life.

So that on the appointed day, I heard Miss Cora and Wynona leave the house, and I rolled myself out of the bed. But when my feet touched the floor, it was like I didn't have any bones in my legs to hold me up! Somehow or other, I managed to get to the chifforobe and pulled out my black dress and put it on without even a petticoat under it. Then I went to the dresser to try and do something with my hair—it must be a sight!

But oh, what I did see in the mirror!

Took me a few minutes to realize it was my own face—but my hair gone the color of old cotton that's been left in the field and my skin as gray as ashes. And my eyes like terrible black fires but with no light coming from them.

But I had a funeral to get through, and I was going to do exactly that, no matter what. No matter what. Even if I had to crawl, I was going.

So I finally wobbled my way to the parlor, and my black purse hanging on my arm felt like it weighed fifty pounds. There, Lauralee was sitting, working on her crocheting. When she saw me, she looked up in a way that told me right off she didn't have the faintest idea of what was going on. Those beautiful blue eyes, just as clear and pure as a morning sky, and she smiled at me and said in a sleepy kind of way, "I'm glad you're feeling better, Pet. But where you going?"

"I have to do something," I croaked. "I won't be gone long."

"Oh. All right then. Take care." She smiled and went right back to her crocheting.

201

And there was no way in this world I was gonna tell her I was on my way to her baby's funeral, and I don't think Lauralee ever again remembered a single thing about Hope.

But maybe blessings come in very strange forms, I say.

It was such a hard time I had, getting down the front steps one at a time and staggering my way over to the Baptist Church. Almost like a dream I was walking along in as I got closer and closer and heard the singing and knew what was going on. When I finally got to the church, I went up the steps and it was like climbing a big mountain, and the heavy front door was almost more than I could open. But I got it open anyway.

Once I was inside, I couldn't see any of the people or anything else in this whole world—except for that tiny white casket in front of the altar.

And when I saw that, I almost collapsed into the back pew.

Miss Addie saw me come in, and she got up out of her seat and came and sat beside me and held me in her arms and rocked me back and forth, and all the while, the preacher was saying beautiful things, like "Suffer the little children to come unto me, and forbid them not, for of such is the kingdom of Heaven."

I couldn't have gotten through that without Miss Addie. God rest her soul!

When it came time to take that white box out to the cemetery, folks hesitated. Because there wasn't any menfolks in our family left to carry it. So two of those good men in the church started forward to do what had to be done—pick up that box by the handles on either side.

But Miss Cora got up real sudden-like and walked forward and almost bumped one of them men out of the way. She took hold of the handle on one side of the casket and helped to lift it—just as tender as if that baby was only taking a nap in there.

Maybe Miss Cora was thinking that Wynona would come and take the handle on the other side, but Wynona couldn't. She was sitting there like a ghost, her face as white as a sheet and her eyes looking at nothing at all. Just sitting there wringing her lace-trimmed handkerchief over and over and over again.

So when they brought Hope down that long aisle, it was Miss Cora on one side of the casket and a good, kind man from the church on the other; and that's the way they came, so slowly. As if they were bringing that sweet little baby to me.

When they got right to where I was sitting in the back pew, still leaning against Miss Addie, Miss Cora saw me, and she stopped.

I wobbled to my feet and stood there, waiting for whatever was coming. Because it was all my fault. All my fault we'd lost that baby.

Miss Cora studied me for a long time, and then she turned to the man from the church who was holding the other side of that box and said, "Thank you very much, but we'll take her from here. She's our flesh and blood."

I stumbled over to the side of that white box and put my hands on the handle. But I was so weak. So weak. Still, I was bound and determined to do what needed doing. I just prayed to myself, "Dear Lord, please help me do what has to be done." And before the words even got finished, Miss Addie was there beside me, taking some of the weight of that heavy box.

That's what Miss Addie did for me. Because Miss Cora wanting me to help carry that baby was her way of saying she didn't blame me for nothing. And I needed that—oh, how I needed that!

So walking along together, Miss Cora and Miss Addie and me, we carried Hope to her final resting place.

At the cemetery, I watched Miss Cora and hurt so bad for her—knowing how everything she hoped for the future was gone. All the things that baby would have meant to her—no matter who its daddy had been. More than just carrying the family blood into a future none of us would ever see. Much more. Because sooner or later, Hope would have been the one to inherit Miss Cora's mama's velvet side chairs, and she was the one who would have told Miss Cora's stories to her own grandchildren, and written in all the new family stories, and somehow would have taken some part of us into the future. And Miss Hope would have done a good job of moving our family forward a bit. I know she would have done that.

But she wasn't going to do it now. Not in that tiny white box that went down and down into the red earth.

That's why, a few years later, when I found out that my very own baby was going to come, I went away to Minnie Louise's and stayed there until Lizzy was born; and when I left there to come back to this house, I left my baby girl with Minnie Louise.

Because I'd done all the killing I was ever going to do. And a killing it would have been, sure enough, if I'd kept my baby, Lizzy, with me.

They had all lost too much already. And all because of me.

Miss Addie was the only one ever knew why I'd really left my baby. And when she saw me for the first time after I had left Lizzy, she put her arms around me and held me just like I was a little baby myself. And she cried with me.

*M*innie Louise called me on the phone two days after we got home from Camp Meeting.

"Youall see that thing in the paper?" she asked.

"Thing?"

I just couldn't quite make a connection there, because ever since I'd thought back over what happened to Hope, I'd been feeling sore all over. Kind of bruised, I guess; just the way I usually feel in the springtime after I've used the old grass sling to knock down the brown stubble of the last summer's garden so we can turn the soil and get a new garden going.

But I sure hadn't done any slinging lately, of course. Our garden, even though it had wilted a little from not being watered while we were gone, was putting forth a big harvest of yellow crookneck squash and field peas, spicy radishes and sweet carrots. But I was still feeling sore and tired, and another thing was that I couldn't seem to tear my mind away from whatever I was thinking about whenever anyone said something to me. So that even between the ringing of the phone and my going all the way into the dining room to answer it, even then I didn't have enough time to pull away from feeling the handle of the sling in my hands or from seeing Hope's sweet face among the fallen stalks.

So . . . "Thing?" I said again to Minnie Louise. "What thing?"

"You *know* what thing!" she shouted. "That open-house thing this weekend, and it right across the street from youall!"

"Oh."

"Well, did you?"

"Did I *what?*"

"*SEE* it!" she was almost yelling.

"Oh . . . yes," I finally managed to say.

"And?" Minnie Louise persisted.

"And?" I parroted. *Dear Lord, please help me to find my tongue!*

"And . . ." Minnie Louise continued. "Isn't that about the worst thing you ever heard?"

"Well," I stumbled. "I guess it is." *Strange! How could I have forgotten so fast?*

"When I think about what all's gonna be going on from now on in sweet old Miss Addie's house, I just wanta cry!" Minnie Louise moaned.

"Yes," I said. There was a silence on the other end of the phone, and then she said, "Whatsa matter with you?" Because Minnie Louise liked for me to commiserate with her when she thought something was awful, but I just couldn't seem to work up a head of steam for it. "Pet? I said whatsa matter with you?" she repeated.

"I . . . I guess I'm still tired from Camp Meeting," I said at last. And there! The words were coming, thank the dear Lord, even if they weren't quite the truth.

"Well, I'm not ashamed to tell you I'm worried about you. You just aren't yourself. Not one little bit! No, ma'am!"

"I'm just tired," I repeated.

"No," Minnie Louise protested, almost gently. "You haven't been yourself since Miss Addie passed on. And I guess what with Miss Cora scaring you so bad by running off with that old Maggie woman and then youall having to come home to what's going on right across the street, it's just been too much for you."

Too much for me? I was thinking. *Something that could be too much for me?*

"Tell you what," Minnie Louise was saying. "Let's us go off and do a little fishing. That'll fix you up."

"Fishing?"

"Will you please stop repeating every single word I say?"

"Every single word . . . well, I don't think I rightly want to go fishing right now," I tried to protest. "There's too much to be done around here, what with us having been gone and all."

"Then what'd you want that old wasp nest for?" she growled. "You bring those wasp grubs, and I'll come by and pick you up in a few minutes."

And before I could speak another word, she hung up.

So there I was, standing out by the street, looking at Mr. Grower's sign and holding that bread wrapper full of wasp grubs and wondering how on earth Minnie Louise could make me do something I really didn't feel like doing. Same thing as how she got Miss Addie to eat a little something, I suppose. Because when Minnie Louise got her mind set on something, you might as well save your breath.

But when I saw her familiar old truck coming down the street, I thought that maybe she was right, because for some reason, just the sight of it gladdened my heart. The two cane poles sticking out of the back, and Minnie Louise reaching over and opening the passenger-side door before the truck even came to a complete stop.

"Let's go," she smiled. "Those hungry old fish are just waiting for us!" And that's how she made it sound like we were going on a picnic or something. So despite her hair-trigger temper and that maddening stick-to-it-ness of hers, Minnie Louise sure enough had a gift for making something very ordinary, like fishing, seem like something special.

As I slid into the seat, avoiding the tear in the upholstery, I wondered for a moment if Minnie Louise had managed to pass that along to Lizzy. I sure hoped so.

We had the creek bank all to ourselves that day, and within only an hour or two, we had seven pan-sized bass on our stringer, all of them still swimming around a little in a shallow place near the bank, but held by the stringer running through their mouths and out their gills.

Minnie Louise hadn't started in on me, and I say thank goodness for that, because just sitting there in the quiet watching the red and white bobber on my line, and waiting for it to go under was what I must have needed the most.

Minnie Louise's bobber went under in one sharp, strong movement, and she landed yet another bass, this one a little bigger than the others.

"They sure do love those old wasp grubs," she said, unhooking the fish and putting him on the stringer.

"Best fish bait in the whole world," I said. "Just not very easy to come by is all. Sure not as easy as digging a few worms, that's for sure."

Minnie Louise was studying my face, so I figured she'd been quiet as long as she could stand it, and I knew more questions about my "not being myself" were on the way.

"Pet, can I ask you something?"

I smiled, because I really couldn't help it. Minnie Louise could try and be so doggoned serious, but she just didn't know how funny I thought that was.

"Well, if I said *no*, would it stop you?" I asked.

"Guess not," she admitted, putting another grub on her hook and tossing it into that slow-moving, black creek.

"Then I guess you better go ahead."

"Well, I just wondered if maybe you're scared of . . . you know."

"Heavens, Minnie Louise!" I complained. "I *don't* know and I *won't* know until you spit it out!"

"Of dying."

Why, I was surprised as could be at that. So I couldn't speak for a minute or so. But I thought of that great horse my grandmama rode away on, her laughing and blowing me a kiss. And then I thought of sweet Miss Addie and how her face was shining when she reached up and took hold of her papa's hand. Then I thought about what it would probably be like for me, when Death came, and I figured right quick that the Lord would likely send my own Mama Sunrise to fetch me home. I could imagine myself walking down a long, lonely road, all tuckered out and filled with aches and pains. Then I would look up, and there, in the middle of the road, would be Mama Sunrise. Big as a mountain and strong as a bear, with that red rag wrapped around her head and those strong, white teeth shining in her dark face. I could see her arms go wide open, just waiting for me to run to them, be wrapped in her strength and her love.

"No, Minnie Louise," I laughed. "I'm not afraid of dying. How come you to ask such a thing?"

"Well, I just thought what you went through with Miss Addie got you started in to thinking about it, that's all. We're none of us getting any younger."

"That's the truth," I agreed.

For long moments, Minnie Louise said nothing else, and we just sat there together in the deep shade, watching those little bobbers floating in the water. Mine bobbed just a little.

"Think I'm going to get a bite in a minute or so," I said.

"Sometimes I'm scared of dying," Minnie Louise said out of a clear blue sky.

I glanced at her sharply, and her eyes bored right back at me. "I'm scared because of Lizzy and her not knowing what's what. And after I'm gone and you're gone, there's not going to be nobody left in all this earth who can tell her the truth."

So there it was—Minnie Louise was going to start in on me about Lizzy. Again.

"I'll talk to Lizzy," I heard myself saying, even though the words sounded strange to my ears. "But I've got to talk to Miss Cora first. I've got to get that taken care of. Soon."

"Whatchu got to talk to her about?" Minnie Louise pounced on my words.

"Something I promised Miss Addie," I said, and then I stopped. Because I sure wasn't about to share everything with Minnie Louise right then and there. Too afraid she'd spill it all to Miss Delia, before I got a chance to do what had to be done.

"Don't you go asking me any more about it right now," I said. "When I've done what needs doing, I'll tell you all about it."

"You promise?" Minnie Louise demanded, with her eyes gleaming and her ears fairly twitching in anticipation.

"I promise." Just then my bobber went straight under the water, and I started in to landing the biggest fish we'd seen all day long.

That evening, I fried up all that good bass, and we had a big supper from it. I would have made hushpuppies too, but Wynona

209

started in to fussing about how all that cooking was going to heat up the whole house. So we settled for fresh, sliced tomatoes and good white bread to go with our pan-fried fish.

"I'm going," Miss Cora announced at the breakfast table on the day of Mr. Grower's open house. "I'm going because I have to know what he's done to Addie's house."

"You do as you like," Wynona said. "But I can't go with you over there. Open house for a funeral parlor, for Heaven's sake! Whoever heard of such a thing? And Miss Rosa told me yesterday he's hired a bus and is sending it over to Twilight Hills, to bring all those old folks over. At least, all those who can still walk?" Her voice rose into a question, as if to say: Isn't that one of the most awful things you ever heard of?

And it was, of course.

I paused in pouring myself another cup of coffee, and Lauralee halted her fork right in midair.

"Most completely tasteless thing I ever heard of," Miss Cora pronounced. "But I'm going anyway. I'm going over there and see what he's done to Addie's house, because I can't stand just wondering about it. I have to know."

A silence then, so we were like lonely little flowers planted apart from each other. Well, I sure couldn't stand that.

"I'll go with you," I said. "But only to the porch. I don't want to go in and see all those old people caught up in it, them talking all polite, like it doesn't bother them to be there!" I fairly spat out the words.

Miss Cora and Wynona stared at me, because I guess they'd never heard me sounding so angry-like. And for the life of me, I couldn't figure out why I was so mad about that. I really couldn't.

But while I was trying to figure things out, I glanced over at Lauralee, and I think I saw her smile just the least little bit. I was almost positive of it. And that surprised me even more than the rough sound my own voice had carried. So I took a deep breath and carefully lowered my voice.

"Better the way it was in the old days, when people didn't get sent off to some old-folks home but passed over in their own beds, with their children and grandchildren and maybe even great-grandchildren gathered all around them, just like flowers growing right up out of the floor around the bed."

Of course, just as I said that, I remembered Miss Addie, who passed over with no one but me there with her. But maybe that had been enough. I certainly hoped so.

At exactly three o'clock that afternoon, Miss Cora and I started across the street to Mr. Grower's open house. Miss Cora was wearing her black crepe dress, just as if she were going to a funeral, and I was wearing a church dress and a clean apron. Across Miss Addie's yard we went, and up the steps one at a time, with Miss Cora leaning on my arm and clutching a white handkerchief in her hand. The porch was newly painted, a deep gray enamel that was all shiny, like it was still wet; and red and white balloons that were tied to the pillars by the steps hung there all swollen in the hot sunshine.

"Tackiest thing I ever saw in my life," Miss Cora muttered as we came up the steps.

"Can you go on in by yourself now?" I asked. Because I didn't want to go into that house ever again. Not without Miss Addie being there.

"Of course I can," she snorted, so I left her at the door and went along the wraparound porch to the side. Far at the end, I sat down in a newly painted, uncomfortable chair. To wait.

I was thinking that I'd always thought Mr. Grower was a fool, and now I knew it for sure. I could so easily imagine him inside Miss Addie's lovely old house, grinning and bowing and rubbing his hands together.

Just like a big old vulture.

Later, much later, Miss Cora told me what happened inside: how she was met at the door by fourteen-year-old Lena Anderson, a high-school cheerleader wearing a red and white cheerleading outfit—Mercy!—skirt way too short and white sweater with a big red "R" on it. But Miss Cora said as soon as she reviewed Lena's lineage—mother a Singleton, married to old Miss Vonnie's youngest boy—she understood. Not really Lena's fault. Blood, that's what it was. Blood.

Lena bounced up to Miss Cora, pinned a red carnation on Miss Cora's dress while she babbled away about how glad she was that Miss Cora had come, and "You just help yourself to punch and cookies" and "Do you need any help getting it?" and "Where would you like to sit?"

And the whole time Lena was cackling and chirruping, Miss Cora was gazing around her at the grand old vestibule—the heart-of-pine floors and the grand banister of the staircase.

All of a sudden, Miss Cora remembered seeing Miss Addie on her wedding day, coming down the graceful stairs and wearing a beautiful white satin wedding dress. And peeking out from beneath the hem, as she came down, those lovely white kid shoes. And Miss Cora said she could even breathe the perfume of gardenias in Miss Addie's wedding bouquet.

"Miss Cora?" Lena's voice again. "I'll be glad to fix you a glass of fruit punch and bring it to you, so you just come on, please, ma'am, and have a seat right in here." Lena took Miss Cora's arm with young, pink-nailed hands that didn't like touching the aged skin and guided her across the vestibule and through the big, double doors to what had been Addie's grand parlor, where now, chairs were placed in groups of four or five around a fireplace filled with enormous, bilious-green, plastic ferns and the same kind of ferns at each tall front window and clumped around the bases of the fake mahogany tables.

Sitting in the chairs were the people from Twilight Hills, wearing clothes that were too big for them, and some of the women with their stockings rolled down below their child-sized knees and wearing felt bedroom shoes. All of them talking and smiling and holding glasses of punch and dabbing their mouths with the tiny paper napkins. And in the middle of it all, Mr. Grower, in a stiff new suit, smiling too much and rubbing his hands together and bending to hear what they were saying to him.

Them telling him all about a great-grandchild in Lavonia and the bluebell wallpaper in the dining room at Twilight Hills. And the whole time, the faint smell of liniment over everything, and them holding hard, dry cookies on little bitty napkins.

But just that fast, Miss Cora was back in Addie's wedding day, and she heard her say, *"Why, Cora! I'm so glad to see you! Wasn't the*

212

wedding just lovely? Wasn't it? You remember my husband? Here he is! (and aside) Isn't he just the handsomest thing you ever saw in your whole life? Now let's all have some cake and punch and if there's anything else you need, you just ask Pet. Listen, everyone, please. Cora, my dear cousin, has given me Pet to help us out today, and that makes everything so much nicer, don't you think? Pet? I believe these ladies need some more punch, if you please?"

"Don't you think so, Mr. Grower," someone was asking, and Mr. Grower nodding and smiling and rubbing his hands together. Lena thrusting a clear plastic cup of yellow punch into Miss Cora's hands, and Miss Cora found herself sitting in a pale blue chair next to the tall windows where Addie had stood as a child, watching for her papa to come home.

Out on the porch, I sat rocking and gazing across the street at our house. And feeling so dizzy and out-of-place in the strangest kind of way. It just seemed as if the world was turned upside down, me sitting all alone on Miss Addie's porch and looking across the street that way. Everything all looking exactly the same as it had always looked, but with everything now so different. Changed. Gone forever. But then I realized that maybe things didn't look exactly the same. Because there was somebody sitting on the porch at Miss Cora's house. At our house.

And it wasn't Wynona.

And it wasn't Lauralee.

"I'm having a spell, sure enough!" I said, right out loud, because it made sense, didn't it? What with me feeling so out-of-place and lonely?

I rubbed my eyes, trying to clear them, trying to stop the dizziness and bring myself back to the sound, firm earth, but when I looked again, nothing had changed whatsoever. Someone still rocking on our very own porch.

A woman. A great big woman, rocking in slow, enormous sweeps so that the chair seemed to quiver and balance on the tips of its rockers, as if it was gonna fall over backwards! Before it rocked forward again.

And I was thinking: *Who on earth is that sitting on our front porch, just like she owns the whole place?*

A broad, black face, slashed across with a grin, flashing white teeth and strong—like a horse's teeth—and head wrapped up in a blood-red rag and man-shoes that thumped so loud on the porch as she rocked back and forth that I could hear them going CLUMP! all the way across the street.

Mama Sunrise? Coming to get me? My time to go and me sitting all alone on Miss Addie's front porch?

But then her voice came at me, booming across the street just like a big bass drum:

"It's about time, girl!" she hollered at me. "Time you started listening. You carrying all that old stuff around on your back all those years, and you didn't have to, you know. Lord Jesus done forgave your sins and died to pay for them. When you gonna forgive yourself? When you gonna stop whipping yourself about something the Lord done forgave and forgot about a long time ago?"

Inside Miss Addie's house, and sitting to Miss Cora's right in an identical blue chair was an old woman who was slumped against the arm, looking at the floor and with her head bobbing around.

Miss Cora studied her for long, quiet minutes. Then, "Excuse me," Miss Cora said. "Do I know you?"

No response. So louder, "EXCUSE ME, I said. Do I know you?"

The head turned slowly, and the coffee-milk eyes blinked at her. "Ma'am? Was you talkin' to me?"

"Yes, I was talking to you. Do I know you?"

"No'm. Don' think so, less'n you mebbe know the Brown family, other side to Keysville? Them's my peoples."

"No," Miss Cora finally said. "I guess not." And then, she added, "My cousin, Addie, used to live in this house."

"That so?" Polite.

"I do *too* know you," Miss Cora added suddenly. "You're from Great-Uncle Raymond's side of the family. I sure do remember you!"

"*Your* great-uncle?"

"Yes. Of course."

"No'm," the old woman said, smiling shyly and shaking her head. "I shore ain't no kin to you. Why, you is a white lady!"

Miss Cora sat back, noticing for the first time the ash-gray skin that had once been black.

"No'm," the old woman repeated, still smiling and shaking her head. "I shore nuff ain't no kin to you. But I is waiting for my mama to come, and when she do, I'll ask her does she know any of your folks. Yes'm."

Then the voice of someone talking to no one in particular: "My great-granddaughter graduates from Emory this spring. Prettiest little thing you ever saw. Engaged to a medical student now, and she'll be coming home this summer, so she'll come see me. I was saying just the other day that it's time for me to give her the Family Book, what with her graduating and getting married, even though she says she doesn't put much store in old things. But I'll bet you that one of these days she'll come to know how much it means, and she'll thank me. Don't you think so?"

Don't you think so?

Miss Cora stood up, put the plastic cup of punch on her napkin, placed it on the long table against the wall, and went out. As she pulled the door shut behind her, Lena shouted, "You leaving so soon? Well, bye-bye now! Thanks for coming!"

Rah, rah! Sis boom bah!

Out on the porch, she found me waiting, but I was lost in some kind of a dream or something. Because I'd been sitting there listening to all the things Mama Sunrise was hollering to me and thinking about what I promised Miss Addie I'd do.

Yes'm.

Without a word, Miss Cora sat down in the chair next to me. And that kind of waked me up a little.

"That was fast," I said. "How was it?"

"Terrible," Miss Cora said, shaking her head. "Just terrible."

I reached over and patted her hand. "I was afraid that's the way it would be. Let's us go on home. There's somebody sitting on our porch I want you to meet."

"Let me rest a few minutes first," Miss Cora said. "Try and get my head straight. I can't go see anybody until I get my head straight. Why, I got the worst feeling in the whole world in there. Like I didn't know whether I was in a funeral parlor, and it was today, or whether I was in this house a long time ago, on the day of Addie's wedding and watching her come down the staircase in that beautiful satin gown and wearing those white kid shoes her mama sent all the way to Charleston for."

I waited, a little impatiently, for her to get done with talking about it. She took a deep breath.

"Sometimes I forget about shoes," she said, as if I could understand what she was talking about. "They're so important, and sometimes I forget about that."

Well, I was kind of studying her out of the corner of my eye, thinking that maybe she was only sad and confused, what with going into Miss Addie's house, but what on earth was going to happen when we got back across the street and she saw who was sitting there, rocking and talking just as big as day?

"First time I ever knew about shoes was at the funeral for some cousin of my grandmama's. Why, I was just a girl, and I was supposed to be praying like everyone else. But even though I had my head bowed, my eyes were open, and I was looking down at my feet, just to make sure they were still there and that I wasn't the one dead and gone. And I got to looking at the feet of my great-aunt, who was standing right there next to me—her clumpy, old-lady shoes that had a shape to them where the leather had stretched around her corns. I was so young, you see, and I couldn't imagine how old ladies could bear wearing ugly shoes like that. And on the other side of me, the new, shiny-black patent leather shoes of my littlest cousin, Jessica, from Rockmart."

I just sat there and listened and kept rubbing Miss Cora's hand, waiting for her to get all the words out and maybe feel better because of it.

"That's when I knew it for the first time, Pet," she said earnestly, looking deep into my eyes as if to assure herself that I was hearing what she said. "A whole row of us, you see. All different ages and all wearing different shoes, but somehow all the same. And our feet planted good and solid on the earth."

She heaved the deepest sigh I ever heard. "Oh, I can't say it right. Because I guess it can't be said. Just that it's who we are and who we come from. And that's the most important thing— who we come from. Because that's who we are. And it's why I have to find that old grave, Pet, even though I know all of you are right impatient about it. But one day a long, long time ago, folks stood around and saw that man into the earth, whoever he was. And he was blood of their blood and bone of their bone. That's what you take away from every funeral you ever go to. And that's what you will leave behind for the ones who follow you."

Still, I waited, rubbing her hand and feeling a lump coming into my throat.

"Well!" Miss Cora seemed to shrug off whatever that feeling had been. "And listen, Pet, it wasn't just Addie I saw in there and her coming down that staircase on her wedding day, but I think I saw Aunt Frances too. Can that be?"

"No, ma'am," I said, as gently as I could. "She's gone, Miss Cora. Been gone a long time." I was looking across the street to where Mama Sunrise was still rocking away on our porch but not saying a word.

"Well . . . maybe I knew all along it wasn't Aunt Frances," Miss Cora finally admitted. "But I did so want it to be her. She's gone, you say?"

"Yes'm."

"Seems like everyone's gone now. And we'll be gone too, and who's going to carry it on for us?" Miss Cora asked in a most sincere voice, recalling the woman who said that her great-granddaughter was graduating from Emory.

"Carry it on?" I asked. "Carry what on?"

"Why, the family. This family. Where'd they all go? Why isn't there someone left to go on with it? You know what I mean. To talk about us. Tell our stories. Who's going to tell our stories when we're all gone?"

I didn't answer. Because I was watching Mama Sunrise again, and now she had a little baby in her arms, and the rocking was softer and far more gentle, and she was looking down into the baby's face and smiling at her with those big strong teeth.

"Where'd they all go?" Miss Cora repeated the question, and this time, she aimed it at me just like a cannonball. "Pet! I'm talking to you! Where'd they all go, and why isn't there somebody left to go on with it?" The anger coming up in her voice.

"Because . . ." I started, *and from across the street, Mama Sunrise looked up and hollered, "This is it! Tell her! Tell her NOW! Tell her how she talks about her blamed family all the time and how she just hung all over that old Maggie Brown's neck and made out like she was her Aunt Frances. And never once in all these years, you've been right under her nose, Pet, did she ever think you was somebody kin to her!"*

"Because why?" Miss Cora pressed.

"Tell her what all you done for that family. YOUR family! Go on now, and do as I say!" Mama Sunrise hollered.

"But . . ."

"Tell her about what you done!"

"Oh!"

"Pet!" Miss Cora said. "What's the matter with you? Are you having a spell? Answer me!"

"And tell her about her family what's left. It sure won't be pretty, I'll tell you that right off. But it's got to be said! So go on now and say it!" Mama Sunrise shouted, and Miss Addie, who—somehow!—had come and sat down next to Mama Sunrise was smiling and nodding her head to me.

"Because you've forgotten about Hope," I breathed, feeling all the hairs come up on the back of my neck.

"What?"

"I thought so. You've clean forgotten all about it."

Miss Cora sat there facing me and with an expression of pure and absolute revelation on her face. "Hope! Where is she?"

"Gone," I said. "Been gone for years and years. Don't you remember? Her hardly four months old and that fever?"

And Miss Cora remembered. For the first time in all those years. Or, at least, she remembered all she could handle for that little moment.

"The baby! The baby's gone? Wynona's little girl?"

Her voice liked to have broken my heart. Sounded just like a woman moaning in the birth-pains. But wasn't going to be no baby coming from this pain, sure enough! Only a memory that maybe should have been left alone.

"You remember Mr. Adkins?" I floated the question into the air, where it hung for an instant like a falling leaf.

She thought for a few minutes. "No," she finally said. "Should I? Who was he?"

"Nobody," I said.

But Mama Sunrise started to hollering at me again from across the street: *"Well, if she don't remember him, she don't remember what all you done for your family. What you done for Hope and what it cost you to do it. No, she'll hug old Maggie's neck, but she's never hugged yours!"*

"The baby!" Miss Cora moaned. "How could I forget? And her my own flesh and blood?"

"There's lots of things you forget, Miss Cora," I said. "Even about flesh and blood; and lots of things I forget too because we never talked about them. All your going on and on about family all the time and you didn't once in all those years remember about me. How I'm family too."

There. I'd said it. And right out loud.

"Well, of course you're family. Of course you are. You've been with us forever."

"That's not what you mean!" Mama Sunrise insisted, and Miss Addie nodded her head vigorously. *"You tell her—that's not what you mean! Tell her now!"*

"That's not what I mean," I repeated, holding my breath.

Miss Cora was looking at me hard and never even blinking. And I was watching across the street and listening to Mama Sunrise saying, *"Well, good for you! Took you long enough, you know!"*

Miss Cora seemed to be listening to someone too. Someone out of the past.

Touch his hand, Mama. He's crying. Did he go to Dilsey, Mama? Instead of you?

I was thinking: Now you've got it right. How he came to the little room off the back porch one midnight, and my mama waked up to see him standing in the doorway. She told me all about it. About the white man in the black room and him a solid shaft of hunger and cold. Master of his own house, and alone, staring at her with those deep, sad eyes. And she took him into her bed just the way her mama, my grandmama, took him into her bed when he was just a child and afraid of the dark and look-

219

ing at her exactly the same way. My mama pulled the warm covers up over his shoulders and held him close against her until he stopped shivering.

Then . . . she was so surprised when he began reaching for her the way a man reaches for a woman. And that cold, lonely reaching is what brought me into this world.

Miss Cora was still staring at me. I watched as she studied the curve of my jaw and all the bone-shape under my skin. And my eyes.

Just exactly like his.

And me thinking: *Yes. Because here I am, the result of your papa's loneliness. And your mama's coldness. That's how come him to turn to my mama and not yours. Me—black, fatherless, and born out of loneliness—but the one who loves you and Wynona and Lauralee more than any other person on the face of this earth.*

Finally, I said, "You knew it a long time ago, and you forgot it because you wanted to forget it. But you've got to remember it now. Because what you're needing in the worst kind of way is knowing this family's gonna go on, just like everything goes on. Even through somebody like me."

"No! Not *that* way!" Miss Cora croaked like an old frog.

And I could see her remembering more: a whisper. Who's whispering in the dining room? Just beyond the door? *"Well, Anne, sometimes it happens. Lots of good women have had to forgive it. So just pretend it didn't happen. Thank goodness she's clean, at least. So now you just forgive him and forget about it."*

"Yes," I said. "That way. Because there's Samantha."

"Samantha?"

Well, that was something to see, I tell you. Me watching Miss Cora as she came across a memory of a painting she'd seen one time, of a pale little girl smiling and leaning back in a swing, with sunlight across her cheek and roses behind her and pink ribbons in her yellow hair.

"My granddaughter," I said.

She stared at me while she seemed to find from long ago a faraway image of a little black girl in a lavender dress and with white satin ribbons tied among all the tiny braids of hair.

Like lost white gulls floating on a midnight sea. Hetti? Betty? Lizzy?

"Lizzy?"

"No, ma'am. Lizzy's girl, Samantha. And she's so bright, she's going to the University of Georgia this fall. And she's ours—yours and mine."

"What?"

"I said she's ours—yours and mine," I repeated slowly, staying lock-eyed with her for long minutes. It was an awful hard thing for me to do, looking right at her and watching her pulling so hard against the truth.

"I'm sorry if I hurt you," I said. "But you have to know. I promised . . . Miss Addie . . . that I would tell you the truth."

"You leave sweet Addie out of this!" Miss Cora shouted, and she startled me so bad, I almost fell out of my chair.

"She said you needed to know the family's going to go on," I barely whispered. "And now you know it."

But Miss Cora's jaw was as square as a block of granite, and I knew she'd shut herself up in a silence neither one of us was going to be able to get through.

"Let's go on home," I said at last, getting up and standing in front of her. Finally, she let me help her up from the low chair, and she leaned against me as we went back across the street.

And when we got to the porch, all the chairs were empty.

*E*vening came, and we took our usual places on the porch, sitting together just like always.

Across the street, light poured out of the front windows of Miss Addie's house, and a shadow moved against that light—Mr. Grower probably walking around picking up napkins and plastic glasses and adjusting the smoked glass ashtrays just so on those fake mahogany tables.

On the porch, two tired old balloons drooped in the dusk.

Miss Cora hadn't said a word all afternoon, and neither had I. Once, I saw Wynona silently mouth to Lauralee, "What's wrong with them?" But Lauralee just looked at her.

"Think I'll fix some iced tea," Wynona said, getting up as she spoke. "Would youall like some?"

"I'll fix it, if you want," I offered.

"No, thank you," Wynona answered. "I'll fix it for us. Lauralee?" She turned to her sister. "Would you help me?"

Lauralee said nothing, but she followed Wynona, pausing for only a moment to look right at me. But I couldn't tell what was in those eyes. Nothing sad, that much I knew. Then she went into the house.

The very minute they were gone, Miss Cora scooted her chair around so she was facing me.

"I just can't believe it's all come down to this!" she said. Her voice was hoarse-sounding and hurried. "How on earth could

I have forgotten about Hope? She was everything—the only thing left that mattered!"

"I know you feel that way, but you're wrong," I said, a little cautiously. "She was a wonderful, beautiful little girl. But she wasn't *everything*. And I don't want to see you go making yourself sick about it after all these years. Not a bit of sense in us trying to make it all fit together so we can understand."

We sat in silence for a while, with Miss Cora letting out a big sigh. And then finally, she said, "I want you to bring Samantha here so I can see her."

"You *what?*"

"What I just said, just as clear as day."

"But why?"

Miss Cora sat for a few minutes in stony silence, before she whispered, "I'm going to give the Family Book to her."

"You're *what?*" Why, I couldn't believe my ears! Seems like all I could hear were little popping sounds, like green tips of new vines reaching upward!

"You're getting as deaf as a post, aren't you?" Miss Cora snorted. "Just as plain as I can say it again, I'm going to give the Family Book to Samantha. But Heaven knows, this isn't the way I wanted it to be! I just don't know what else to do. Somebody in the family has to have it, or else one of these days, when we're all dead and gone, folks we don't even know will come in and clean out everything, and either they'll throw it out or else put it away in a box up in the attic, and nobody will take care of it and build on it. So I'm giving it to Samantha because she'll care. She has to care!"

She was silent for a few moments then, but finally she said, "I didn't want it to be this way! Why, when I think of what might have been. . . ."

"Well, that sure doesn't do any good," I piped up. "Some things are and some things aren't, and we have to take it any way it comes."

But I sure made her mad with that!

"I don't believe that!" she fairly shouted. "Why, you sound like being good and trying hard doesn't mean a thing! Especially being good and trying hard for your family. And I know good and well that family is everything. All there is that matters. And you know it too!"

"No," I insisted. "Not everything. But I guess it's all we're going to get while we're on this earth. And I say we better learn how to love each other, because we don't get any choices about family. Just have to go along with whatever we're given. We don't get any more choice than a creek gets about where it's trying to go all the time."

"Why, you don't even know where it's trying to go!" Miss Cora yelped, clearly delighted for the conversation to turn so suddenly in her favor.

"I do too!" I insisted. "You told me all about it. Down to the Savannah River and then out into the ocean. You told me all about that a thousand and one times. I've sat right here on this very porch and heard you tell it over and over and over again. So I know because *you* told me."

I hadn't realized I was beginning to shout, so I lowered my voice and added, "But my knowing where it goes isn't what makes it go there."

Miss Cora could hardly speak a word. But I could tell exactly what she was thinking: *What on earth is the world coming to? Going to be made up of nothing but uppity people who don't know who they are and what their place is. And then what will happen?*

But before Miss Cora could go ahead with that thought, another one came crowding in behind it—that she most certainly would give the Family Book to you, Samantha. A beautiful, black young woman who is bright and ambitious, and who's going to be in school at the University of Georgia. Because you're the only one left now to carry it all forward. And in all of our born days, who would ever have thought such a thing could happen?

"I'm sorry, Cora," I said. "I didn't mean to speak so rough-like to you. I like your stories. I always have."

And it didn't slip by her that I'd left off her honorific. Cora, I had called her. Simply Cora. At last!

But the silence sat between us again, like an old dog that scratches fleas and smells bad. And I think she was trying to decide what to do. She wasn't one to humble herself, not her. So

224

maybe she was deciding that this was the end of it, the end of everything we had been through together or that we could ever mean to each other.

Because she had the most pained look on her face that I've ever seen. Like she was hurting more even than when she remembered about Hope being gone and when she thought there wasn't nobody left to carry it all forward—except for a child she'd never seen in her life. A black child. The great-granddaughter of her own papa's indiscretion.

But she was remembering other things too—hands, maybe—all the black hands she had watched for her whole life long. Hands that kneaded and stirred and smoothed and soothed. And more: my strong black finger on the twin triggers of that double-barreled shotgun all those years ago, and the muzzle of the gun swinging upward and away from where it had been pointing.

At that little baby Lauralee was carrying.

Cora looked at me, and I knew then that she'd finally remembered every bit of it. The whole thing about Mr. Adkins and what he did. And what all I did, to try and save this family.

And more—I think she remembered right then and there how she was the very one who brought me into the world. Remembered the black thighs—my mama's thighs—and how they trembled. And her own pale hands, white as lilies, lifting me out of the wet purple flower and into this world.

Then Miss Anne's voice coming back through all the years, saying, "Well, isn't that silly! Why would anybody want to give that little thing an African name, for Heaven's sake? Pet's a perfectly good name, so just don't pay any attention to Dilsey, and she'll soon forget about it. It's just an uppity streak Dilsey's got."

To me she said, "What *is* your name? Your real name?"

"Sunrise," I answered easily, thinking about my great-grandmama and her big strong bones inside the old wall down at the cemetery. Her, whose name was Sunrise. "It was my great-grandmama's name. And it's my name too," I said. "It's my name!"

We heard the faraway sound of Wynona laughing at something she and Lauralee were doing in the kitchen. Or maybe even laughing at us. Then the sound of ice clinking into the tall glasses.

Cora sighed. "And what is Samantha's real name?" she asked.

"Samantha."

"Well, that's something, at least!"

Because Cora and I both knew at last that blood is blood and family is family. No matter what. And I guess we were thinking about all the years that had gone by and Cora's mama's rocking chair and the hard work of just being alive, of going on with it, no matter what, and maybe she was deciding right then and there that I was right. That maybe we don't have a thing to do with it. That what God asks of us is to take whatever He gives us and do the best we can with it and thank Him for it, no matter what it is. No matter how much it hurts.

I sat there watching her, and somehow, I could see the broad Savannah River I'd never seen myself, but that she'd told me about so many times—where our papa had taken her, and it was a breathing sheet of silver light, always moving.

"All right," she said at last. "You're Sunrise and I'm Cora and she's Samantha. So it's all settled. Now let's drop the subject."

"All right," I said.

Because what I know is this: Nobody's ever gonna care what we called each other. Because one of these days, nobody will even remember our names. And that doesn't matter. Not one little bit. Our names will just be faded out so bad on some old leaning tombstones that no one will be able to read the writing anyway.

So the only thing that's going to last is how we loved each other—any way we could, and no matter what.

Postlogue

So, Samantha—baby girl—I hope you've listened to everything I've been telling you about all the things that happened to us.

About the summer when Wynona said I was getting funny from everything that had happened—what with Miss Addie passing on and her house being made into a funeral parlor—and all of it going on right across the street from us, and Miss Cora driving us crazy about looking for that old grave. Her even running away with that old Maggie Brown woman and scaring us half to death. Wynona said it had turned me into a different person.

But, honey, she hadn't seen nothing yet!

Because right at the end of the summer, it got worse. Much worse. Because there came an evening after we were home from Camp Meeting, when I took a deep breath and pulled Miss Addie's old green rocking chair out of the back corner of the porch and brought it right up beside Cora's very own chair. And sat down in it. Right where everyone who drove by in the street could see us. No black woman had ever done such a thing before, not in this small town where the old ways of things hang on so hard.

"Who on earth has ever heard of such a thing?" I heard Wynona whispering to Lauralee, but she never said a word to me about it.

"Just look at that, would you?" the people would say. "Her sitting right there on the front porch, like she's one of the family or something! Craziest thing I ever heard of. And what's the world coming to, when folks don't remember who they are and what their place is?"

And that wasn't all.

Cora put a whole big bunch of new pages in the Family Book, and she asked me all kinds of questions about my mama and my grandmama and Mama Sunrise and me and the ones who came after me, and she wrote down everything I told her.

And even that wasn't all.

Because one day when Wynona wasn't keeping an eye on us, we called the Stephens Stoneworks out on the Waynesboro Highway and ordered a tombstone and never told a soul what we were doing. Lauralee heard us on the phone in the dining room, but she just passed right on by. And she was smiling.

When the stone was ready, we had it delivered down to Brushy Creek Cemetery about the second week in September and set up inside that last old wall of the slave cemetery. We slipped away and drove down there all by ourselves too. And I had never driven a car before in my entire life, but I did it that day.

What confused everybody the most, I think, was that they thought the stone didn't even have anybody's name on it. Just one word: Sunrise. When word got around town about that, folks drove all the way down to Brushy Creek Cemetery on Sunday afternoons, just to see it. Like it was a tourist attraction or something.

I'll take you down there tomorrow, Samantha, and show it to you.

Anyway—that's the kind of craziness that went on all summer. Cora and me sitting together every evening, rocking and talking. And just being with each other.

Wynona said I was getting to where I had "spells" almost all the time, and maybe she was right. Because when we were all there together on that porch—Cora and me and Wynona and Lauralee—it wasn't just us. But Miss Anne and the aunts, and my mama and my grandmama.

And Mama Sunrise and Hope.

And Lizzy, your sweet mama.

And you, Samantha, her baby girl.

Like all that water in the creek joining up with the Savannah River and heading toward the ocean.

The long line of rocking chairs tilted back and facing the twilight and all our stories, like strong, green vines rising up out of the black earth and curling and twining and holding on.

And my sister, Cora, reaching up and putting her hands into the stars.

Augusta Trobaugh earned the Master of Arts degree in English from the University of Georgia, with a concentration in American and Southern literature. Her first novel, *Praise Jerusalem!*, was a semi-finalist in the 1993 Pirate's Alley Faulkner Competition. Trobaugh's work has been funded through the Georgia Council of the Arts, and she has been nominated for Georgia Author of the Year.

PRAISE JERUSALEM!

A Novel by

Augusta Trobaugh

THREE SOUTHERN WOMEN *journey to Jerusalem, Georgia, in hope of finding utopia. Along the way, they must overcome social, economic, and racial estrangements that isolate them from each other.*

The journey taken by these three leads them to some difficult and surprising revelations about themselves and their culture and provides them with the courage they need for facing an ever-changing future with courage and dignity.

In this colorful, evocative story, Augusta Trobaugh furthers the legacy of the great Southern novel as she explores three women's search for ultimate happiness.

"A touching and often amusing novel."
— LIBRARY JOURNAL

"A perfect balance of richness and delicacy."
— BAILEY WHITE, NPR COMMENTATOR

Paper (6 x 9)   **288 pages**
0-8010-5814-7   **Fiction**
$12.99